INDUSTRIAL BIOTECHNOLOGY in Non-Aligned and Other Developing Countries

Current Status and Future Prospects

About the Centre

The Centre for Science and Technology of the Non-Aligned and Other Developing Countries (NAM S&Centre) is an inter-governmental organisation with a membership of 47 countries spread over Asia, Africa, Middle East and Latin America. Besides this, 12 S&T agencies and academic/research institutions of Bolivia, Botswana, Brazil, India, Nigeria and Turkey are the members of the S&T-Industry Network of the Centre. The Centre was set up in 1989 to promote South-South cooperation through mutually beneficial partnerships among scientists and technologists and scientific organisations in developing countries. It implements a variety of programmes including international workshops, meetings, roundtables, training courses and collaborative projects and brings out scientific publications, including a quarterly Newsletter. It is also implementing 5 Fellowship schemes, namely, NAM S&T Centre Research Fellowship, Joint NAM S&T Centre – ICCBS Karachi Fellowship, Joint CSIR/CFTRI (Diamond Jubilee)–NAM S&T Centre Fellowship, Joint NAM S&T Centre – ZMT Bremen Fellowship and Research Training Fellowship for Developing Country Scientists (RTF-DCS) in Indian institutions. These activities provide, among others, the opportunity for scientist-to-scientist contact and interaction, training and expert assistance, familiarising the scientific community on the latest developments and techniques in the subject areas, and identification of technologies for transfer between member countries. The Centre has so far brought out 59 publications and has organised 91 international workshops and training programmes.

For further details, please visit www.namstct.org or write to the Director, NAM S&T Centre, Core 6A, 2nd Floor, India Habitat Centre, Lodhi Road, New Delhi-110003, India (Phone: +91-11-24645134/24644974; Fax: +91-11-24644973; E-mail: namstcentre@gmail.com; namstct@bol.net.in).

INDUSTRIAL BIOTECHNOLOGY in Non-Aligned and Other Developing Countries

Current Status and Future Prospects

— *Editors* —
Maranda Esterhuizen-Londt
Abdelfattah Badr

CENTRE FOR SCIENCE & TECHNOLOGY OF THE NON-ALIGNED AND OTHER DEVELOPING COUNTRIES (NAM S&T CENTRE)

2014
DAYA PUBLISHING HOUSE®
A Division of
ASTRAL INTERNATIONAL PVT. LTD.
New Delhi – 110 002

ISBN 9789351302711

Centre for Science and Technology of the Non-Aligned and Other Developing Countries (NAM S&T Centre)
Core-6A, 2nd Floor, India Habitat Centre, Lodhi Road,
New Delhi-110 003 (India)
Phone: +91-11-24644974, 24645134, Fax: +91-11-24644973
E-mail: namstct@gmail.com
Website: www.namstct.org

Published by : **Daya Publishing House®**
A Division of
Astral International Pvt. Ltd.
– ISO 9001:2008 Certified Company –
4760-61/23, Ansari Road, Darya Ganj
New Delhi-110 002
Ph. 011-43549197, 23278134
E-mail: info@astralint.com
Website: www.astralint.com

Laser Typesetting : **Classic Computer Services**, Delhi - 110 035

Printed at : **Thomson Press India Limited**

PRINTED IN INDIA

Foreword

Biotechnology is a powerful enabler for transformational economic reform in the developing world. From finding solutions for environmental sustainability through green technologies to developing vaccines to prevent infectious diseases; from improving agricultural productivity through genetic enhancement to developing alternate biofuels that provide independence from fossil fuels, Biotechnology helps address a plethora of present day global challenges.

Let's start with the role of Industrial Biotechnology in Bio-pharmaceutical production. Microbial & mammalian cell based fermentation supports the production of antibiotics, vaccines, and therapeutics such as recombinant proteins and monoclonal antibodies, which have brought about a paradigm change in treating both acute and chronic diseases. Biotechnology based drugs and vaccines have provided lifesaving solutions to a plethora of medical conditions from Cancer and Diabetes to Hepatitis. Recombinant Human Insulin and Insulin analogs have replaced animal derived Insulins to greatly improve Diabetes management, while recombinant Hepatitis B vaccines have played a lifesaving role and drugs like Erythropoetin and Herceptin have even cured cancer patients. Today Biopharmaceuticals or biologics account for half the list of top 10 best-selling drugs worldwide.

Industrial Biotechnology also plays an important role in developing Biofuels as an alternate to fossil fuel. Developing countries like India and Brazil are increasingly turning to Biofuels to attain energy independence. Using novel enzyme technologies, a number of bio-materials like sugarcane bagasse, corn, sorghum and other cereals have been converted into fuel alcohol. More recently, micro algae and seaweed are also being harnessed as a more sustainable option for biofuels. Many countries have already started blending Biofuels like Bio-ethanol with fossil fuel as a way to reduce their dependence on oil imports. The future bodes well for renewable energy where Biofuels will play a key role.

Another area where Industrial biotechnology offers great promise is in the area of regeneration of contaminated land and polluted water bodies. 'Bioremediation' using living microbes which utilize their unique enzyme systems, can metabolize and remove pollutants from contaminated soil or groundwater. Such microbial metabolism can also be adopted for 'Bioregeneration' and 'Bioaugmentation' that speeds up the rate of degradation of organic wastes and pollutants. Oil spills are frequently being mopped up by genetically engineered microbes.

In the area of agriculture, Biotechnology can usher in a second green revolution by providing scientific techniques that optimize the use of available resources without placing additional demands on land or water to boost yields. These solutions can improve the quality of the agricultural produce with disease-free and nutritionally enhanced varieties of crops. The early benefits of biotechnology are already being reaped by Indian and Chinese farmers as they increasingly opt for Genetically Modified Bt cotton seeds to enhance productivity. Countries like Bangladesh have recently adopted genetically altered crops like Bt Brinjal to boost productivity and reduce pesticide usage, a boon to farmers.

Most importantly, the adoption of industrial biotechnology can lead to the creation of a plethora of jobs for engineers, scientists, technicians and entrepreneurs.

Clearly, the opportunity is enormous. Governments the world over will need to play an enabling role by creating suitable physical, financial, legislative, and regulatory infrastructure so that the private sector can invest in building the necessary manufacturing capacity.

I was most interested to learn that the Centre for Science and Technology of the Non-Aligned and Other Developing Countries (NAM S&T Centre) organized the First Winter School on Industrial Biotechnology in Egypt from December 2 - December 6, 2012 jointly with the National Research Centre of Egypt; Arab Biotechnology Association; Federation of Arab Scientific Research Councils; University of Technology, Malaysia; and Arab Society for Genetic Engineering and Biotechnology.

The importance of such an event cannot be emphasized enough as it highlights how Industrial Biotechnology can be applied across sectors to provide a sustainable foundation for developing countries to transition from agrarian to industrial economies in a sustainable way. It also helps knowledge sharing on the evolving developments in Industrial Biotechnology from developing countries.

This book "Industrial Biotechnology in Non-Aligned and Other Developing Countries: Current Status and Future Prospects" is an outcome of this important event. It features 16 scientific and technical papers written by experts and professionals from 13 different countries.

I would like to compliment the NAM S&T Centre, particularly its Director, Prof. Arun Kulshreshtha, and his team, for their initiative in bringing out this very important and relevant publication.

I am sure this book will greatly help to showcase the capabilities of Industrial Biotechnology in improving the efficiency of modern industrial processes as well as curbing their potential environmental impact through greener solutions. Additionally, I believe it will also highlight the Biotechnology led research and development programmes being conducted across developing countries.

Dr. Kiran Mazumdar-Shaw

Chairman & Managing Director,
Biocon Pharmaceuticals,
Bengaluru, India
E-mail: kiran.mazumdar@biocon.com

Preface

Biotechnology may be simply defined as the use of living organisms or their products to make products of commercial value. Practices of biotechnology go back centuries and examples of biotechnological applications in the past include the use of microbes to produce cheese and beverages as well as use of selective breeding of plants and livestock to breed more productive forms. In the recent decades renewed interest in biotechnology has made it one of the most important scientific and technological developments that have greatly influence various aspects of human life. This is due to the advent of gene technology that may simply be defined as the manipulation of living organisms with deliberate handling of DNA for the identification and modification of specific genes and moving genes between organisms in order to obtain new traits or produce a new product. The impact of the availability of new genetic and genomic tools is also highly relevant for industrial, medical, agricultural and environmental applications of biotechnology. However, biotechnology is based on a multidisciplinary approach, including such disciplines as biology, organic chemistry, biochemistry, microbiology, proteomics, bioinformatics and bio-engineering. Since the recent development of an advanced set of genomics tools, there are wider prospects of fully exploring and implementing the possibilities of these tools in biotechnology.

Very few areas of research have undergone such a dramatic development as biotechnology in the recent few decades. Almost every single aspect of life science research is affected by the progress that has been achieved in biotechnology. The global scientific community as well as international and regional organizations has identified biotechnology as a technology that had improved health care, environmental management, poverty alleviation, maintenance of food security, and industrial development. For this reason, biotechnology has become a hot spot of major interest nationally, regionally and globally. Workshops have been organized to bring together the leading scientists, young investigators and students active in the field of biotechnology. In addition to these workshops, training courses have been specifically designed to address the needs of students and young researchers and new educational programs have been initiated in almost all the countries of the world.

Industrial biotechnology, also known as white biotechnology is concerned with the utilization of various aspects of biotechnology for environmental friendly production, processing and commercialization of various types of products such as chemicals, pharmaceuticals, enzymes, food, feed, detergents, paper, pulp, textiles and other material of industrial applications that can be used to improve human life. Industrial biotechnology approaches, processes, methods and products are widely applied in other fields of biotechnology such as biomedical, pharmaceutical, agricultural, forensic, and environmental. Biomolecules produced by using industrial processes are used for disease diagnosis, and production of new pharmaceutical compounds in microorganisms, plants, and animals. Kits and reagents produced via industrial processing of biomolecules are widely applied in agricultural research and in basic scientific studies. In addition, engineered biomolecules are widely used to combat pollution, keeping the environment clean. In addition, bioenergy (such as biofuels or biogas) has emerged as one of the fast growing fields of biotechnology in recent years.

More in depth research on industrial biotechnology is essential to fully explore the widerange of possibilities to transform industrial biotechnology knowledge into sustainable, competitive, innovative and commercial industrial products. It is evident that industrial biotechnology must be explored to unravel the wide range of possibilities that would provide a more sustainable foundation for developing a more industry based economy in developing countries that have been dependent on exporting their raw material and natural resources to the industrialized countries at cheap price. Whilst considering the vast potential that exists in biotechnology, the decision-making and priority setting in industrial biotechnology research, and development and commercialization must be coordinated for the benefit of each country and its people. The development of biotechnology has received strong government patronage at the initial stages owing to its multi-disciplinary nature and heavy investment costs. In developing countries where investments are hard to secure, small and medium scale enterprises can help in promoting and advancing industrial biotechnologies. An effective foundation for intergovernmental cooperation and promotion of partnerships amongst developing countries in an open and transparent manner may be urgent in order to increase awareness and adopt common policies to implementing industrial biotechnology achievements for the welfare of their peoples.

This book "Industrial Biotechnology in Non-Aligned and Other Developing Countries: Current Status and Future Prospects" contains various articles dealing with biotechnology, in general and with industrial biotechnology in particular, in these countries. Some articles are of general nature and report on the biotechnology research and development and the status of biotechnology and prospects of industrial biotechnology and its role in the economic growth in some countries. The majority of the articles however, are research reports on experimental research on various aspects of biotechnology such as the production of industrial compounds, antimicrobial substances and enzymes from plant and microbial sources. The book also contains review articles on rather sophisticated biotechnological processes such as bioreactors and bioprocess. The majority of the articles are based on presentations to the First Winter School on Industrial Biotechnology held in Cairo, Egypt in December 2-6, 2012 by the Centre for Science and Technology of the Non-Aligned and Developing Countries in cooperation with the Egyptian Academy of Science and Technology and the National Research Centre in Cairo and the Arab Biotechnology Association. However, the book also contains some invited papers from experts in advanced research in the area of industrial biotechnology.

We are grateful to Professor Arun P. Kulshreshtha, Director of the NAM S&T Centre in New Delhi, India for nominating us to edit this book. We also thank Ms. Isha Sehgal, Research Assistant and In-Charge of Publication in the NAM S&T Centre.

Professor Abdelfattah Badr
Faculty of Science, Helwan University,
Post code 11790 Cairo, Egypt

Dr. Maranda Esterhuizen-Londt
InnoVenton Nelson Mandela Metropolitan University
Port Elizabeth, 6001, South Africa

Introduction

Industrial biotechnology, popularly known as white biotechnology, involves the successful utilisation of various aspects of biotechnology for the environment friendly production and processing of chemicals, pharmaceuticals, materials and bio-energy. It is being widely considered as the solution to find alternatives for the diminishing amount of fossil resources such as oil and natural gas and thus symbolises its importance in providing clean and sustainable processes. Industrial Biotechnology makes an efficient use of enzymes and micro-organisms to produce bio-based products in sectors such as chemicals, food and feed, detergents, paper and pulp, textiles and bio-energy (such as bio-fuels or biogas) by incorporating renewable raw materials. This has been one of the most promising and innovative approaches towards lowering greenhouse gas emissions. Most recently, the World Wide Fund for Nature (WWF) has confirmed about the potential of industrial biotechnology to cut CO_2 emissions and hence its significance in building a greener economy.

Industrial Biotechnology, although already successfully established in some sectors, is still in its infancy. More in-depth knowledge is essential to fully explore the wide-range of possibilities of Industrial Biotechnology and to transform the traditional chemical and chemical-related sector to a sustainable, competitive, innovative and sophisticated sector. And to achieve this, a multidisciplinary approach is required, including such areas as biotechnology, organic chemistry, biochemistry, microbiology, genomics, proteomics, bio-informatics and process engineering. Since in last few years an advanced set of genomics tools have become available, there are wider prospects of fully exploring and implementing the possibilities of these tools. It is evident that the Industrial Biotechnology sector must be explored to unravel the wide range of possibilities so as to provide a more sustainable foundation for the developing world's transition from an agrarian to an industrial economy.

In order to enhance and develop the research skills of the young and senior scholars in various aspects of industrial biotechnology and to deliberate on the recent developments in this field in the developing countries, the Centre for Science and Technology of the Non-Aligned and Other Developing Countries (NAM S&T Centre) jointly with the Science and Technology Development Fund (STDF) of Egypt organised the First International Winter School on Industrial Biotechnology at the National Research Centre (NRC), Giza, Egypt during 2–6 December, 2012. The Winter School was sponsored by the Academy of Scientific Research and Technology (ASRT) of Egypt; Arab Biotechnology Association (ABA); Federation of Arab Scientific Research Councils (FASRC); University of Technology, Malaysia; and Arab Society for Genetic Engineering and Biotechnology. The Winter School was attended by 65 participants from 18 countries including Colombia, Ethiopia, The Gambia, India, Indonesia, Malaysia, Myanmar, Nepal, Nigeria, Pakistan, South Africa, Sri Lanka, Sudan, Togo, Uganda, Vietnam, Zimbabwe, and 38 participants from the host country Egypt.

This publication contains 16 scientific papers and country status reports presented at the First Winter School on Industrial Biotechnology and also papers contributed by other invited experts on the subject.

I gratefully acknowledge the dynamic involvement and untiring efforts of Dr. Maranda Esterhuizen – Londt, InnoVenton Nelson Mandela Metropolitan University, Institute for Chemical Technology and Downstream Chemicals Technology Station, Summerstrand Campus (North), South Africa and Prof. Dr. Abdelfattah Badr, Professor of Genetics and Biosystematics, Botany and Microbiology Department, Faculty of Science, Helwan University, Cairo, Egypt for technical editing of this publication. Last but not the least, valuable services provided by the entire team of the NAM S&T Centre, in particular, Mr. M. Bandyopadhyay for overall supervision, and Ms. Parul Sehgal and Mr. Pankaj Buttan in compiling the presented papers, liaising with the authors and editors, and giving a final shape to the volume. I hope that this book will be a relevant step forward in giving maximum exposure towards the updated research and development that are being conducted in this field across the developing countries.

Prof. Dr. Arun P. Kulshreshtha

Director and Executive Head,

NAM S&T Centre

Contents

Foreword *v*
Dr. Kiran Mazumdar-Shaw

Preface *ix*
Professor Abdelfattah Badr and Dr. Maranda Esterhuizen-Londt

Introduction *xiii*
Prof. Dr. Arun P. Kulshreshtha

1. **High Value Products from Brown Sugar Cake (Panela) by Means of a Biorefinery: Colombian Case** 1
Javier A. Dávila and Carlos A. Cardona (Colombia)

2. **The Role of Industrial Biotechnology for the Economic Growth of Ethiopia** 17
Teshome Sahilemariam Ashagre (Ethiopia)

3. **Binding of Serum Albumins with Nanoparticles: A Short Review** 25
S. Naveenraj and S. Anandan (India)

4. **High Throughput Refolding and Purification of Recombinant Asparaginase from Inclusion Bodies of *E. coli*** 41
Parul Sehgal (India)

5. **Measurement and Control of Cultivation Parameters during Mammalian Cell Cultivation and Their Impact on Bioprocess Performance** 55
Hesham A. El Enshasy (Malaysia)

6. **Antinociceptive Activity of Haruan (*Channa striatus*) Traditional Extract** 65
Zuleen Delina Fasya Binti Abdul Ghani and Abdul Manan Bin Mat Jais (Malaysia)

7. **The Pathogenicity of *Beauveria bassiana* on *Spodoptera litura* in Cotton Field** 91
Kyi Pyar Win, Weine Nway Nway Oo and Mya Mya Oo (Myanmar)

8. **Status of Biotechnology and Prospects of Biotechnology Related Small and Medium Size Enterprises in Nepal** 99
Chiranjivi Regmi (Nepal)

9. **Temporary Immersion Bioreactors in Nigeria for *In vitro* Propagation of Plants: Status and Prospects** 109
M.T. Abdulkareem, A.A. Adekunle, O.A. Adetunji and J.M. Madu (Nigeria)

10. **Optimisation of Alpha-amylase Production by *Bacillus subtilis*: A Local Isolate Grown on Cassava Starch** 119
O.A. Adetunji, B.O. Solomon, M.T. Abdulkareem, A.A. Adekunle, M. Madu Josephine, R.E. Okonji, T.F. Adepoju, O.A. Adesina and S.K. Layokun (Nigeria)

11. **Some Traditional Fermented Foods: Current Status and Future Prospects in Nigeria** 135
A.A. Adekunle, O.A. Adetunji, G.B. Olukotun, M.T. Abdulkareem and J.M. Madu (Nigeria)

12. **Recent Technical Advancements in the Areas of Industrial Biotechnology in Pakistan** 145
Mudassir Asrar and Saima Nasir (Pakistan)

13. **Large Scale Cultivation of a Mixed Microbial Consortium for Biofuel Production** 155
Maranda Esterhuizen-Londt and Ben Zeelie (South Africa)

14. **Alpha Amylase Production Using Cassava Root Extract** 163
S.L. Dalpatadu, A.K. Nanayakkara, N.V. Chandrasekharan and S.G. Senaratne (Sri Lanka)

15. **Research and Application of Biotechnology for Food Industry in Vietnam** 175
Do Thi Thuy Le (Vietnam)

16. **Status of Biotechnology in Zimbabwe: Towards a More Sustainable Biotechnology Era in Zimbabwe** 183
Muvhunzi Faith and Mufandaedza Jonathan (Zimbabwe)

Chapter 1

High Value Products from Brown Sugar Cake (Panela) by Means of a Biorefinery: Colombian Case

Javier A. Dávila and Carlos A. Cardona***

Biotechnology and Agroindustry Institute, Department of Chemical Engineering, Universidad Nacional de Colombia, Cra 27 No. 64-60 Manizales Colombia

ABSTRACT

The biorefinery concept is analogous to that of oil refinery which fractionates biomass into a family of products. The typical biorefinery products are biofuels, biomolecules, natural chemicals, biomaterials and foodstuff. The conceptual design of biorefineries is based on the study of different sources as raw materials and in this context the panela sugarcane *(Saccharum officinarum L.)* is one of the most important raw materials that can be used in a biorefinery. This work presents a biorefinery from brown sugar cake (Panela) using the remaining bagasse in its process. Simulation and analysis were carried out to produce Gibberellic Acid as a biomolecule from a biorefinery using panela sugarcane bagasse as raw material. Aspen Plus software was used as simulation tool and a pass conversion of 83.82 per cent was obtained for the glucose in the fermentation while the total conversion was 97.35 per cent. The rate of production of Gibberellic acid (at 99.1 per cent of purity) was 26.76 kg per batch. According to the economic analysis, the production of Gibberellic acid using panela sugarcane bagasse is feasible obtaining competitive prices. The Potential Environmental Impact (PEI)

E-mail: *ccardonaal@unal.edu.co; **jadavilar@unal.edu.co

for the most appropriate scheme was analyzed using the software Waste Algorithm Reduction (WAR) developed by the U.S. Environmental Protection Agency (EPA) demonstrating the effect generated by the process on the environment.

Keywords: *Panela sugarcane, Biorefinery, Simulation, Gibberellic acid, Environmental impact, Economic analysis.*

1. INTRODUCTION

Colombia is the second major producer of panela (brown sugar cake) in the world after India. In Colombia, the average production of panela during the last 12 years was 1,307,315 tonnes per year; meanwhile India produces approximately 1,600,000 tonnes per year (Tarrazona, 2011). In Colombia, there are at least 70,000 producers of panela and 266,559 hectares are used to produce sugarcane to the panela production. Colombia is located in a tropical region and thus has excellent conditions for the cultivation of sugarcane for the panela production. Figure 1.1 shows the location of Colombia and its regions in which the panela is produced (Ministerio de Agricultura, 2010).

The principal product from panela sugarcane is the panela which is a brown sugar cake used to make a typical drink. However, products such as juices, biofuels,

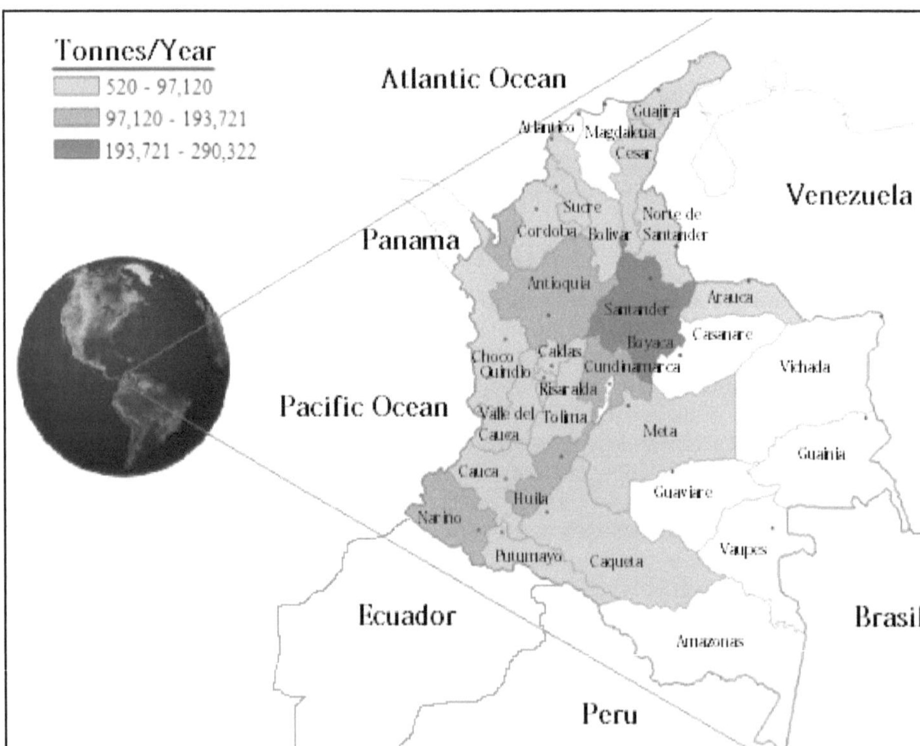

Figure 1.1: Production of Panela in Colombia (Adapted from Tarrazona, 2011).

and drinks among others can be obtained from the remaining material such as the bagasse, cachaza and others.

The biorefinery concept is analogous to that of oil refinery which fractionates biomass into a family of products. The main products of a biorefinery are biofuels, biomolecules, natural chemicals, biomaterials and foodstuff (Moncada *et al.*, 2012). In other words, the biorefinery concept implies the production of multiple products with different applications from the same raw material.

Biorefineries conceptual design is based on the study of different sources as raw materials. Raw materials can be classified as first, second and third generation feedstocks which correspond to food security, agroindustrial residues (lignocellulosic biomass) and algae respectively (Stoeglehner *et al.*, 2009).

Depending on the generation of the raw material selected, it is possible to establish a sequence for producing different high value products, preserving the food security as the principal one. After the production of food security products, the remaining streams can be used to obtain other products but integrating all the process from the same raw material in the same scheme of production.

Even if the solid wastes have high lignin, cellulose and hemicellulose contents, it is possible to integrate a cogeneration system to the process. In this manner it is possible to supply some energetic requirements of the process with the generated electricity and at the same time obtain steam at different levels (high, medium and low pressure) for covering a fraction of the heat needed by the process. On the other hand, lignocellulosic biomass can also be used to obtain glucose by means of acid hydrolysis and use this sugar in different fermentative processes to obtain different biomolecules.

One of the biomolecules with high value is Gibberellic Acid (GA3). This compound has important applications due to its effective use in agriculture, nurseries, tissue culture, tea garden, etc (Ruchi *et al.*, 2005a). GA3 has the capacity of controlling many developmental plant processes such as the induction of hydrolytic enzymes activity during seed germination, stem elongation, induction of flowering, improvement of crop yield, overcoming dwarfism and retards leaves and fruit senescence among others.

In 2006, the volume of GA3 produced was 50 tonnes with its major uses in the grape industry (Thirumalai *et al.*, 2012). Typically, GA3 is produced by submerged fermentation using *Gibberella fujikuroi*, an ascomycetous fungus (Ruchi *et al.*, 2005a; Subhash *et al.*, 2005; Nhujak *et al.*, 2005). GA3 also has been produced using immobilized *Gibberella fujikuroi* mycelium in fluidized bioreactors reaching a production of three times greater than the reported submerged and solid fermentations (Escamilla *et al.*, 2000). Solid stage fermentation has been developed with *Gibberella fujikuroi* employing the water activity to increase the yield of the fermentation, reaching 4.8 g of GA3 per kg in dry basis (Corona *et al.*, 2005).

Glucose is the most common substrate used in the production of GA3 with which the mathematical models are developed (Ruchi *et al.*, 2005a, Ruchi *et al.*, 2005b). Different mathematical models have been used to describe the concentration profiles of all compounds involved in the fermentation. A non-structured model has been used to describe the behavior of glucose and nitrogen consumption in GA3 and bikaverin production (Chavez *et al.*, 2008).

However, more complex models have been used to predict the concentration profile behaviour during the fermentation with *Gibberella fujikuroi* in bioreactors, evaluating pH and initial C/N (Carbon/Nitrogen) ratio (Subhash *et al.*, 2005). Other models have been developed for solid state fermentations using *Gibberella fujikuroi* under limited nitrogen conditions, finding that the fungus does not assimilate nitrogen source and urea, directly (Gelmi *et al.*, 2002).

GA3 has also been produced using *Gibberella fujikuroi* cells immobilized on the surface of fibrous carriers with copolymers obtained by a radiation polymerization technique (Lu *et al.*, 1995). With this technique it was found that the fermentation time was not an important variable over the GA3 produced while the glucose concentration was a key parameter in GA3 production.

Separation of GA3 is complex due to other compounds produced in fermentation such as other Gibberellic acids (GA1, GA4, GA7, GA13) or secondary metabolites. GA3 is also unstable in the aqueous phase under fermentation conditions. In this sense, GA3 has been separated from fermentation broths using an emulsion liquid membrane (ELM) reaching yields of approximately 68 per cent if compounds such as SPAN 80, n-heptane, Aliquat 336 and water in oil emulsion made of KCl aqueous solution are used (Berrios *et al.*, 2010).

GA3 has been separated by extractive fermentation using a 65 per cent (v/v) of polyalkoxilate (Genapol 2822) and water mixture as solvent. With this technique approximately 400 hours are necessary with the extraction process beginning only at 130 hours (Hollmann *et al.*, 1995). Moreover, the amount of GA3 can be improved by 150 per cent without incurring in higher recovery costs (Hollmann *et al.*, 1990).

Isolation of GA3 also has been carried out based on acid base extraction of gibberellins from a water phase containing ammonium ions. This method allows the separation of GA3 with purity above 75 per cent, practically free of GA4, GA7, GA9, GA13 and GA3-isolactone (Rachev *et al.*, 1993).

Taking into account the high importance of GA3 and its complex production and separation processes, this work presents the GA3 production as an important part of a biorefinery from brown sugar cake bagasse (panela) as raw material in the Colombian context. Additionally, techno-economic and environmental analyses are shown to evaluate the state of the art of this method to produce GA3.

2. MATERIALS AND METHODS

2.1. Panela Sugarcane Biorefinery

The proposed biorefinery scheme from panela sugarcane is shown in Figure 1.2 in which different products can be obtained, beginning with those that belong to ensuring food security. Additionally, other products as biomolecules, biomaterials and biofuels can be obtained.

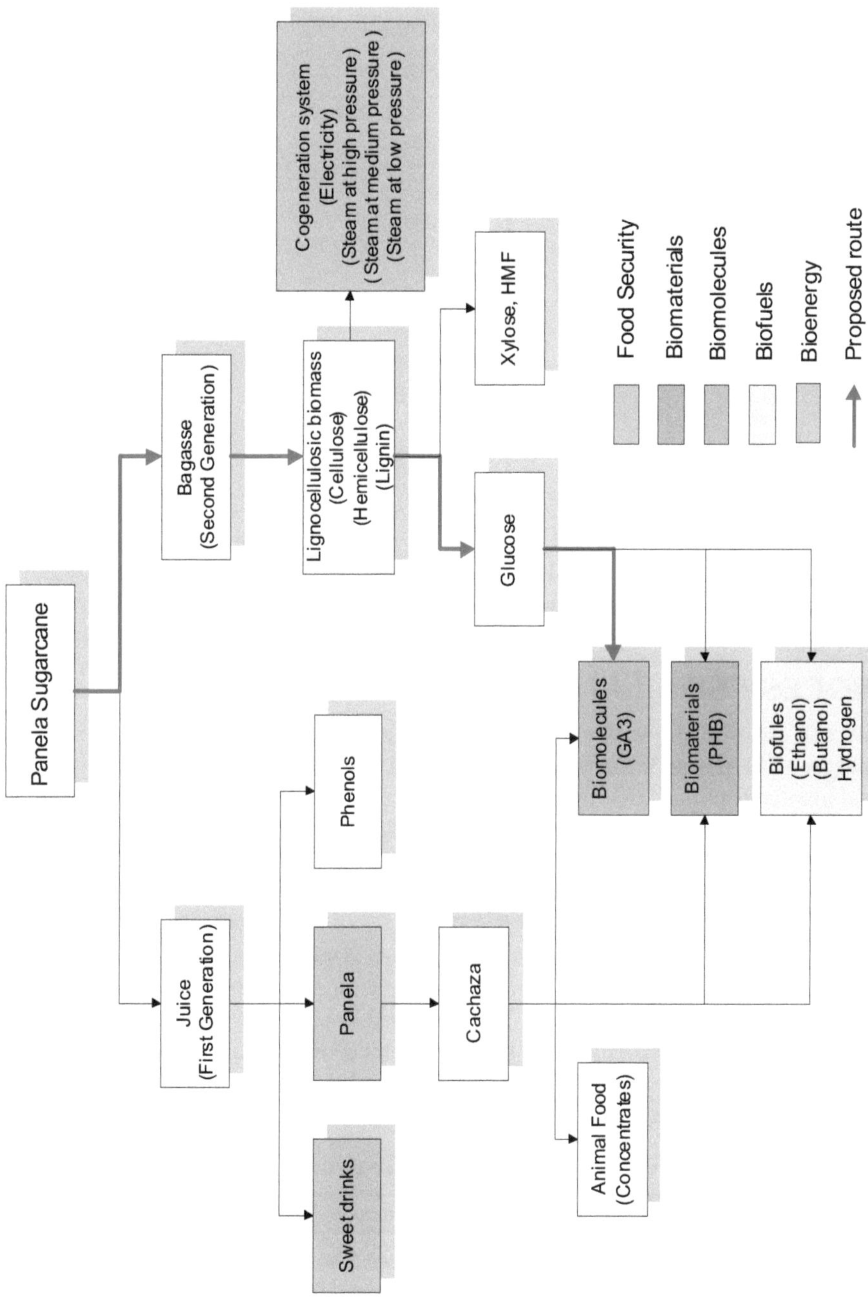

Figure 1.2: A Proposed Scheme for a Panela Sugarcane Biorefinery (Red lines means the route proposed in this work).

2.2. GA3 Fermentation Model

The most typical model used to describe the concentration behaviour during the fermentation is shown in the equations (1) to (4). With this model, it is possible to represent the concentration profiles of GA3, bikaverin, nitrogen and residual glucose (Ma. Del Carmen *et al.*, 2008).

$$\frac{dX}{dt} = kXe^{\mu t} \tag{1}$$

$$\frac{dS}{dt} = -\frac{1}{Y_{X/S}}\frac{dX}{dt} - m_S X \tag{2}$$

$$\frac{dN}{dt} = -\frac{1}{Y_{X/n}}\frac{dX}{dt} - m_n X \tag{3}$$

$$\frac{dP}{dt} = \alpha\frac{dX}{dt} + \beta X \tag{4}$$

Where X, S, N and P correspond to biomass, substrate, nitrogen and product concentrations respectively. μ, k, α; β, m_s, m_n, Yx/s and Yx/n are specific growth rate, kinetic parameter related to initial specific growth rate, Leudeking Piret constant, maintenance coefficient for substrate and nitrogen yield factor for substrate and nitrogen respectively.

3. PROCESS SIMULATION

Process simulation was carried out using Aspen Plus V7.1 (AspenTech: Cambridge, MA). Some of the physicochemical properties were obtained from the National Institute of Standards of Technology (NIST). The activity model used for the liquid phase was NRTL and Hayden O'Conell equation was employed for the vapour phase (NRTL-HOC).

3.1. Raw Material and Pretreatment

The lignocellulosic raw material used was panela sugarcane bagasse *(Saccharum officinarum L.)* remaining after panela production in Colombia. This residue represents 25 per cent of the total processed cane. This lignocellulosic material has high cellulose and hemicellulose content which can be transformed into sugars to be used in GA3 production by fermentation with *Gibberella fujikuroi*. Table 1.1 shows the composition of panela sugarcane bagasse as given by Aguilar (2011).

Table 1.1: Composition of Panela Sugarcane Bagasse.

Compound	*(per cent)*	*Compound*	*(per cent)*
Cellulose	29.02	Hemicellulose	16.82
Lignin	13.82	Acetate	2.17
Ash	2.54	Extracts	18.69
Water	16.94		

Figure 1.3 shows a scheme of the proposed process for the simulation of GA3 production from panela sugarcane bagasse. This process is composed by pretreatment, hydrolysis, fermentation and separation sections.

For producing GA3, the lignocellulosic material was firstly crushed to obtain particles below 45 mm, then a filtration was made to separate the solids (cellulose, hemicellulose and lignin) while the remaining water contains some phenolic compounds which can be used in other processes.

Acid hydrolysis was performed using H_2SO_4. In this step, different reactions can be present and some of them produce toxic compounds for the fermentation. The various bonds in cellulose, hemicellulose and lignin can be broken to form glucose, xylose, mannose, galactose and phenolic compounds (Villalobos *et al.*, 2010). Also, the sugars produced can form toxic compounds such as furfural, hydroxy-methylfurfural (HMF) and some acids such as formic and levulinic acid. Figure 1.4 shows the possible reactions of cellulose, hemicellulose and lignin in a lignocellulosic material.

The reactions denoted as (5) to (9) occur in an acid hydrolysis process of lignocellulosic materials as biomass in which cellulose ($C_6H_{10}O_5$) and hemicellulose ($C_5H_8O_4$) can produce glucose ($C_6H_{12}O_6$) and xylose ($C_5H_{10}O_5$). However, these sugars can produce at the same time hydroxymethylfurfural HMF ($C_6H_6O_3$), levulinic acid ($C_5H_8O_3$), formic acid (CH_2O_2) and furfural ($C_5H_4O_2$) (Wyman *et al.*, 2012; Girisuta *et al.*, 2007).

$$C_6H_{10}O_5 + H_2O \rightarrow C_6H_{12}O_6 \quad (5)$$

$$C_5H_8O_5 + H_2O \rightarrow C_5H_{10}O_5 \quad (6)$$

$$C_6H_{12}O_6 \rightarrow C_6H_6O_3 + H_2O \quad (7)$$

$$C_6H_6O_3 + 2H_2O \rightarrow C_5H_8O_3 + CH_2O_2 \quad (8)$$

$$C_5H_{10}O_5 \rightarrow C_5H_4O_2 + 3H_2O \quad (9)$$

After the hydrolysis process, detoxification was made using Ca $(OH)_2$ to separate HMF, lignin and $CaSO_4$.

3.2. Fermentation

Fermentation was carried out at 30°C using glucose as substrate and *Gibberella fujikuroi* as microorganism. The conditions of the fermentation were taken from the concentration profiles reported by (Escamilla *et al.*, 2000). From these profiles, the yield of GA3 was extracted (0.093 gr of GA3/gr of glucose).

In this fermentation process, a C/N (Glucose–C, NH_4Cl–N) ratio of 36.8 was used and a pH of 5 was necessary. The microorganism used was *Gibberella fujikuroi* strain CDBB H-984. KH_2PO_4 and $MgSO_4$ were used as nutrients (Escamilla *et al.*, 2000).

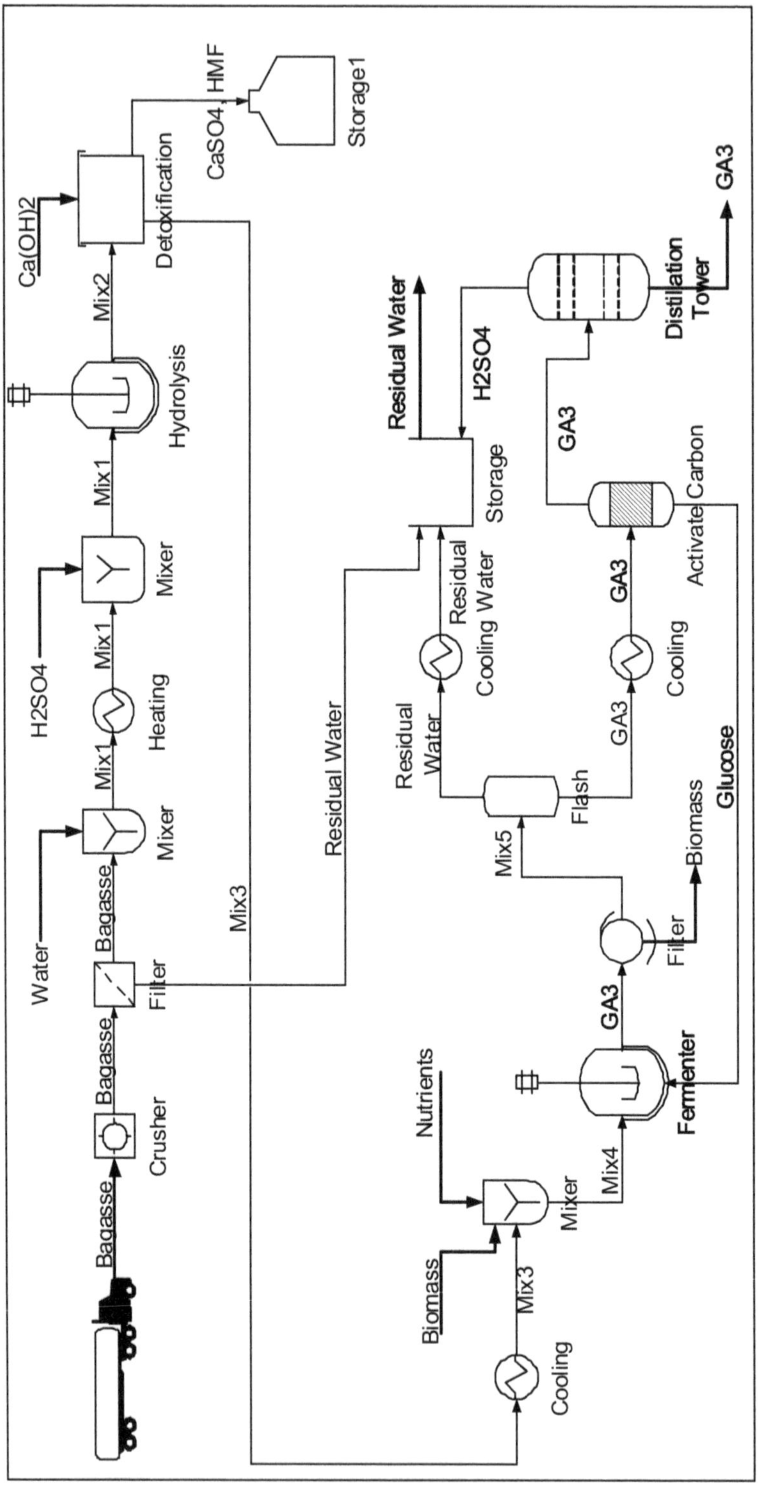

Figure 1.3: Scheme of the Proposed Process for the Simulation of GA3 Production.

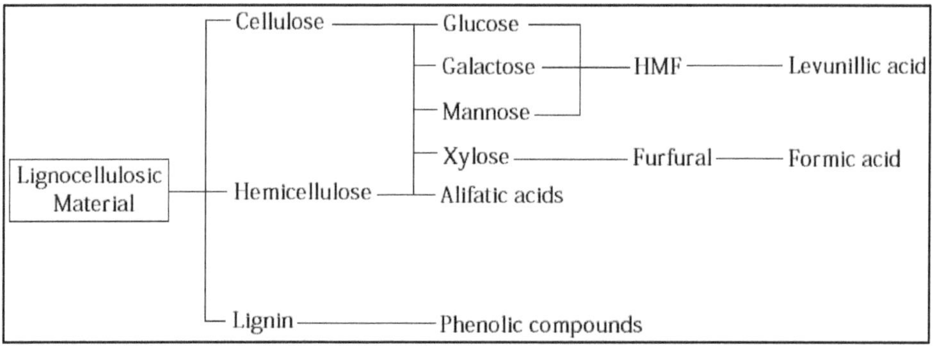

Figure 1.4: Diagram Illustrating Possible Reactions in an Acid Hydrolysis Process of Cellulose, Hemicellulose and Lignin in a Lignocellulosic Material.

3.3. Separation

The separation of GA3 was initiated with filtration of the fermentation broth to separate the biomass and the water was evaporated from the remaining liquid stream. After that, the liquid stream was sent to a filter using activated carbon (20 per cent, w/v) for removing the residual glucose (or other similar sugars) or protein impurities (Qiang *et al.*, 2010). The residual sugar (glucose) was recycled to the fermentation process while the separated GA3 was distilled into two streams, corresponding to a GA3 purified (99.1 per cent of purity) and diluted H_2SO_4 (20 per cent of purity).

4. RESULTS AND DISCUSSION

Table 1.2 shows the results obtained from the simulation. GA3 (26.76 kg) at 99.1 per cent of purity was obtained from the panela sugarcane bagasse (1 ton). From fermentation, 27.49 kg of GA3 was obtained. Gypsum with HMF traces and a residual water stream with 98 per cent (in mass fraction) were obtained as byproducts. According to the simulation and data used, the glucose pass conversion in the fermentation was 83.82 per cent while the total conversion was 97.35 per cent.

Table 1.2: Results to GA3 Production Simulated.

Stream	*Flow (Kg)*	*Stream*	*Flow (Kg)*
Bagasse (inlet)	1,000	Water (inlet)	30,000
H_2SO_4 (inlet)	600	Ca $(OH)_2$ (inlet)	66
NH_4Cl (inlet)	2.39	Residual water (outlet)	31,203
GA3 concentrated (outlet)	26.76	Gypsum (outlet)	415.12
Biomass (outlet)	26.08		

Taking into account that the fermentation is carried out in 190 hours (Escamilla *et al.*, 2000), according to the principal operations and the time required to complete them, Figure 1.5 shows the Gantt diagram with which the total time of the batch is calculated as 217.3 hours (222 hours approximately). In this order, the total batches per year (8000 hours) are 36.

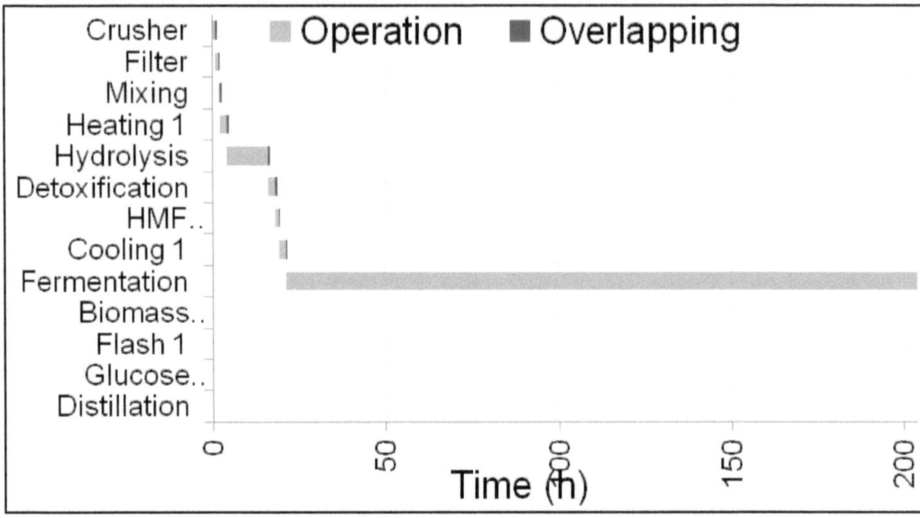

Figure 1.5: Gantt Diagram Illustrating the Major Operations and their Timing during the GA3 Production.

4.1. Economic Analysis

The economic analysis was made using the Aspen Process Economic Analyzer software. Labor, operational and utilities costs according to the laws in Colombia are shown in Table 1.3. Additionally, tax and interest rates were taken as 33 per cent and 17 per cent respectively. The total production costs considers total raw material cost, total utilities cost, operating labor cost, maintenance cost, operating charges, plant overhead and general and administrative cost. Figure 1.6 shows the distribution of the total costs to GA3 production.

Table 1.3: Operational Cost to Gibberellic Acid Production.

Item	*Cost (USD)*	*Item*	*Cost (USD)*
Operator (h)	2.14	Supervisor (h)	4.29
Electricity (KWh)	0.1	Potable water (m^3)	1.252
Fuel (ton)	26.81		

The total cost of GA3 production in the proposed process was 15,575 USD/kg while the sale cost of GA3 ranges between 34,400 USD/kg and 55,600 USD/kg (Chem 2012, Sigma 2012, Cole 2012, Lab 2012, Fisher 2012). In this way, the techno-ecomonical evaluation reveals that the production of GA3 is possible using panela sugarcane as raw material.

4.2. Environmental Impact

The environmental impact assessment was made using Waste Algorithm Reduction (WAR) developed by the U.S. Environmental Protection Agency (EPA) which evaluates eight environmental impact categories: Human Toxicity Potential

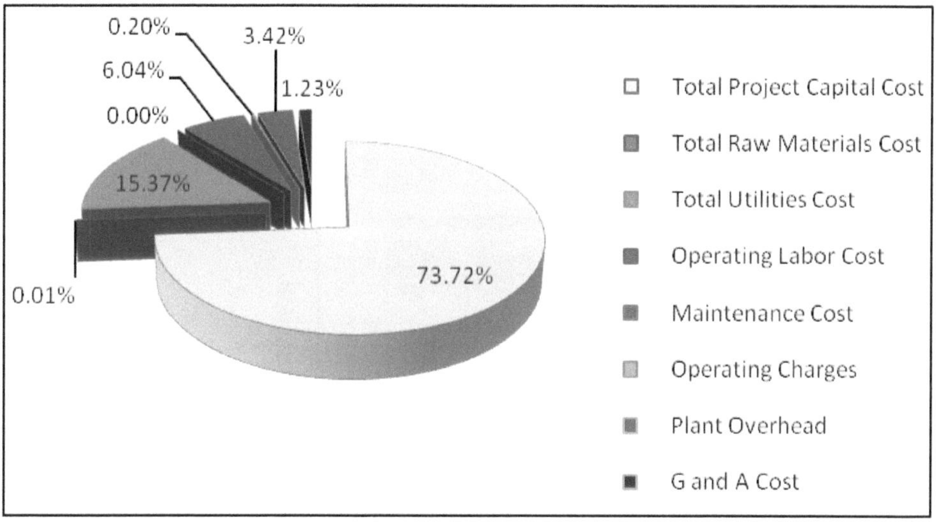

Figure 1.6: Diagram Showing the Distribution of the Costs to the GA3 Production.

by Ingestion (HTPI), Human tToxicity Potential by Dermal and Inhalation Exposure (HTPE), Terrestrial Toxicity Potential (TTP), Aquatic Toxicity Potential (ATP), Global Warming Potential (GWP), Ozone Depletion Potential (ODP), Photochemical Oxidation Potential (PCOP), and Acidification Potential (AP).

The Potential Environmental Impact (PEI) of the process is calculated per kilogram of product and the leaving impact from the process was evaluated. Figure 1.7 shows the leaving impact which demonstrates that the total PEI cannot be mitigated due to that fact that some substances can become toxic such as sulfuric acid, other acids, furfural and HMF. The categories GWP and AP are the more affected due to the sulfuric acid and other acids resulting from the process. In general, the leaving environmental impact is not reduced indicating that this process is not environmental friendly from the point of view of Acidification Potential (AP).

CONCLUSIONS

The economic analysis of the Gibberellic acid production from panela sugarcane shows that this process is viable obtaining competitive prices per kg of GA3.

This process provides Gibberellic acid with a purity of 99.1 per cent that can cover a wide market due to its widespread applications.

The environmental impact evaluation of this process demonstrates that it is not environmental friendly from the point of view of acidification potential due to the acids such as sulphuric acid which contributes to this category of impact.

This process demonstrated how sugarcane bagasse can be used a lignocellulosic residue from a typical industry in Colombia. The panela sugarcane bagasse provides the required glucose to produce GA3 in an economic way.

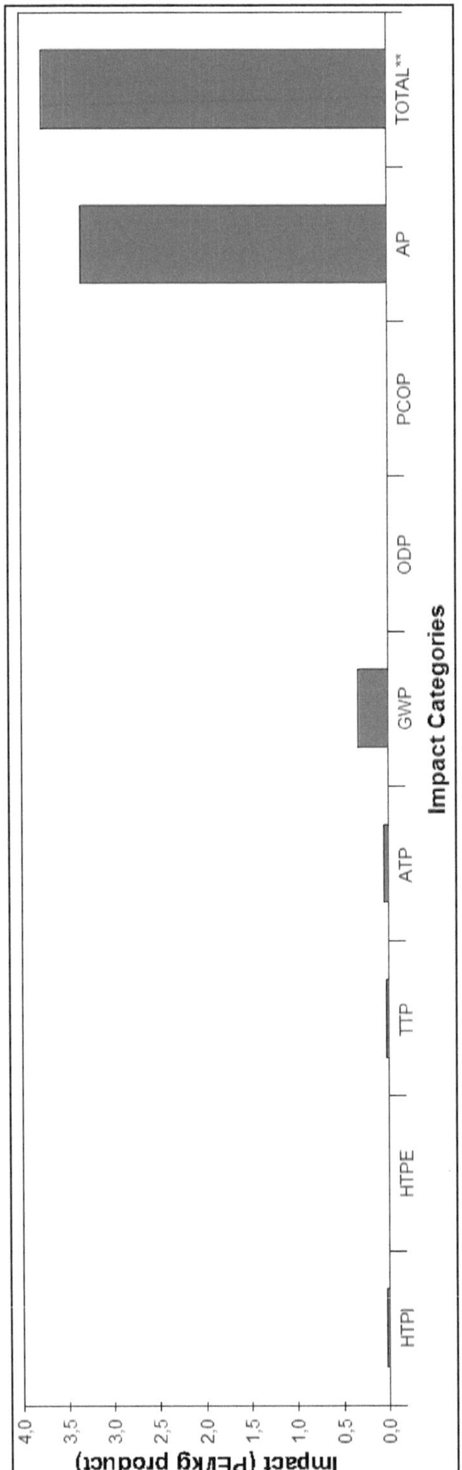

Figure 1.7: Diagram Illustrating the Value of Impact Categories in the GA3 Production.

REFERENCES

1. Aguilar Valencia Diana Maria. Ethanol production from panelera cane bagasse using a hybrid fermentation and pervaporation system. Universidad Nacional de Colombia, 2011. Available in www.bdigital.unal.edu.co/4443/1/8109501.2011.pdf.

2. Berrios Julio, Pyle D. Leo, Aroca German. Gibberellic acid extraction from aqueous solutions and fermentation broths by using emulsion liquid membranes. Journal of Membrane Science 348 (2010) 91 – 98.

3. Chavez Parga Ma. del Carmen, Gonzalez Ortega Omar, Negrete Rodriguez Ma. de la Luz X., Galindo Vallarino Irma, Gonzalez Alatorre Guillermo, Escamilla Silva Eleazar M. Kinetic of the gibberellic acid and bikaverin production in an airlift bioreactor. Process Biochemistry 43 (2008) 855 – 860.

4. Chem-Info. Gibberellic acid 99 per cent. Sell and Buy. http: //www.chem-info.com/trade/sell/Gibberellic-acid,-99-789111.html. (Accessed 13 Nov. 2012).

5. Cole Parmer. Gibberellic acid 99 per cent. Sell and Buy. http: //www.coleparmer.com/buy/product/39479-gibberellic-acid-99-5g-yo-8834793.html. (Accessed 13 Nov. 2012).

6. Corona Andres, Saez Doris, Agosin Eduardo. Effect of water activity on gibberellic acid production by *Gibberella fujikuroi* under solid-state fermentation conditions. Process Biochemistry 40 (2005) 2655 – 2658.

7. Escamilla S. Eleazar M., Dendooven Luc, Magan Ignacio P., Parra S., De la Torre M. Optimization of gibberellic acid production by immobilized *Gibberella fujikuroi* mycelium in fluidized bioreactors. Journal of Biotechnology 76 (2000) 147 – 155.

8. Fisher Scientific. Gibberellic acid 99 per cent. Sell and Buy. https: //www._shersci.ca/coupon.do?cid=138311. (Accessed 13 Nov. 2012).

9. Gelmi Claudio, Perez Correa Ricardo, Agosin Eduardo. Modelling *Gibberella fujikuroi* growth and GA3 production in solid state fermentation. Process Biochemistry 37 (2002) 1033 – 1040.

10. Girisuta B., Janssen L. P. B. M., Heeres H. J. Kinetic Study on the Acid-Catalyzed Hydrolysis of Cellulose to Levulinic Acid. Ind. Eng. Chem. Res. 2007, 46, 1696 – 1708.

11. Hollmann, D., Merrettig Bruns, U., Miiller, U., Onken, U. Secondary metabolites by extractive fermentation, p. 567–576. Separations for biotechnology, vol. 2. Elsevier Applied Science, London (1990).

12. Hollmann Dirk, Switalski Jiirn, Geipel Sven, Onken Ulfert. Extractive Fermentation of Gibberellic Acid by *Gibberella fujikuroi*. Journal of Fermentation and Bioenoineering. Vol. 79, No. 6, 594–600. 1995.

13. Lab Life. Gibberellic acid 99 per cent. Sell and Buy. http: //www.lablife.org/p?a=productsshowid=48222lastquery=vendor per cent 3DFisher per cent 2BScienti_c per cent 26tproductsorderdesc per cent 3Dfalse per cent

26tproductsorder per cent 3Dname per cent 26tproductsstart per cent 3D135720. (Accessed 13 Nov. 2012).

14. Lu Z. X., Xie Z. C., Kumakurab M. Production of Gibberellic Acid in *Gibberella fujikuroi* Adhered onto Polymeric Fibrous Carriers. Process Biochemistry, Vol. 30. No. 7. pp. 661–665, 1995.
15. Ma. del Carmen Chavez-Parga, Omar Gonzalez-Ortega, Ma. de la Luz X. Negrete-Rodriguez, Irma Galindo Vallarino, Guillermo Gonzalez Alatorre, Eleazar M. Escamilla-Silva Kinetic of the gibberellic acid and bikaverin production in an airlift bioreactor. Process Biochemistry 43 (2008) 855–860.
16. Ministerio de Agricultura y desarrollo Rural. Anuario Estadístico del Sector Agropecuario y Pesquero 2010. Bogota Colombia. ISBN 978-958-97128-8-7.
17. Moncada Jonathan, Mahmoud M. El-Halwagi, Cardona Carlos A. Techno-economic analysis for a sugarcane biorefinery: Colombian case. Bioresource Technology Vol. 135, May 2013, Pages 533–543 (2012).
18. Nhujak Thumnoon, Srisa Art Monpichar, Kanyarat Kalampakorn, Tolieng Vasana, Petsom Amorn. Determination of Gibberellic Acid in Fermentation Broth and Commercial Products by Micellar Electrokinetic Chromatography. J. Agric. Food Chem. 2005, 53, 1884 – 1889.
19. Qiang Li, Dan Wanga, Yong Wub, Wangliang Li, Yunjian Zhang, Jianmin Xing, Zhiguo Su. One step recovery of succinic acid from fermentation broths by crystallization. Separation and Purification Technology 72 (2010) 294 – 300.
20. Rachev R. CH., Pavlova Rousesva R., Bojkova S. V., Gancheva V. K. Isolation of gibberellic acid produced by *Fusarium moniliforme*. Journal of Natural Products Vol. 56, No. 7, pp. 1168–1170, July 1993.
21. Ruchi Shukla, Subhash Chand, Ashok Kumar Srivastava. Improvement of gibberellic acid production using a model based fed-batch cultivation of Gibberella fujikuroi. Process Biochemistry 40 (2005a) 2045 – 2050.
22. Ruchi Shukla, Subhash Chand, Ashok K. Srivastava. Batch kinetics and modeling of gibberellic acid production by *Gibberella fujikuroi*. Enzyme and Microbial Technology 36 (2005b) 492 – 497.
23. Sigma Aldrich. Gibberellic acid 99 per cent. Sell and Buy. http: // www.sigmaaldrich.com/catalog/product/sigma/g7645?lang=enregion=CO. (Accessed 13 Nov. 2012).
24. Stoeglehner, G., Narodoslawsky, M., 2009. How sustainable are biofuels? Answers and further questions arising from an ecological footprint perspective. Bioresour. Technol. 100 (16), 3825–3830.
25. Subhash Chand, Ruchi Shukla, Ashok K. Srivastava. Batch kinetics and modeling of gibberellic acid production by *Gibberella fujikuroi*. Enzyme and Microbial Technology 36 (2005) 492 – 497.
26. Tarazona Parra German Alberto. Manejo fitosanitario del Cultivo de la Ca a Panelera. Instituto Colombiano de Agricultura ICA. 2011. Available in http: // es.scribd.com/doc/125487865/Cartilla-Cana-ICA-Final. Accessed 20 Nov 2012.

27. Thirumalai Anusha P. Gomoto Ryan. Gibberellic acid production by solid state fermentation using mixed substrate coffee huks and cassava bagasse. http: // www.slideshare.net/anush88/gibberellic-acid-production (Accessed 6 Jan. 2013).

28. Villalobos C. Victoria A. Comparacion de Pretratamientos en Residuos Forestales para la Produccion de Bioetanol de Segunda Generacion: Hidrolisis Acida y Liquidos Ionicos. Departamento de Ingenieria Quimica y Biotecnologia. Universidad de Chile. 2010.

29. Wyman Charles E., Decker Stephen R., Himmel Michael E., Brady John W., Skopec Catherine E., Viikari Liisa. Hydrolysis of Cellulose and Hemicellulose. Polysaccharides, Structural diversity and functional versatility 1 (2005) 1023 – 1062.

Chapter 2

The Role of Industrial Biotechnology for the Economic Growth of Ethiopia

*Teshome Sahilemariam Ashagre**

Ministry of Science and Technology,
Addis Ababa, Ethiopia

ABSTRACT

Developing countries like Ethiopia have not benefited much from modern use of biotechnology. In many cases they tend to strongly stick to traditional ways of agricultural production and old industrial processes. Besides low level of production and productivity, which emanates from such historical practices, remains unsolved due to lack of technological accumulation capability.

The lag in agricultural productivity, environmental degradation and low levels of industrial development has all proved incompatible with the growing needs of the ever-increasing population. Such challenges should not be left aside if we need to attain better standards of living. With the current and future challenges and trends, it becomes inevitable to seek for better ways of tackling these problems. Developing new technologies or adapting or utilizing the already developed biotechnologies can solve these problems in an efficient and effective manner.

Bearing this fact in mind, the Ministry of Science and Technology of Ethiopia has taken the responsibility for developing means and mechanisms of coordinating the scattered activities, in order to, mobilize and concert the minimal available resources and there by avoid unnecessary duplications of efforts to improve efficient utilization of the limited experts in the area of bio -technology. In addition, the Ministry will implement the policy directives of the government and monitor and regulate biotechnology and bio- safety issues and

* E-mail: teshomesmariam@yahoo.com

activities in the country, availing the necessary budget and opportunities for capacity building pertinent to biotechnology.

In this regard, the National Science, Technology and Innovation Policy of Ethiopia, which was issued in 2012, identified biotechnology as one of the priority programs of the country. In the green paper of the document it is clearly stipulated that the application of biotechnology in the field of agriculture and industry play a paramount role in enhancing productivity and by and large contribute for the economic development of Ethiopia.

Bioconversion, detoxification, safe waste treatment and intended conversion of waste into valuable products are possible through biotechnological means. Improved industrial processing and use of various enzymes, microorganisms and their components would give an advantage in saving foreign exchange. Besides, the use of industrial biotechnology in industries contributes in having diversified products with prolonged shelf life to meet consumer demands. All of these should be done wisely in a coherent and sustainable manner.

Keywords: *Biotechnology, Technology accumulation capability, Enzymes, Bioconversion, Biodiesel.*

1. INTRODUCTION

Using industrial biotechnology to develop capacity in the leather, textile, pulp and paper, detergent, and starch industries is highly essential in order to become one of the middle income countries within 10 years time. Just because recent developments in industrial biotechnology, *i.e.* the use of enzymes or microorganisms for industrial processes, has offered a viable option to decrease costs, enhance competitiveness and avoid environmental pollution. Besides, widespread use of enzymes in industrial processes, in addition to lowering the level of pollution could improve product quality and or process efficiency. Thus, availability of enzymes locally with affordable price and with expert support on their use is expected to have significant contribution in the economic growth.

For products where enzymes are already in use (such as bating agents in the leather industry), the new enzymes will be compared with commercial enzymes and the best will be selected and promoted for use in the country.For processes where enzymes are not used (usually for reason of cost), factories will be encouraged to transfer the technology and adopt them or promote foreign investors with the knowledge and capability to do the job in the country.

Under the Plan for Accelerated and Sustained Development to End Poverty (PASDEP), implemented from 2005/06 to 2009/10, Ethiopia achieved rapid economic growth and laid a foundation for future growth by making substantial investments in infrastructure and human capital. Based on its experience with implementation of PASDEP, the government has formulated the next five year plan, the Growth and Transformation Plan (GTP), for 2010/11–2014/15. The GTP is envisaged to sustain rapid and broad based economic growth and contribute to Ethiopia's goal of becoming a middle-income economy by 2020–2023. Economic growth and other development targets set in the GTP are even higher than those in PASDEP and earlier plans. Achieving these targets, however, will require very large productivity growth and huge amounts of financial resources are anticipated to be secured from increased domestic saving mobilization, foreign direct investment, and foreign borrowing.

Biotechnology is one of the technologies that has a potential to tackle the existing and emerging problems and is considered a priority area for the implementation of the Growth and Transformation Plan of the country. Biotechnology is an umbrella term that covers abroad spectrum of scientific tools and techniques, ranging from traditional uses of living organisms such as yeast in bread or bacteria in yoghurt to more advanced techniques such as plant tissue culture, genetic transformation, recombinant DNA, cell fusion, embryo manipulation, etc. Biotechnology uses living organisms, or part of living organisms, to make new products or provide new methods of production. Biopesticides, bio-fertilizers, bio fuels, bioremediation etc., are the contribution of modern biotechnology keeping environment eco friendly and sustainable.

Today in Ethiopia many type of enzymes, additives, colorants de colorants, dyes,hardening and softening agents utilized in tanneries, plastic, paper and pulp, sugar, food beverage alcohol, acid, etc. manufacturing industries are all imported expending substantial amount of foreign currency. On the other hand, there are plenty of by-products not utilized properly. However, opportunities to develop these imported items locally and also to scale up and improve industrial production and productivity both in quality and product diversity are plenty. The diverse microbial strains indigenous to country could be exploited to this effect and the tremendous benefits to follow should encourage us to develop national capability in biotechnology in order to address our current and future needs.

3. STATUS OF INDUSTRIAL BIOTECHNOLOGY IN ETHIOPIA

Ethiopia has adopted a national economic policy that focuses mainly on implementing the Agricultural Development Led Industrialization (ADLI). The objectives of ADLI include promotion of economic efficiency and growth; development of domestic technological capacities and capabilities for the promotion and development of small and intermediate (and capital goods) industries.

One of the key indicators of the socioeconomic development and technological progress of a country is the contribution of the industrial sector to the economy. Instead, science and technology is identified as the major driving force behind industrialization. The role of industry in the Ethiopian economy is envisaged to grow rapidly. Biotechnology is identified as the major priority technology area to be vigorously pursued to realize agricultural development led industrialization of Ethiopia.

On the basis of Ethiopia's economic development policy, all agricultural products and by products have to find their way as industrial raw materials. Agro industries from cottage to higher levels could therefore be developed. For all requirements for improved and optimum productivity, production and product diversity therefore innovative and novel procedures and catalysts, such as enzymes are essential. Enzymes of wide specificity, utmost efficiency and best performance could be developed employing biotechnology as a tool. They could serve improved production and packaging to an excellent level where products could also be exported. Exports usually need to be of high quality to meet international requirements. Poor products could also be improved and enhanced in this way. For instance, good quality health foods, coffee, tea, vanilla, fruits, vegetables, meat, dairy and dairy products of prolonged shelf life could be produced by employing safe biotechnological means. This alternative therefore adds value to the price of these goods in the global market. Novel industrial products for health, agricultural, and other commercial utilities could thus be developed and utilized using such a technology reducing production cost and time while enhancing efficiency and quality.

3.1. Addis Ababa University Department of Biology

The department has been conducting research for almost 3 decades. More than 20 species of aerobic microorganisms, which perform the bioconversion, have already been isolated and their biochemical, biological and cultural characteristics studied. Besides this a biopolymer project has been going on quite for a long time. The major objective of this, project was to isolate different types of fungi and bacteria that can degrade lignocellulosics whose main polymers are cellulose, hemicelluloses, pectin, xylans, lignin and other minor organic molecules.

The department has isolated the following cellulase for various industrial applications:

- ✰ Cellululase (for the removal of lignocellulosic waste in cotton processing, production of SCP, alchol and organic acids)
- ✰ Proteases (for production of animal feed from feather, additives for detergents, removl of hairs from leather)
- ✰ Xylanases (for bleaching of kraft pulp in paper industries, hydrolysis of zylan from cellulosic wastes)
- ✰ Amylase (for the degradation of starch for deferent industrial uses)

Moreover, Addis Ababa University has established the Department of Biotechnology in 2006 in the Faculty of Natural science. The department has post graduate program and particularly giving emphasis on industrial biotechnology and conducting research in enzyme and microbial technology and biofuel.

3.2. Pulp and Paper

Pulp and paper production has three major types: pulping, bleaching and paper production. However, in Ethiopian process of the pulp and paper industry includes bleaching, chemical recovery and by product recovery. Until recently, the use of enzymes in this industry was not considered. However there are interesting possibilities in the pulp and paper industry. Two example applications that have been made possible by new enzyme development are enzymatic deinking of waste paper and bleach boosting.

3.3. Food Industries

3.3.1. Kaliti Food Share Company

Kaliti Food Share Company is one of the oldest food processing enterprises mainly producing wheat flour, bread, biscuits and pasta.

Yeast is one of the major biotechnological inputs in the production of the bakery products. Baker's yeast *(Saccharomyces cerevisiae)* utilizes sugars for its energy requirement during the fermentation process and in doing so produces carbon dioxide and alcohol as by-products. It is this property that makes this yeast and lactic acid bacteria, are widely used as an aerating agents to enhances flavor, which is one of the important qualities in bakeries.In addition to this other inputs, such as bread quality improver, that facilitates the dough to raise the volume of the bread, produce good quality crumb and enhance the keeping properties of the end product are also imported. There is a research effort to apply the enzyme amylase for future product diversification.

3.3.2. Fafa Food Share Company

Fafa and Cerifam, (baby foods) are some of the products produced by the factory of the Share company. Cerifam is a precooked baby food similar to the imported product Cerilac. Amylase is applied in the processing of Cerifam, and is capable of converting starch into simple sugars. In this case the product develops better flavor and reduces the bulk density of this specific product, which results in a low consistency and a high calorie density supplementary food.

3.3.3. Dairy Development Enterprise

According to available information, the milk yield per animal (cow) in Ethiopia is very low and this has led to high cost of milk besides hampering the development of the dairy industry. Major constraints observed were lack of a research and development scheme as well as skilled manpower for product diversification, less developed infrastructure for milk collection and storage, and shortage in the supply of milk.

An active starter culture, in Gouda cheese processing, performs three important functions: 1) acid production, 2) desired, characteristic flavour development, and 3) prevention of the growth of undesirable microorganisms that may survive heat treatments (pasteurization) or contaminate the product.

3.4. Meat Industry

Presently Elfora Agro-industries PLC is the major livestock and poultry products' processor and producer in the country. It produces beef, edible offal, chicken, eggs, canned corned beef, beef in jelly, meat, vegetable sauces, and others for local and foreign markets. It was reported that no biotechnological inputs and processes are used except chemical preservatives, such as, monosodium glutamate and pectic carbohydrates are utilized for flavor development, as enhancer, and for gel formation, respectively.

3.5. Merti Fruits and Vegetable Processing Factory

The factory has imported pectic enzymes for trial purpose in clarification of juices. Pectic enzymes are used to facilitate processing of juice extraction and to aid in the separation of the flocculent precipitate by sedimentation, filtration, or centrifugation. The need for enzymatic treatment varies with the type of fruit and associated difficulties during production.

3.6. Meta-Abo Brewing

The beverage industries in Ethiopia, including alcohol production schemes, breweries and wineries use yeast (*Saccharomyces* spp.) and enzymes to breakdown starch into smaller molecules that can be converted into alcohol and carbon-dioxide.

In fact, the modern breweries use enzymes instead of malt to breakdown starch materials into fermentable sugars. Enzymes present in malt and in adjuncts (maize or rice) degrade the starch and protein from the malt itself giving rise to simple sugars, amino acids, and short chain peptides that can be used by the yeast for the production of alcohol, carbon dioxide, favourites, and new yeast cells.

The enzymes alpha-amylase and beta-amylase are commonly used in brewing and are highly specific as they act only on one substance and affect only one type of chemical reaction. In addition, hexamethylene tetraamine is used to enhance the fermentation process.

The yeast used by the brewing industry is *Saccharomyces cerevisae*. This is imported in dry powder form and cultured for further use. The yeast treatment, which involves yeast propagation (production of new yeast), pitching of yeast to wort, storage of production yeast and discharge of surplus and spent yeast, is done in the brewing factories.

3.7. Addis Ababa Abattoir's Bio fertilizer Project

Bio fertilizers are cultures of microorganisms, which benefit plants by providing nitrogen or phosphorus or rapidly mineralize organic materials. The Addis Ababa Abattoir implemented a project to produce natural organic fertilizer from bones (source of phosphorus, P), horns and hooves (source of nitrogen, N). The project has the following objectives: cleaning up the bad odor produced by the accumulation of waste materials from the abattoir and conversion of waste materials into a useful product, *i.e.* organic fertilizer using different strains of bacteria. The function of the bacteria is to convert the insoluble phosphorous into P_2O_5, a soluble form. However, since the available P in the organic fertilizer is less as compared to the commercially available DAP, three times the dose of the inorganic fertilizer should be applied. Three types of products with different contents of P and N are produced.

3.8. Bio-fuel

In order to ensure that the country's development and national fuel security, it is important to increase fuel utilization and substituting the demand by locally produced fuels such as bio-fuel. The country has issued the national bio fuel strategy.This document "The Ethiopian Bio fuel Development and Utilization Strategy " is targeted for supply of fuels from locally produced bio fuel and the objective of the strategy is to ensure the production of bio fuel without affecting food self sufficiency, import substitution and improve balance of payment. The two most important biofuels are bio ethanol and biodiesel.

3.8.1. Bio-ethanol

Ethiopia has three sugar industries which are run and administered by Sugar Corporation. Beyond producing sugar these industries are also producing ethanol for the domestic market. Currently the country has started to blend ethanol (5 per cent) with gasoline. The corporation began to install nine more sugar industries throughout the country to satisfy the domestic need and further export to some neighboring countries.

3.8.2. Bio-diesel

Although production of bio-diesel is not yet started, various types of plant species which can be used for producing bio-diesel grow in the country. The major crops for biodiesel feedstock are Jatropha *curcas*, castor crop and palm tree. Favorable air condition and suitable soil type for bio-diesel development is available. Jatropha, which is a very important feed-stock for bio-diesel grows in many parts of the country and used as a hedge and medicinal plant. The Jatropha plant is growing in different areas of Ethiopia, mainly in dry areas and also it grows at mid and high altitudes. In Ethiopia *Jatropha curcas* may be produced at cheaper cost than other countries. Another plant which grows in many parts of Ethiopia and important feed-stock for producing bio-diesel is castor oil.

4. CONCLUSION

Biotechnology development in Ethiopia is still at its infancy. Most of the work revolves around classical biotechnology involving traditional liquors, selection of plants, animals and microorganisms for different purposes. Modern biotechnology involving recombinant DNA technology in the production of GMOs is not adopted yet. Even though, Biotechnology has been identified as one of the priority areas of the Government Industrial Technological capability building and should be undertaken in a prioritized, coordinated and focused manner to align the activities with the national development objectives and to efficiently use the limited resources. The experiences of successful countries also show that they developed priority programs in the areas where they were convinced that they could bring break through. The priority programs in fact differ from country to country, depending on the level of the economic development and the need of the country. Based on the immediate and near future needs of Ethiopia, industrial and agricultural biotechnology has an enormous impact for the country development.

5. ABBREVIATION

ADLI: Agriculture Development Led Industrialization

DNA: Deoxyribonucleic acid

GMO: Genetically modified Organism

GTP: Growth and Transformation Plan

PASDEP: Plan for Accelerated and Sustained Development to End Poverty

REFERENCES

1. Science and technology Policy of Ethiopia (2011)
2. Industrial Biotechnology and Climate Change, opportunities and challenges (2011), p. 8

3. Convention on biological diversity united nations (1992),p.3
4. Bangladesh National Biotechnology Policy (2011),final draft
5. The Ethiopian Biofuel Development and Utilization Strategy *(2007)*
6. National Biotechnology policy and Strategy (volume 1), draft document.
7. Engida Ermias, Tamru Seneshaw, Ethiopia's Growth and Transformation Plan: A Computable General Equilibrium Analysis of Alternative Financing Options (2011), IFPRI-ADDIS ABABA

Chapter 3

Binding of Serum Albumins with Nanoparticles: A Short Review

*S. Naveenraj and S. Anandan**

Nanomaterials and Solar Energy Conversion Lab, Department of Chemistry, National Institute of Technology, Tiruchirappalli – 620 015

ABSTRACT

In the past decade, tremendous attention has been focused on understanding the biomolecule-nanoparticle interactions owing to their significance in the field of bionanotechnology. Among the various techniques available, the optical technique become the most appropriate to study their interactions. In this review, we provide a snapshot range of activities which are emphasized for their key research activity, the bioconjugates, formed from the biomolecule-nanoparticle interactions, highlight the similar sizes of their nanoparticle and biomolecular building blocks and show how the combination can result in tightly controlled assemblies that could have quite interesting biological, electronic, and plasmonic properties.

Keywords: *Nanoparticles, Serum albumins, Binding interaction, Fluorescence quenching.*

1. Introduction

In the recent years, the emerging field of bionanotechnology has undergone a dramatic evolution due to its unique approach in probing and controlling a wide variety of biological and medical processes at nanometer scale (Paciotti *et al.*, 2006). Due to the large surface-to-volume ratio, the size controlled nanoparticles are amenable to bioconjugation with biomolecules which makes it suitable for various innovative

*E-mail: sanand@nitt.edu; sanand99@yahoo.com

biomedical applications (diagnostic and therapy) (Luo and Stutzenburger, 2008). Hence understanding the interactions between nanoparticles and biomolecules becomes more significant.

Although many methods are available to study the nanoparticles' interaction, optical techniques play a vital role due to its sensitiveness, rapidness, abundant theoretical foundations, selectiveness and relative ease (Li *et al.*, 2005; Gao *et al.*, 2004) over the conventional approaches such as affinity and size exclusion chromatography, high-performance liquid chromatography, capillary electrophoresis, equilibrium dialysis, ultrafiltration and ultracentrifugation (Gao *et al.*, 2004; Bian *et al.*, 2004). These methods suffer from lack of sensitivity, long analysis time or both and use of biomolecule concentration far in excess (Kandagal *et al.*, 2006). From the measurements and analyses of the fluorescence emission spectra, the fluorescence lifetime, fluorescence polarization, etc., an incalculable amount of information can be acquired about the structural fluctuations and the microenvironment changes surrounding the fluorophore in the protein. Hence, fluorescence spectroscopy plays a pivotal role in the investigation of interactions between the nanoparticle and receptor biomolecules since it allows non-intrusive substances in low concentration under physiological conditions (due to the quenching measurement of biomolecule fluorescence; fluorescence is defined as the emission of radiation as a molecule returns to its ground state from an excited electronic state) (Wang *et al.*, 2007). This quenching measurement reveals the accessibility of quenchers to protein's fluorophore groups which in turn helps us to understand the binding mechanisms and the nature of the binding phenomenon (Barbero *et al.*, 2009). As stated by Silva (2004), fluorescence quenching, refers to any process that decreases the fluorescence intensity of a sample, may result from variety of processes such as excited state reactions, molecular rearrangements, energy transfers, ground-state complex formation (static quenching) and collisional processes (dynamic collision).

Here we review some of the recent literature on biomolecule–nanoparticle interactions using the optical techniques in light of the fact that the nanoparticles have enormous therapeutic potential as it binds with serum albumins in their in-vivo studies. The review is organized as follows. A description of (i) Serum Albumins such as Human Serum Albumin (HSA) and Bovine Serum Albumin (BSA); and (ii) the biological applications of metal nanoparticles, semiconductor nanoparticles and metal doped semiconductor nanoparticles and their binding capability towards biomolecules is given.

2. SERUM ALBUMINS (HSA AND BSA)

Serum Albumins such as HSA and BSA are the most abundant proteins in the systemic circulation comprising 52- 60 per cent in plasma. It is synthesized by the liver and possesses a half-life in circulation of about 19 days. It consists of amino acid chains forming a single polypeptide with well-known sequence, which contains three homologous α-helices domains (I-III) that assembles to form a heart shaped molecule (Lemiesz *et al.*, 1999). Each domain contains 10 helices and is divided into anti-parallel six-helix and four domains (A and B) extensively cross-linked by disulfide bridges. Both HSA and BSA are 66kDa globular protein molecule of manifold functions and applications. They are also capable of binding reversibly with a large variety of endogeneous and exogeneous ligands even though their principal function is to transport metabolites such as nutrients, hormones, and fatty acids (Klajnert and Bryszewska, 2002; Zhao *et al.*, 2005). Apart from an important role in maintaining colloidal osmotic pressure in blood, they can play a dominant role in drug disposition and efficacy since it increases the apparent solubility of hydrophobic drugs in plasma (Maiti *et al.*, 2006). Crystal structure analyses have revealed that HSA contains 585 amino acid residues with only one tryptophan (Trp), which is responsible for their fluorescence, located at position 214 along the chain whereas BSA contains 582 amino acid residues with two tryptophans located in positions 134 and 212. Trp-212 is in chemical microenvironment similar to that Trp-214 in HSA and Trp-134 is located at the surface of the molecule (Viallet *et al.*, 2000). The absorption peak maximum of serum albumins is around 280 nm. The intrinsic fluorescence of serum albumins appears at 340 nm when excited at 280 nm which is originating from tryptophan (Trp), tyrosine (Tyr), and phenylalanine (Phe) residues. Intrinsic fluorescence characteristics are very sensitive to its microenvironment. Actually, the intrinsic fluorescence of serum albumin were mainly contributed by the Trp residue alone due to the low quantum yield of Phe residue and the total quenching of Tyr residue (when it is self-ionized or nearby an amino group, carboxylic acid, or trp). It would be ultimately weakened if there is a slight change of the local surroundings of serum albumins, such as conformational transition, biomolecular binding, and denaturation (Gao *et al.*, 2005).

3. BINDING CAPABILITY OF METAL NANOPARTICLES WITH BIOMOLECULES.

Gold nanoparticles hold a great promise for biology and medicine due to their interesting size tunable optical properties. They are one of the noble metal plasmon-resonant nanoparticles where the production of an optical signal for the bright intense colors of solutions occurs upon the excitation of collective coherent oscillations of free electrons at the metals surface (Heltzel *et al.*, 2008; Schrand *et al.*, 2008). Their biocompatibility and stability make it an excellent candidature intended as unique versatile highly efficient drug delivery vectors with no noticeable toxicity for various biomedical applications such as in-vivo photodynamic cancer therapy (Cheng *et al.*, 2008), medical diagnostic tool for the sensitive and specific biodetection of HIV-1 in plasma (Lee *et al.*, 2004), cell imaging tool due to its sensitive detection of physiological changes of Adenosine triphosphate (ATP) concentrations in live cells (Zheng *et al.*, 2009) and heterodyne high sensitive detection tool to distinguish between various kinds of virus types (Mitra *et al.*, 2010). Simple conjugation of gold nanoparticles onto therapeutically inactive monovalent small organic molecules converts them into highly active drugs of small molecule coated gold nanoparticles. This highly active drug effectively inhibits HIV-1 fusion to human T cells (Bowman *et al.*, 2008).

Vast applications of gold nanoparticles make its interaction with serum albumins a vital one. The binding of serum albumins with gold nanoparticles synthesized using $NaBH_4$ reduction method and sonochemical reduction method were investigated using optical techniques by Gao *et al.* (2005) and Naveenraj *et al.* (2010) respectively.

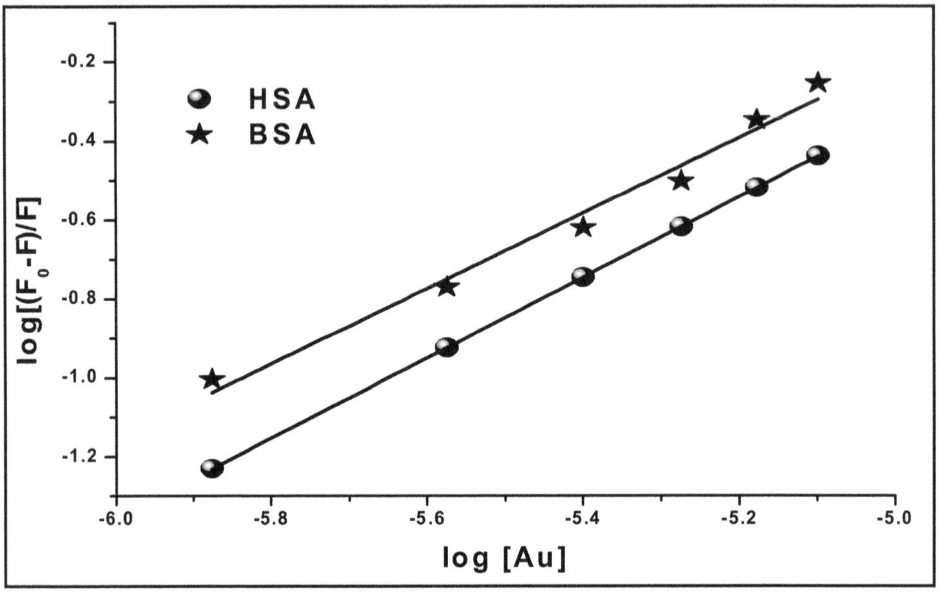

Figure 3.1: Modified Stern-Volmer Plot for Serum Albumins in the Presence of Sonochemically Synthesized Gold Nanoparticles. (From ref. Naveenraj *et al.*, 2010).

The effect of these gold nanoparticles, synthesized by different methods, on the fluorescence spectra of serum albumins showed gradual decrease in the fluorescence intensity of serum albumins without changing their emission maximum and shape of the band indicates the formation of non-fluorescent ground state complexes (static quenching mechanism). The same fluorescence quenching trend was observed for the binding of gold nanospheres and gold nanorods with BSA in the study conducted by Iosin *et al.* (2009). The binding constant of sonochemically synthesized gold nanoparticles with HSA deduced from the modified Stern-Volmer plot (Figure 3.1) was found to be about 1.5 times greater than that of BSA. This indicated that the affinity of HSA was more than that of BSA towards gold nanoparticles synthesized by sonochemical reduction whereas in the case of gold nanoparticles synthesized by $NaBH_4$ reduction method, BSA showed more affinity than that of HSA. This difference in binding affinity can be attributed to the fact that sonochemically synthesized nanoparticles have a high surface area and high crystalline structure which induces a huge binding interaction with biomolecules and also causes rapid transfer of drugs to the tissues. In addition to this, the sonochemically synthesized nanoparticles were similar in size and shape which was evident from its high resolution transmission electron micrograph illustrated in Figure 3.2a and Atomic Force Micrograph illustrated in Figure 3.2b.

In the size comparative study conducted by Pramanik *et al.* (2008), they use gold nanoparticles with diameters of 8, 10, 16, 25, 34, 41, 47, 55 and 70 nm. These were synthesized just by varying the [Au]/citrate ratio. The Stern- Volmer constant, K_{SV}, increased with decrease in the size of gold nanoparticles (Figure 3.3) and this suggests

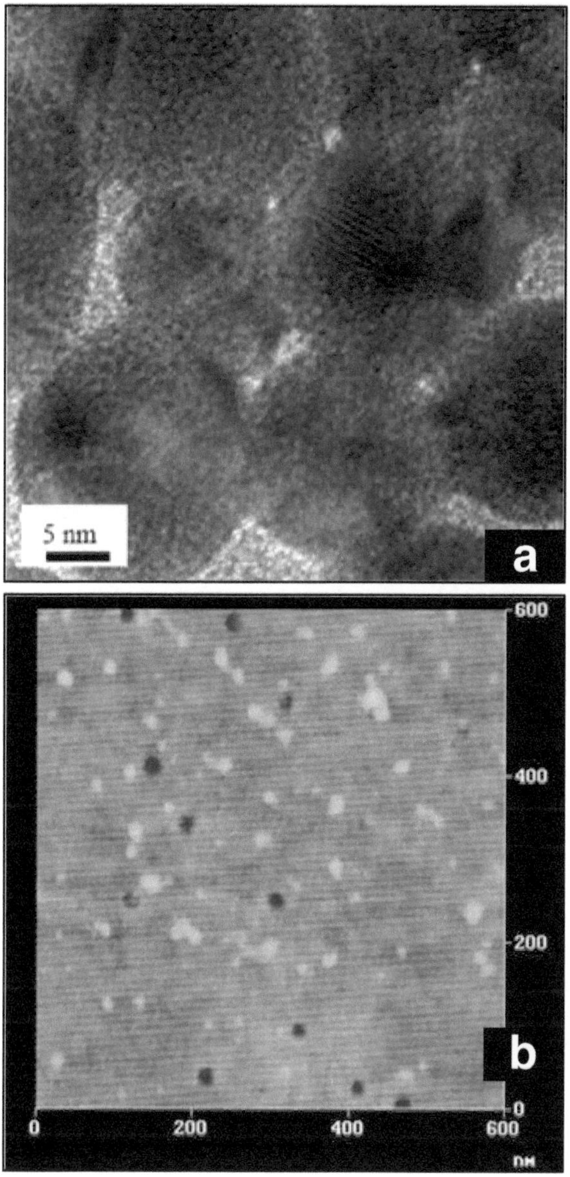

Figure 3.2: High Resolution Transmission Electron Micrograph (a) and Atomic Force Micrograph (b) of Sonochemically Synthesized Gold Nanoparticles. (From ref. Naveenraj *et al.*, 2010).

that the smaller particles quench the fluorescence more efficiently, indicating that smaller particles will have more binding interaction because of the fact that the smaller the size larger the surface area.

The interaction of silver nanoparticles with serum albumins was studied owing to the fact that silver nanoparticles have potential antimicrobial and antiplatelet/

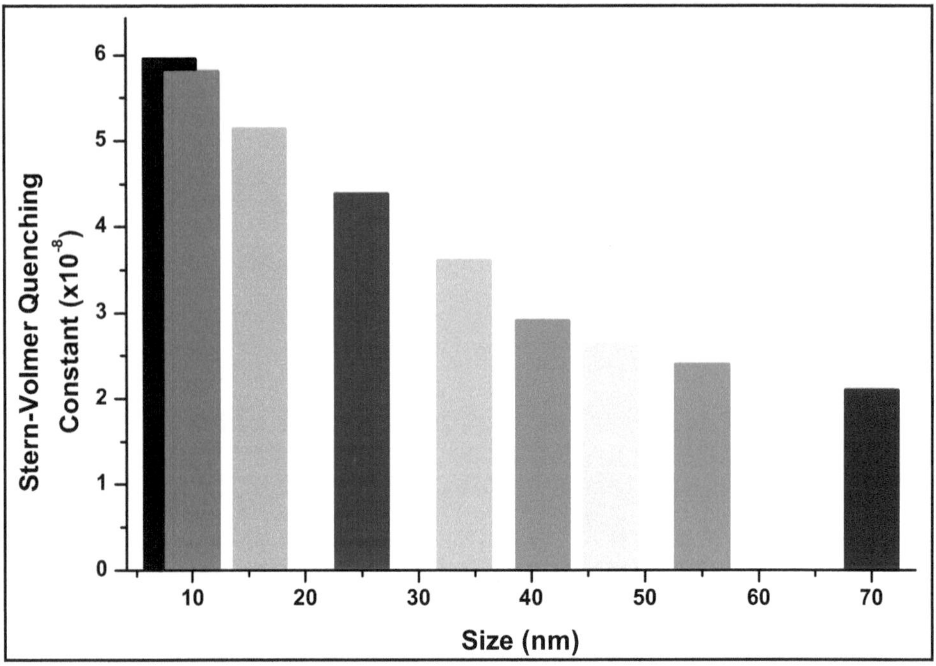

Figure 3.3: Histogram Showing the Change in the Size of Gold Nanoparticles with Respect to their Stern-Volmer Quenching Constants. (Using ref. Pramanik *et al.*, 2008).

antithrombolytic properties. The silver nanoparticles decrease the fluorescence of serum albumins with a blue shift in their emission maximum (Figure 3.4) which indicates the decrease in the polarity or increase in the hydrophobicity near the binding site of serum albumins. From the study conducted by Mariam *et al.* (2011), the obtained non-linear Stern-Volmer plots indicated that the quenching mechanism follows a combination of both static and dynamic quenching. A similar phenomenon of quenching mechanism was followed in the study conducted by Manivel and Anandan (2012) which was confirmed from the fluorescence lifetime and absorption studies. In the comparative study conducted by these authors, the binding constants suggested that BSA has more affinity towards silver nanoparticles than that of HSA which is pictographically shown in Figure 3.5.

4. BINDING CAPABILITY OF SEMICONDUCTOR AND METAL DOPED SEMICONDUCTOR NANOPARTICLES WITH BIOMOLECULES

Not only metal nanoparticles but also research on semiconductor nanocrystals (Quantum dots) enthused over the past decade from electronic materials and physics to biological and biomedical areas (Elaissari, 2008) due to their unique photophysical properties. Semiconductor TiO_2 nanoparticles, a well-known photocatalyst in the deactivation of microorganisms and viruses, of various sizes and morphologies exhibit

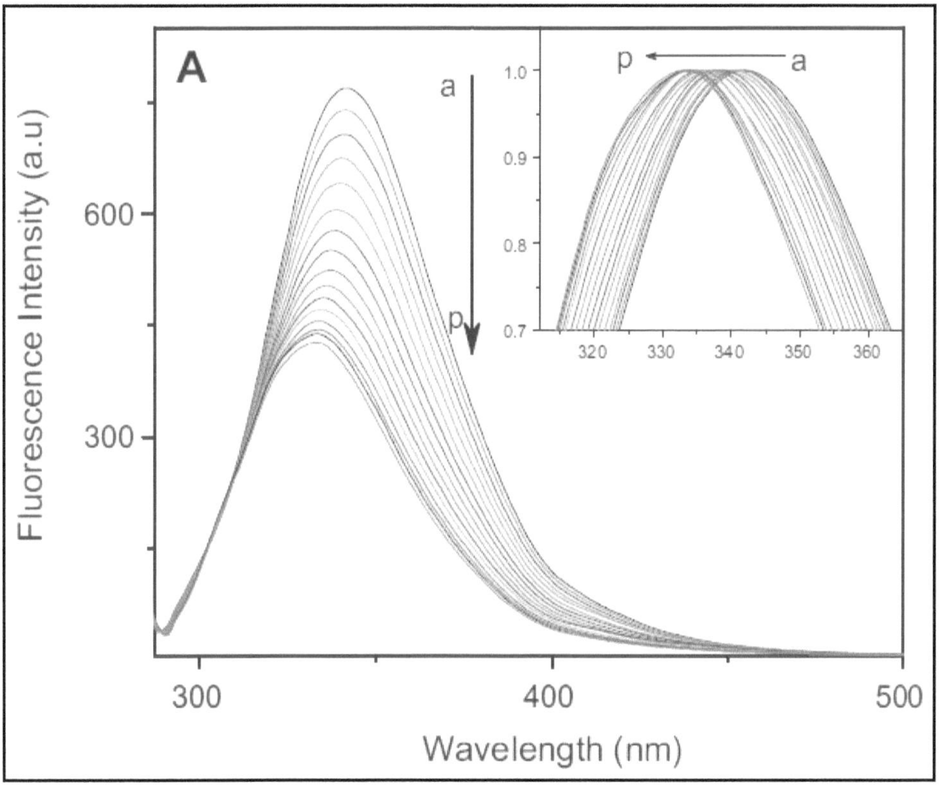

Figure 3.4: Fluorescence Spectra Showing the Quenching of Intrinsic Fluorescence of BSA, as Increase in Concentration of Silica Coated Silver Nanoparticles. (*a–p* = 4, 8, 12, 16, 20, 24, 28, 32, 36, 40, 44, 48, 52, 56 and 60 × 10 $^{-6}$ M); Inset represents the normalized fluorescence intensity showing shift in fluorescence wave length. (From ref. Manivel and Anandan, 2012).

cytotoxicity towards some tumors under ultraviolet light (UV) excitation. However, interaction of nano-sized TiO_2 complexed with an antibody (nanosized TiO_2/antibody complex) makes it a visible light-induced photo-toxin towards human brain cancer cells (Rozhkova *et al.*, 2009). Even in the dark condition, TiO_2 nanoparticles deform the tumor cell colony pattern by arresting their growth (Sungkaworn *et al.*, 2006). Owing to its bactericidal properties, either on their own or upon illuminated with UV light, it is used in many products including fabrics (Manchikanti and Bandopadhyay, 2010) and filters (Salata, 2004). Further it is used as a food colorant, additive in many cosmetic creams, and pharmaceutical excipient (Sun *et al.*, 2009). It has been hypothesized that the doping of transition metal nanoparticles to Titania improves the light absorption capability of TiO_2. This also increases its carrier lifetime by scavenging the electrons from the surface of the semiconductor and this shows unusual enhancement in their biological activities (Patil *et al.*, 2008). Pt-TiO_2 showed efficient cytotoxicity towards microbial cells in water when irradiated with a near-UV light. Pt-TiO_2 and Au-TiO_2 nanocrystals showed an effective cytotoxic effect towards the

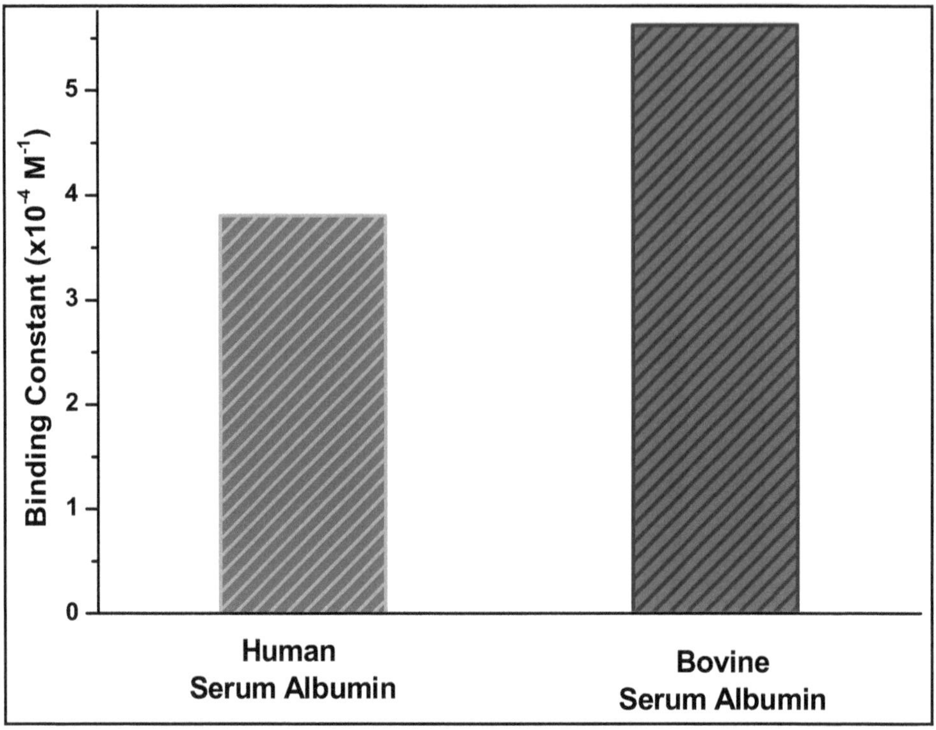

Figure 3.5: Histogram Showing the Affinity of Serum Albumins (HSA and BSA) towards Silica Coated Ag Nanoparticles using their Binding Constants. (Using ref. Manivel and Anandan, 2012).

killing of the cancer cells with near-UV light irradiation than that of undoped TiO_2 nanoparticles (Lazau *et al.*, 2007).

Due to these remarkable applications of TiO_2 nanoparticles, the interaction of commercially available TiO_2 nanoparticles (20 nm) and TiO_2 nanoparticles synthesized by hydrolysis method (1.4 nm) with human serum albumin were investigated by Sun *et al.* (2009) and Kathiravan *et al.* (2009b). The effect of commercially available TiO_2 nanoparticles on the fluorescence spectra of HSA showed a decrease in fluorescence intensity with a red shift in emission maxima whereas TiO_2 nanoparticles synthesized by hydrolysis method showed a decrease in fluorescence intensity without any shift in emission maxima. In both cases, the quenching followed static mechanism *i.e.*, the formation of ground state complex. The synchronous fluorescence spectra results indicated that the commercially available TiO_2 nanoparticles disturbed both the environments of tyrosine and tryptophan residues present in HSA whereas the TiO_2 nanoparticles synthesized by hydrolysis method only affected the microenvironment of tyrosine residues in HSA due to their variation in size.

The binding ability of TiO_2 nanoparticles and Ag doped TiO_2 with serum albumins were investigated using optical techniques by Kathiravan *et al.* (2009 a and

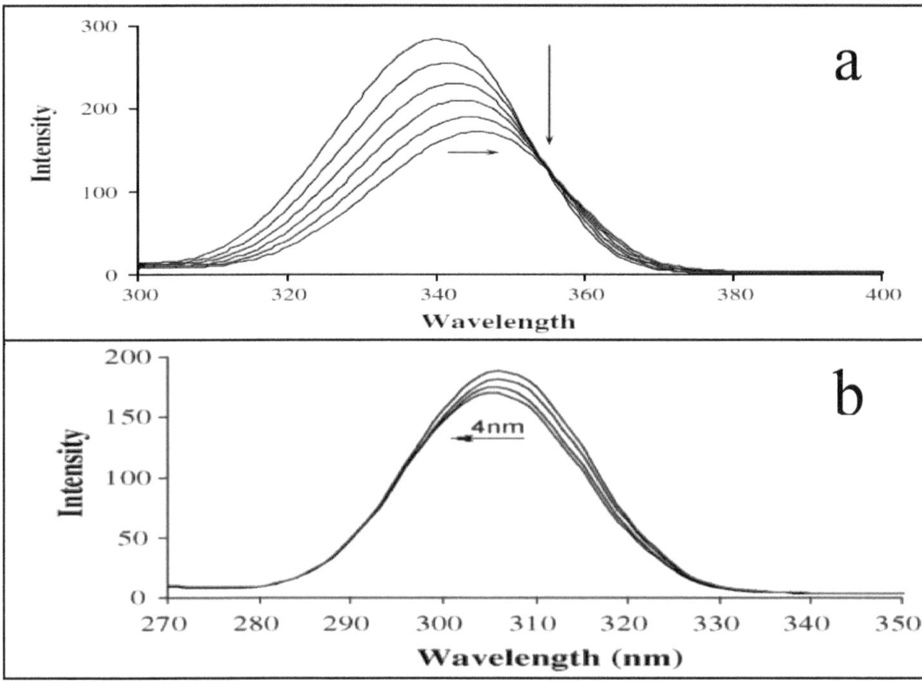

Figure 3.6: Synchronous Fluorescence Spectrum of HSA with $\Delta\lambda$= 15 nm in the Absence and Presence of Colloidal $AgTiO_2$ (a) and Colloidal TiO_2 (b) in the Concentration Range of 0–3×10^{-5} M. (From ref. Kathiravan *et al.*, 2009 a and b).

b). They inferred that both TiO_2 and $AgTiO_2$ nanoparticles quenched the fluorescence without any shift in the emission maxima. Lifetime measurements confirm that both nanoparticles followed static quenching mechanism. In the synchronous fluorescence spectra of serum albumins at $\Delta\lambda$= 60 nm, there was no shift in the emission wavelength which confirmed the absence of a binding site near tryptophan residue. In the synchronous fluorescence spectra ($\Delta\lambda$= 15 nm) of serum albumins, $AgTiO_2$ addition showed a red shift (Figure 3.6a) indicating the binding site was near the tyrosine region and the environment was more polar (or less hydrophobic) and more exposed to the solvent molecules (Wang *et al.*, 2007). Pure TiO_2 nanoparticles showed a blue shift (Figure 3.6b) indicating the binding site is also near tyrosine region but it is in less polar (or more hydrophobic) environment and less exposed to the solvent molecules.

The interaction of Wurzite structured ZnO nanoparticles with BSA was investigated by Bhogale *et al.* (2013) and Kathiravan *et al.* (2009c) for their antimicrobial, cancer cells imaging and photodynamic therapy applications since it is biocompatible, chemically stable and non-toxic. ZnO nanoparticles formed non-fluorescent ground state complex with BSA. In the study conducted by Bhogale *et al.* (2013), ZnO nanoparticles quenched BSA with a blue shift in the emission maximum whereas no shift was observed in the study conducted by Kathiravan *et al.* (2009c). In the study conducted by Bhogale *et al.* (2013), synchronous fluorescence spectra suggested that the ZnO nanoparticles perturb the microenvironment close to both the tyrosine and tryptophan residues of BSA whereas only tryptophan microenvironment is changed in the study conducted by Kathiravan *et al.* (2009c).

Due to the applications of CdTe quantum dots (QDs) in the field of bio-imaging, immunofluorescence and phototherapy, the interaction of CdTe QDs with BSA were recently investigated. In the size comparative binding study conducted by Liang *et al.* (2008), TGA stabilized CdTe QDs of sizes 1.8, 2.6 and 3.1 nm were used. These nanoparticles were synthesized just by varying the reaction time in the same reaction. On increasing the size of TGA stabilized CdTe QDs, their binding interaction with BSA increased with a decrease in the number of QDs 'n' binding per molecule of BSA. This behaviour of CdTe QDs is probably due to the changes of relative size between BSA and CdTe QDs during their binding. In the study conducted by Idowu *et al.* (2008), CdTe QDs of sizes 2.3, 3.0 and 3.2 nm were synthesized by varying the stabilizers mercaptopropionic acid (MPA), L-cysteine (CYS), and thioglycolic acid (TGA). The Stern-Volmer quenching constants (Figure 3.7) suggested that the binding ability of these QDs with BSA follows the order: QD (TGA) > QD (CYS) > QD (MPA) which in turn suggested that the increase in size increased the binding ability of QDs. However, in the study conducted by Wang *et al.* (2012), CdTe QDs of mean

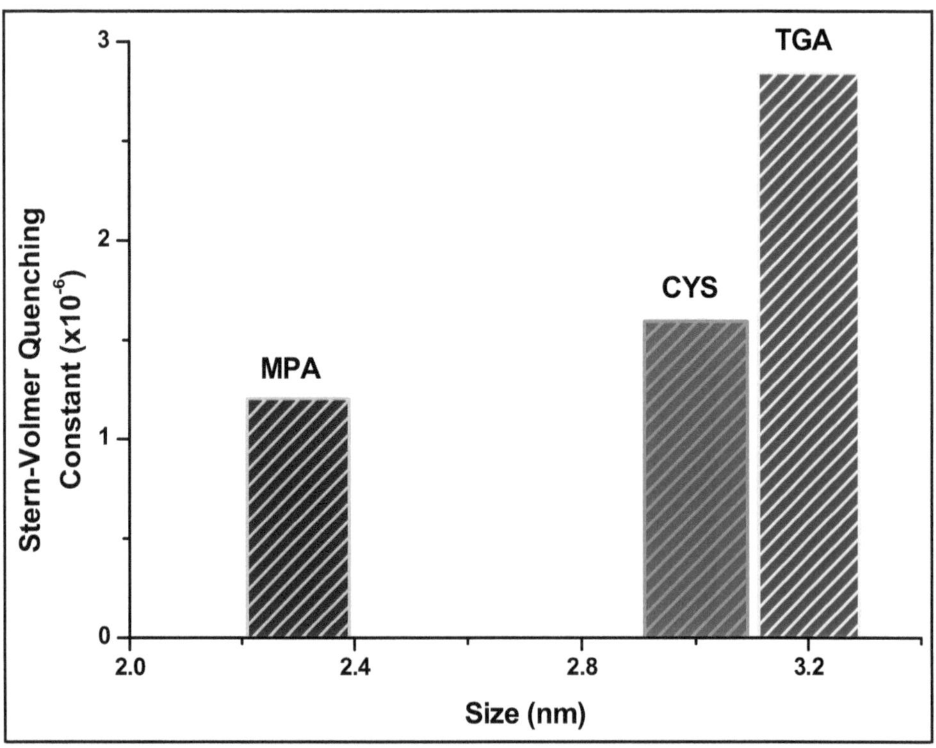

Figure 3.7: Histogram Showing the Affinity of Various Sized CdTe Nanoparticles Synthesized using different Stabilizing Agents Towards BSA. (Using ref. Idowu *et al.*, 2008).

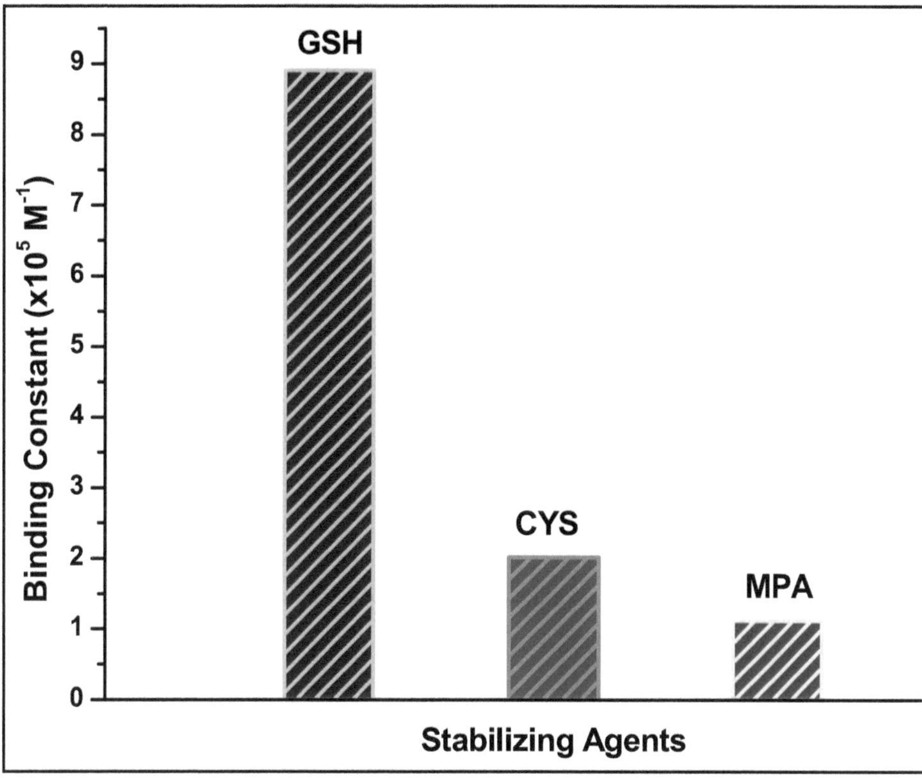

Figure 3.8: Histogram Showing the Affinity of same Sized (3.2 nm) CdTe Nanoparticles Synthesized using different Stabilizing Agents towards BSA. (Using ref., Wang *et al.*, 2012).

diameter 3.2 nm were synthesized by varying the stabilizers MPA, CYS, and Glutathione (GSH). The binding ability of these QDs with BSA (Figure 3.8) followed the order: QD (GSH) > QD (CYS) > QD (MPA) which suggested that the interaction depends on the capping agent of QDs. Xiao *et al.* (2010) investigated the interaction of 2.04 nm green-emitting QDs (G-QDs) and 3.79 nm red-emitting QDs (R-QDs) with HSA. The binding constant suggested that the size of CdTe QDs affected the affinity for HSA and the increasing size of QDs enhanced the binding force with HSA.

Owing to the applications of CdS nanoparticles in the field of biology and medicine, the interaction studies of CdS nanoparticles with BSA becomes vital and were investigated by Jhonsi *et al.* (2009) and Ghali (2010). Starch capped, thioglycerol capped and uncapped CdS nanoparticles interacted with BSA by the formation of ground state complex. Starch capped CdS nanoparticles quenched the fluorescence of BSA with blue shift in the emission maxima whereas thioglycerol capped CdS nanoparticles quenched the fluorescence of BSA with red shift in the emission maxima.

Serum albumins serve as the depot for the interacting nanoparticles and hence these nanoparticles can be circulated through the system in body. The binding affinity of any nanoparticles to serum albumin is one of the major factors that determine the pharmacokinetics of the nanoparticles *i.e.*, time course of absorption, distribution, metabolism, and excretion. In addition to the time course, it also determines the availabilities in various tissues (Ercelen *et al.*, 2005). If the binding affinity is low, even the initial step of pharmacokinetics (absorption) is not feasible. In the case of moderate binding affinity between serum albumins and nanoparticles, the absorption and distribution to tissues are easily feasible. The absorption of nanoparticles is feasible in the case of high binding affinity, but distribution to the required tissues gets decreased due to the more stable complex formation which affects the pharmacokinetics of the nanoparticles (Naveenraj and Anandan, 2013).

6. CONCLUSION

A critical need in the field of nanobiotechnology is the study of binding interactions of various nanoparticles with biomolecules. To accomplish this, the use of optical techniques becomes essential. The studies reviewed here exemplify the symbiotic relationship that nanotechnology shares with biology. Nondestructive nanoparticles attachment to the biomolecules opens up new avenues for medical diagnostic applications, biocompatible, 'smart' and functional nanocomposites, highly effective drug delivery vehicles, and novel therapeutics.

ACKNOWLEDGEMENTS

Authors thank DST-FIST, New Delhi (SR/FT/CSI-190/2008 dated 16th Mar 2008) for the sanction of research fund towards development of new facilities. Author SA thanks NAM S&T Center and DST, New Delhi for nominating him for First Winter School on Industrial Biotechnology held at Cairo, Egypt.

REFERENCES

1. Barbero, N., Barni, E., Barolo, C., Qualiotto, P., Viscardi, G., Napione, L., Pavan, S., Bussolino, F., 2009. A study of the interaction between fluorescein sodium salt and bovine serum albumin by steady-state fluorescence. Dyes Pigm. 80 (3), pp. 307-313.
2. Bhogale, A., Patel, N., Sarpotdar, P., Mariam, J., Dongre, P.M., Miotello, A., Kothari, D.C., 2013. Systematic investigation on the interaction of bovine serum albumin with ZnO nanoparticles using fluorescence spectroscopy. Colloids Surf. B 102, pp. 257-264.
3. Bian, Q., Liu, J., Tian, J., Hu, Z., 2004. Binding of genistein to human serum albumin demonstrated using tryptophan fluorescence quenching. Inter. J. Bio. Macromol. 34 (5), pp. 275-279.
4. Bowman, M.-C., Ballard, T.E., Ackerson, C.J., Feldheim, D.L., Margolis, D.M., Melander, C., 2008. Inhibition of HIV Fusion with Multivalent Gold Nanoparticles. J. Am. Chem. Soc. 130 (22), pp. 6896–6897.
5. Cheng, Y., Samia, A.C., Meyers, J.D., Panagopoulos, I., Fei, B., Burda, C., 2008. Highly Efficient Drug Delivery with Gold Nanoparticle Vectors for *in vivo* Photodynamic Therapy of Cancer. J. Am. Chem. Soc. 130 (32), pp. 10643–10647.

6. Elaissari, A., 2008. Colloidal Nanoparticles in Biotechnology. John Wiley and Sons Inc.

7. Ercelen, S., Klymchenko, A.S., M´ely, Y., Demchenko, A.P., 2005. The binding of novel two-color fluorescence probe FA to serum albumins of different species. Inter. J. Biol. Macromol. 35 (5), pp. 231-242.

8. Gao, D., Tian, Y., Bi, S., Chen, Y., Yu, A., Zhang, H., 2005. Studies on the interaction of colloidal gold and serum albumins by spectral methods. Spectrochim Acta A 62 (4-5), pp. 1203-1208.

9. Gao, H., Lei, L., Liu, J., Kong, Q., Chen, X., Hu, Z., 2004. The study on the interaction between human serum albumin and a new reagent with antitumour activity by spectrophotometric methods. J. Photochem. Photobio. A Chem. 167 (2-3), pp. 213-221.

10. Ghali, M., 2010. Static quenching of bovine serum albumin conjugated with small size CdS nanocrystalline quantum dots. J. Lumin. 130 (7), pp. 1254-1257.

11. Heltzel, A., Theppakuttai, S., Chen, S.C., Howell, J.R., 2008. Surface plasmon-based nanopatterning assisted by gold nanospheres. Nanotechnol. 19 (2), 025305 pp. 1-6.

12. Hu, Y.-J., Li, W., Liu, Y., Dong, J.-X., Qu, S.-S., 2005. Fluorometric investigation of the interaction between methylene blue and human serum albumin. J. Pharm. Biomed. Anal. 39 (3-4), pp. 740-745.

13. Idowu, M., Lamprecht, E., Nyokong, T., 2008. Interaction of water-soluble thiol capped CdTe quantum dots and bovine serum albumin. J. Photochem. Photobio. A 198 (1), pp. 7-12.

14. Iosin, M., Toderas, F., Baldeck, P.L., Astilean, S., 2009. Study of protein–gold nanoparticle conjugates by uorescence and surface-enhanced Raman scattering. J. Mol. Struct. 924–926, pp. 196-200.

15. Jhonsi, M.A., Kathiravan, A., Renganathan, R., 2009. Spectroscopic studies on the interaction of colloidal capped CdS nanoparticles with bovine serum albumin. Colloids Surf. B 72 (2), pp. 167-172.

16. Kandagal, P.B., Ashoka, S., Seetharamappa, J., Shaikh, S.M.T., Jadegoud, Y., Ijare, O.B., 2006. Study of the interaction of an anticancer drug with human and bovine serum albumin: Spectroscopic approach, J. Pharm. Biomed. Anal. 41 (2), pp. 393-399.

17. Kandagal, P.B., Shaikh, S.M.T., Manjunatha, D.H., Seetharamappa, J., Nagaralli, B.S., 2007. Spectroscopic studies on the binding of bioactive phenothiazine compounds to human serum albumin. J. Photochem. Photobiol. A 189 (1), pp. 121-127.

18. Kathiravan, A., Paramaguru, G., Renganathan, R., 2009c. Study on the binding of colloidal zinc oxide nanoparticles with bovine serum albumin. J. Mo. Struc. 934 (1-3), pp. 129-137.

19. Kathiravan, A., Renganathan, R., 2009b. Interaction of colloidal TiO_2 with human serum albumin: A fluorescence quenching study. Colloids Surf. A 333 (1-3), pp. 91-95.
20. Kathiravan, A., Renganathan, R., Anandan, S., 2009a. Interaction of colloidal $AgTiO_2$ nanoparticles with bovine serum albumin. Polyhedron 28 (1), pp. 157-161.
21. Klajnert, B., Bryszewska, M., 2002. Fluorescence studies on PAMAM dendrimers interactions with bovine serum albumin. Bioelectrochem. 55 (1-2), pp. 33-35.
22. Lazau, C., Mocanu, L., Miron, I., Sfirloaga, P., Tanasie, G., Tatu, C., Gruia, A., Grozescu, I., 2007. Consideration regarding the use of TiO_2 doped nanoparticles in medicine. Digest J. Nanomat. Biostruc. 2 (3), pp. 257-263.
23. Lee, K.B., Kim, E.Y., Mirkin, C.A., Wolinsky, S.M., 2004. The Use of Nanoarrays for Highly Sensitive and Selective Detection of Human Immunodeficiency Virus Type 1 in Plasma. Nano Lett. 4 (10), pp. 1869-1872.
24. Lemiesz, L.T., Keppler, B.K., Kozlowski, H., 1999. Studies on the interactions between human serum albumin and imidazolium [trans-tetrachlorobis (imidazol)ruthenate (III)], J. Inorg. Biochem. 73 (3), pp. 123-128.
25. Li, Y., He, W., Liu, J., Sheng, F., Hu, Z., Chen, X., 2005. Binding of the bioactive component Jatrorrhizine to human serum albumin. Biochim. Biophys. Acta 1722 (1), pp. 15-21.
26. Liang, J., Cheng, Y., Han, H., 2008. Study on the interaction between bovine serum albumin and CdTe quantum dots with spectroscopic techniques. J. Mol. Struc. 892 (1-3), pp. 116-120.
27. Luo, P.G., Stutzenberger, F.J., 2008. Nanotechnology in the Detection and Control of Microorganisms. Adv. in App. Microbio. 63, pp. 145-181.
28. Maiti, T.K., Ghosh, K.S., Dasgupta, S., 2006. Interaction of (-)-epigallocatechin-3-gallate with human serum albumin: Fluorescence, fourier transform infrared, circular dichroism, and docking studies. Proteins 64 (2), pp. 355-362.
29. Manchikanti, P., Bandopadhyay, T.K., 2010. Nanomaterials and Effects on Biological Systems: Development of Effective Regulatory Norms. Nanoethics 4 (1), pp. 77-83.
30. Manivel, A., Anandan, S., 2012. Spectral interaction between silica coated silver nanoparticles and serum albumins. Colloids Surf. A 395, pp. 38-45.
31. Mariam, J., Dongre, P.M., Kothari, D.C., 2011. Study of interaction of silver nanoparticles with bovine serum albumin using fluorescence spectroscopy. J. Fluoresc. 21 (6), pp. 2193-2199.
32. Mitra, A., Deutsch, B., Ignatovich, F., Dykes, C., Novotny, L., 2010. Nano-optofluidic Detection of Single Viruses and Nanoparticles. ACS Nano 4 (3), pp. 1305-1312.
33. Naveenraj, S., Anandan, S., 2013. Binding of serum albumins with bioactive substances – Nanoparticles to drugs. J. Photochem. Photobiol. C 14 (1), pp. 53-71.

34. Naveenraj, S., Anandan, S., Kathiravan, A., Renganathan, R., Ashokkumar, M., 2010. The Interaction of Sonochemically Synthesized Gold Nanoparticles with Serum Albumins. J. Pharm. Biomed. Anal. 53 (3), pp. 804-810.

35. Paciotti, G.F., Kingston, D.G.I., Tamarkin, L., 2006. Colloidal gold nanoparticles: a novel nanoparticle platform for developing multifunctional tumor-targeted drug delivery vectors. Drug Development Res. 67 (1), pp. 47-54.

36. Patil, K.C., Rattan, T., Aruna, S.T., Hegde, M.S., 2008. Chemistry of Nanocrystalline Oxide Materials, World Scientific Publishing Co. Pte. Ltd.

37. Pramanik, S., Banerjee, P., Sarkar, A., Bhattacharya, S.C., 2008. Size-dependent interaction of gold nanoparticles with transport protein: A spectroscopic study. J. Lumin. 128 (12), pp. 1969-1974.

38. Qi, Z.-D., Zhou, B., Xiao, Q., Shi, C., Liu, Y., Dai, J., 2008. Interaction of rofecoxib with human serum albumin: Determination of binding constants and the binding site by spectroscopic methods. J. Photochem. Photobiol. A 193 (2-3), pp. 81-88.

39. Rozhkova, E.A., Ulasov, I., Lai, B., Dimitrijevic, N.M., Lesniak, M.S., Rajh, T., 2009. A High-Performance Nanobio Photocatalyst for Targeted Brain Cancer Therapy. Nano Lett. 9 (9), pp. 3337-3342.

40. Salata, O.V., 2004. Applications of nanoparticles in biology and medicine. J. Nanobiotechn. 2 (3), pp. 1-6.

41. Schrand, A.M., Braydich-Stolle, L.K., Schlager, J.J., Dai, L., Hussain, S.M., 2008. Can silver nanoparticles be useful as potential biological labels? Nanotechnol. 19 (23) 235104.

42. Silva, D., Cortez, C.M., Louro, S.R.W., 2004. Chlorpromazine interactions to sera albumins: A study by the quenching of fluorescence. Spectrochim. Acta A 60 (5), pp. 1215-1223.

43. Sun, W., Du, Y., Chen, J., Kou, J., Yu, B., 2009. Interaction between titanium dioxide nanoparticles and human serum albumin revealed by uorescence spectroscopy in the absence of photoactivation. J. Lumin. 129 (8), pp. 778-783.

44. Sungkaworn, T., Triampo, W., Nalakarn, P., Triampo, D., Tang, I.M., Lenbury, Y., Picha, P., 2006. The Effects of TiO_2 Nanoparticles on Tumor Cell Colonies: Fractal Dimension and Morphological Properties. Inter. J. Biol. Life Sci. 2 (1), pp. 67-74.

45. Viallet, P.M., Vo-Dinh, T., Ribou, A.C., Vigo, J., Salmon, J.M., 2000. Native Fluorescence and Mag-Indo-1-Protein Interaction as Tools for Probing Unfolding and Refolding Sequences of the Bovine Serum Albumin Subdomain in the Presence of Guanidine Hydrochloride. J. Protein Chem. 19 (6), pp. 431-439.

46. Wang, C., Wu, Q., Li, C., Wang, Z., Ma, J., Zang, X., Qin, N., 2007. Interaction of Tetrandrine with Human Serum Albumin: a Fluorescence Quenching Study. Anal. Sci. 23 (4), pp. 429-433.

47. Wang, Q., Zhang, X., Zhou, X., Fang, T., Liu, P., Liu, P., Min, X., Li, X., 2012. Interaction of different thiol-capped CdTe quantum dots with bovine serum albumin. J. Lumin. 132 (7), pp. 1695-1700.

48. Wang, Y.-Q., Zhang, H.-M., Zhang, G.-C., Tao, W.-H., Fei, Z.-H., Liu, Z.-T., 2007. Spectroscopic studies on the interaction between silicotungstic acid and bovine serum albumin. J. Pharm. Biomed. Anal. 43 (5), pp. 1869-1875.

49. Xiao, J., Bai, Y., Wang, J., Chen, Y., Wei, X., 2010. Systematic investigation of the influence of CdTe QDs size on the toxic interaction with human serum albumin by fluorescence quenching method. Spectrochim. Acta A 76 (1), pp. 93-97.

50. Zhao, B., Xie, J., Zhao, J., 2005. Binding of hypocrellin B to human serum albumin and photo-induced interactions. Biochim. Biophys. Acta 1722 (2), pp. 124-130.

51. Zheng, D., Seferos, D.S., Giljohann, D.A., Patel, P.C., Mirkin, C.A., 2009. Aptamer Nano-flares for Molecular Detection in Living Cells. Nano Lett. 9 (9), pp. 3258-3261.

Chapter 4

High Throughput Refolding and Purification of Recombinant Asparaginase from Inclusion Bodies of *E. coli*

*Parul Sehgal**

Research Assistant,
Centre for Science and Technology of the Non-Aligned and Other Developing Countries, (NAM S&T Centre), New Delhi, India

ABSTRACT

L-Asparaginase (E.C 3.5.1.1) a hydrolase enzyme, catalyzes the hydrolysis of L-asparagine into L-aspartate and ammonia molecules. The methodologies adopted in the project were high level expression of L-asparaginase in *E. coli*, isolation and purification of L-asparaginase inclusion bodies from *E. coli*, solubilization of L-asparaginase inclusion bodies and refolding and purification of L-asparaginase using chromatographic methods (DEAE sepharose column). High L-asparaginase expression level was achieved using 1 M IPTG and pure inclusion bodies were produced using mild buffers and solubilized in optimal chaotropic agents. Pure bands of asparaginase of about 37 kDa was achieved by anion exchange chromatography and observed in SDS PAGE. The enzyme obtained has the potential to regulate the cancerous cells of leukemia and lymphoma, the details of which are not a part of this paper. The objective of present study is divided into various sections (a) Kinetic studies of growth of *E. coli* (b) purification of asparaginase protein.

Keywords: *L-Asparaginase, Inclusion bodies, Purification, IPTG, E. coli.*

---

*E-mail: parulsehgal1989@gmail.com

1. INTRODUCTION

The magnitude of the challenge of protein purification becomes clearer when one considers the mixture of macromolecules present in a cell extract. Each protein purification step usually results in some degree of product loss. Therefore, an ideal protein purification strategy is one in which the highest level of purification is reached in the fewest steps. (RR Burgess, 2008)

The selection of which steps to use is dependent on the size, charge, solubility and other properties of the target protein. The advent of genetic engineering has given us the ability to routinely clone genes and overproduce their gene products. This has changed the way we think about protein purification. For most protein purifications, it is no longer necessary to start with large amounts of naturally occurring material. Instead, the gene of interest can be cloned, inserted into a suitable expression vector and the vector transformed into a suitable expression host *(e.g. E. coli)*.

The cells can then be grown, transcription of the gene of interest induced, the cells harvested, the cells broken open and the overproduced recombinant protein purified. By using an expression vector where the target gene has a strong, inducible promoter, it is possible to express the target to levels as high as 20–40 per cent of the total cellular protein. One of the most common problems in over expressing a recombinant protein in *E.coli* is the fact that while large amounts of the protein are produced, most of it is not soluble, but is found as an insoluble inclusion body. (RR Burgess, 2008).

Apparently, the newly synthesized protein, when partially folded into its native structure, exposes some hydrophobic regions and is quite sticky and prone to interaction with other partially folded proteins, leading to aggregation and inclusion body formation.

The most common applications of L-Asparaginase are in acute lymphoblastic leukemia (ALL), Hodgkin disease, acute myelocytic leukemia, acute myelomonocytic leukemia, chronic lymphocytic leukemia, lymphosarcoma treatment, reticulosarcoma and melanosarcoma (Khushoo *et al.*, 2004). Tumor cells have high level of protein synthesis so they need high amount of necessary amino acids such as L-asparagine. Effective depletion of L-asparagine by L- asparaginase results in cytotoxicity for leukemic cells (Basha *et al.*, 2009). Asparaginase acts by lowering critically the concentration of asparagine so that it becomes unavailable to a competing process essential for tumor growth. L-asparaginase in combination with methotrexate and other drugs is highly effective in the therapy of both primary and acute lymphoblastic leukemia of children and adults (Muller and Boos, 1998). Furthermore, new studies have revealed potential application of this enzyme in prevention of acrylamide formation (carcinogenic agent formed due to the heat induced reaction between the α-amino group of the free amino acid asparagine and carbonyl groups of reducing sugars such as glucose.) in fried potatoes and similar food products. Therefore introduction of new fermentation and purification protocols for production of L-asparaginase II will be mandatory to satisfy these demands.

1.1 Role of Recombinant DNA Technology

The ultimate goal of recombinant fermentation research is the cost effective production of desired protein by maximizing the volumetric productivity *i.e.* to obtain highest amount of protein in a given volume in least amount of time. Such bio-processing for recombinant protein using genetically modified organism requires a stable high yielding recombinant culture, a high productive fermentation process and cost effective recovery and purification procedures. *E.coli*, the workhorse of recombinant DNA technology, is being used on a large scale for this purpose.

Extensive information on its physiology, easy genetic manipulation and higher growth rate under controlled environment in the fermenter has attracted the use of *E.coli* for production of wide varieties of recombinant proteins. *E.coli* has been most widely used as host for the expression of recombinant proteins.

1.2 Expression of Recombinant Proteins as Inclusion Bodies

Inclusion bodies are dense particles of aggregated protein found in both cytoplasmic and periplasmic spaces of *E.coli* during the high level expression of foreign protein. Inclusion bodies impose a serious limitation on the production of recombinant proteins. This is a problem that remains critical in the development of biotechnology.

The strategy used to recover bioactive protein from inclusion bodies involves 4 steps: Isolation and purification of IBs from *E.coli* cells, solubilization of the protein aggregates, purification and refolding of the solubilized protein. Among these steps, refolding of the solubilized protein is the most crucial step and needs careful attention for a high recovery of protein. (Tarun K. Ghose, 2003)

1.2.1 Isolation and Purification of Inclusion Bodies

High level expression of recombinant proteins in bacterial cytoplasm leads to the formation of high density (~1.3 g/ml) aggregates called as inclusion bodies (Pattnaik, ý2009). Since these IBs are of higher density, they can be isolated by centrifugation method (Mukhopadhyay, 1997). However, complete lyses of bacterial cells are prerequisite before IBs isolation and purification. Complete lyses of cells are generally accomplished by mechanical and chemical disruption methods. Lysozyme treatment prior to sonication or high pressure disruption steps helps in improved lysis of cells. Beside this, detergents and salts are also used to break down membrane and to remove attached impurities from IBs. This combination of cell disruption techniques guarantees the complete disintegration of cell wall and membrane (Rudolph *et al.*, 1997). After lyses, IBs can be isolated by centrifugation or filtration methods up to 90 per cent homogeneity (Kuivila, 2002). Most of the impurities commonly identified in IBs isolates, however, may originate primarily from incomplete lysis and removal of particulate host material. Therefore, these IBs can be further purified by additional washing steps using EDTA, low concentration of denaturants such as urea or GdmCl and detergents such as Triton X-100, deoxycholate, octylglycoside and sarkosyl (Orsini *et al.*, 1991, Misawa S *et al.*, 1994, Noguchi Y *et al.*, 1996). Furthermore, IBs in their particulate state can be purified by gel filtration methods.

1.2.2 Solubilization of Inclusion Bodies

Solubilization is achieved by the use of denaturing solvents and renaturation of the dissolved protein occurs on removal of the denaturant. Further polishing steps are needed to remove small amounts of contaminating proteins as well as incorrectly folded species. (John A. Smith, 2010)

As inclusion bodies are formed due to the strong hydrophobic interactions between misfolded protein molecules, generally, they require high concentration of denaturing agents for their solubilization. The most commonly used agents for IBs solubilization are chaotropes such as urea and guanidium hydrochloride (GdmCl). Usually higher concentration (6-8 mole/litre) of urea and GdmCl is employed for complete solubilization and denaturation of most of the inclusion body proteins (Fischer *et al.*, 1992, De Bernadez Clark E. 2001). But in some cases, 2 molar concentration of urea has also been found sufficient for solubilization of inclusion bodies (Li *et al.*, 1999). This mild solubilization has been found to be useful in preferential solubilization of IBs proteins since it does not solubilize the impurities and other particulate matter present in IBs.

Apart from chaotropes, detergents have also been used for solubilization of IBs. Cetyl trimethyl ammonium salts (CTAC or CTAB) have been used for solubilization of human growth hormone IBs (Patra *et al.*, 2002).

It has been observed that solubilization conditions greatly affect the yield of bioactive protein during renaturation; the development of an appropriate mild denaturing condition for IBs solubilization can help in achieving high throughput recovery of recombinant proteins (Singh SM and Panda AK, 2005).

1.2.3 Renaturation of Solubilized Recombinant Proteins

Refolding is a process which leads to change in protein conformation from unfolded to folded (native) state. Transfer of protein molecules from high denaturant concentration to aqueous buffer leads to misfolding or aggregation. So, the best way of refolding is in the presence of intermediate concentration of the denaturant, where denaturant concentration is low enough to force protein molecules to collapse, still allow them to stay in solution and be exible to reorganize their structures in to native forms. Inclusion bodies that have been solubilized using suitable denaturants can be renatured by the removal of excess denaturants by either dilution or buffer exchange method such as dialysis and diafiltration. Solubilized proteins are generally refolded in to their native state after removing the chaotropic agents or other salts by dialysis of the proteins in buffers containing reducing and oxidizing agents (Tripathi, 2012).

Renaturation of solubilized proteins involves the removal of denaturing agents for the formation of correct native conformation. It can be achieved by various methods. The classical method used for removal of denaturants is dialysis. In this process, the solubilized protein is dialyzed against renaturation buffer. This is carried out in step gradient manner in which the concentration of denaturants is gradually decreased in renaturation buffer. However, the major impedance observed during this process is aggregation of solubilized protein in transition zone of denaturant concentration.

The other method used for renaturation is dilution methods in which solubilized protein is directly added in the large volume of renaturation buffer. This is most commonly used for renaturation of protein. Dilution of the solubilized proteins in large volume of renaturation buffer lowers the crowding of folding intermediates and consequently reduces the possibility of aggregation of the protein molecules.

Pulsatile renaturation method had also been used for refolding of solubilized IB proteins (Singh, 2005). In this process, small amount of solubilized protein is added into the renaturation buffer at successive time intervals. It helps in refolding of large quantity of protein in smaller volume of refolding buffer. It works on the fact that once a small amount of denatured protein molecules enter in renaturation condition they fold very rapidly and form native structures. These native proteins do not participate in aggregation process with successively incoming denatured proteins or folding intermediates in renaturation buffer. However, this method should not be preferred in case of slow refolding proteins. If the folding behaviour for a protein is known then one can determine, the right amount of denatured protein to be added into the refolding buffer; and the duration of interval between successive addition steps. This is followed by purification step which can also be performed prior to renaturation.

2. L-ASPARAGINASE

L-asparaginase (Amidohydrolase, EC 3.5.1.1) is found in many animal tissues, bacteria, plants (Cornea *et al.*, 2002). It catalyses the conversion of L-Asparagine to Aspartic acid and Ammonia.

The proposed covalent intermediate is formed through nucleophilic attack by the enzyme. There are two isozymes of L-asparaginase; type I is produced by many kind of bacteria such as *E.coli* (Mercado and Arenas 1999), *Erwinia carotovora* (Aghaiypour *et al.*, 2001), *Enterobacter aerogenes* (Mukherjee *et al.*, 2000), *Candida utilis* (Kil *et al.*, 1995), *Staphylococcus aureus* (Muley *et al.*1998), *Thermus thermophilus* (Prista and Kyridio 2001) and it is a cytosolic enzyme with low affinity for L-asparagine. L-asparaginase II is a periplasmic enzyme in Gram-negative bacteria such as *E.coli* and *Erwinia carotovora* with high affinity for substrate so it is widely used as a therapeutic agent.

E.coli synthesizes two types of asparaginases called EcA1 and EcA2 (Campbell *et al.*, 1927). EcA1 is found in cytosol of bacteria and has very low affinity to substrate while EcA2 is present in the periplasm and has higher affinity for the substrate (Marita and Matsuda 1980). All asparaginases consist of four identical subunits A, B, C and D and exist as homotetramers. EcA2 is regulated by the oxygen level in the medium, with the high level of induction under anaerobic conditions (Cedar and Schwartz, 1967, 1968). In contrast, no definite form of regulation has been reported for EcA1, which is considered a constitutive enzyme (Jerlstrom, 1989). Apart from their differing cellular location and regulation, the *E.coli* enzymes differ with respect to their catalytic properties. EcA1 and EcA2 have Km values for asparagine of 3.5 mM and 11.5 mM, respectively (Ho and Milikin, 1970). The active form of EcA1 was reported to be a dimer with a subunit mass of 35.4 kDa (Jerlstrom, 1989) and the active form of EcA2 is a homotetramer with a mass of 4×34.6 kDa (Maita and Matsuda, 1980).

Figure 4.1 shows the rationale for therapy with L-asparaginase.

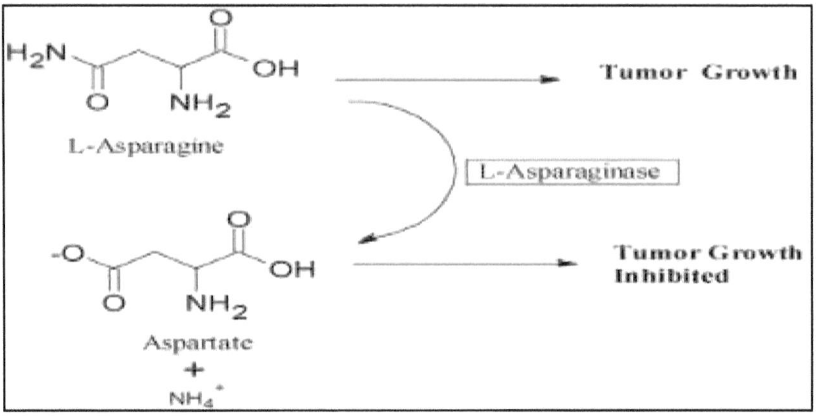

Figure 4.1
(Narta *et al.*, Crit Rev in Oncol/Hem 2007; 61: 2008-12).

3. MATERIALS AND METHOD

3.1. Preparation of Primary Culture of *E. coli*

The culture used here is the LB broth medium, the primary culture was prepared by dissolving 20 ml of LB broth in a 50 ml falcon tube and then 100 mg/ml ampicillin) AMP) was added to make final concentration of 100 µg/ml. One ml r-Asparaginase glycerol stock was added. The medium was incubated at 37°C at 200 convert into g or name the apparatus used rpm and left overnight.

3.2. Preparation of Secondary Culture of *E. coli*

Secondary Culture was prepared by inoculating 1 per cent of primary culture of *E. coli* in 1 litre of LB broth containing 100 µg/ml AMP). The culture was kept at 37°C at 200 rpm in a shaker incubator. The absorbance was noted after every 30 minutes at 600 nm. When the absorbance (optical density, OD) reached 0.6–0.8, induction was carried out with IPTG (from a stock solution of 1 M IPTG) to reach final concentration of 1 mM. The culture was further incubated for a period of 3 hours, after which the culture was harvested to get the cell pellet.

3.3. Growth Kinetics and Expression Levels

The uninduced samples were collected after every 30 minutes and the OD was recorded at 600 nm until it reached between 0.6–0.8. After induction with IPTG, induced samples were collected until the growth became stagnant. All induced and uninduced samples were then harvested by centrifugation at 6000 rpm for 10 min at 4 °C.

The harvested cells were checked for expression of induced and uninduced L-asparaginase by Sodium dodecyl sulphate polyacrylamide gel electrophoresis (SDS-PAGE) (kinetic analysis) (Figures 4.2 and 4.3).

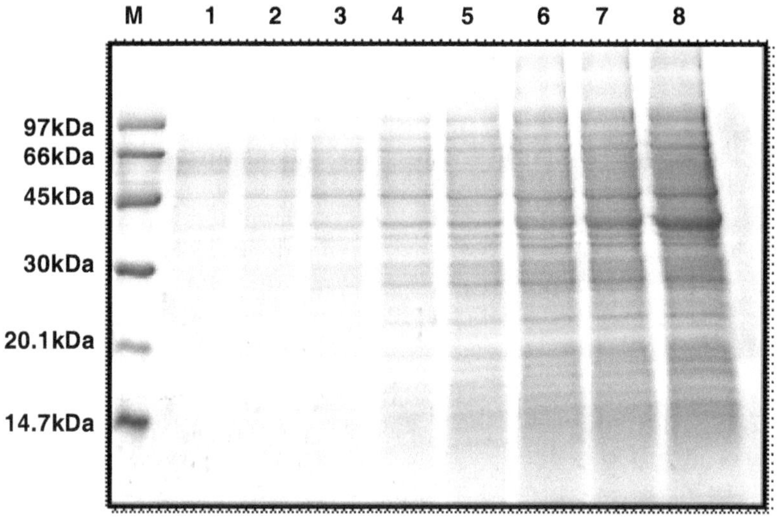

Figure 4.2

LANE M: Low molecular weight marker; LANE 1: UI sample at 0.5 h; LANE 2: UI sample at 1h; LANE 3: UI sample at 1.5 h; LANE 4: UI sample at 2 h; LANE 5: I sample at 2.5 h; LANE 6: I sample at 3 h; LANE 7: I sample at 3.5 h; LANE 8: I sample at 4 h.

UI: uninduced, I: induced

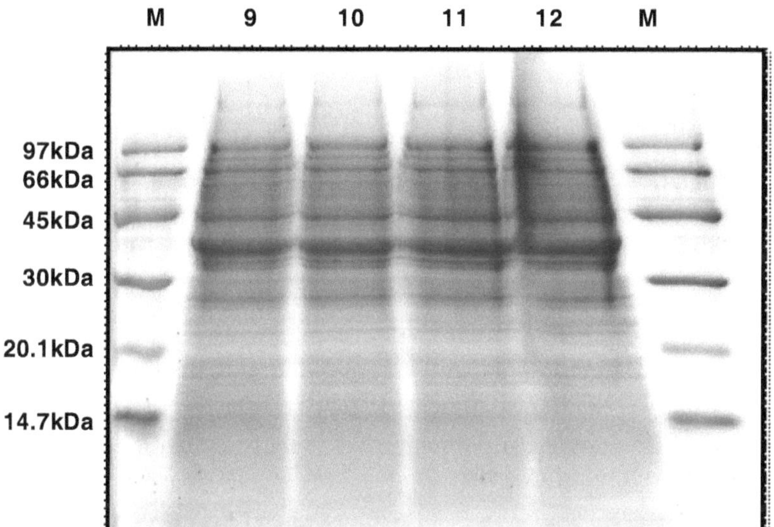

Figure 4.3

LANE M: Low molecular weight marker; LANE 9: I sample at 4.5 h; LANE 10: I sample at 5 h; LANE 11: I sample at 5.5 h; LANE 12: I sample at 6 h.

3.4. Isolation of Inclusion Bodies of Asparaginase from *E. coli* cells

E. coli cells expressing L-asparaginase were harvested and centrifuged (6000 rpm at 4°C for 10 minutes) and the pellet was sonicated. The lysed cells were centrifuged to separate the pellet and the supernatant. Most of the L-asparaginase was in the pellet fraction. Maximum removal of the contaminating cellular proteins was achieved by sonication and washing of L-asparaginase inclusion bodies with Tris-HCl (50 mM), PMSF (1 mM), pH-7. At the end of washing, inclusion bodies contained mostly L-asparaginase (> 85 per cent purity) along with some other impurities. After each Centrifugation at 12000 rpm, 1 ml of supernatant and a small amount of pellet was scraped off and put in 1 ml eppendorfs for expression analysis. (Figure 4.4).

The SDS-PAGE analysis of the various samples obtained at each steps of L-asparaginase inclusion bodies isolation is shown in the Figure 4.5. Recombinant Asparaginase was expressed as inclusion bodies having molecular weight 37 kDa. It was observed that after the first sonication there was little asparaginase in the supernatant. No loss of asparaginase was seen in further washing with Tris buffer and MQ. Inclusion bodies thus obtained were used for solubilization and refolding.

3.5. Expression of L-Asparaginase

After 3 hours of post induction, expression of L-asparaginase was observed to be at maximum. Recombinant L-asparaginase was expressed and analysed on SDS-PAGE as ~37kDa band protein.

3.6. Solubilization of Inclusion Bodies

Inclusion body suspension (500 microlitre) in Milli-Q water was taken and solubilized in 4.5 ml of solubilization buffer (8 M urea, 50 mM Tris- HCl (pH- 8.5), 20 mM 2- mercaptoethanol)

Incubated the above solution at room temperature for 2 hours and then centrifuged at 12000 rpm, 4°C for 20 minutes to remove un-dissolved aggregates and other particulate impurities. Supernatant was collected and used for refolding.

3.7. Refolding of Asparaginase

The solubilized supernatant (5 ml) was refolded in 10 times refolding buffer (5 per cent glycerol, 50 mM Tris HCl (pH- 8.5)) (50 ml) at flow rate of 0.1 ml/min at 4 °C.

Solubilized and refolded supernatants were analysed by SDS-PAGE to check the solubility and refolding. (Figure 4.6)

4. PURIFICATION OF L-ASPARAGINASE BY ION-EXCHANGE CHROMATOGRAPHY, USING AKTA-FPLC

Refolded recombinant asparaginase was purified using DEAE-sepharose anion exchange matrix. The refolded L-asparaginase was subjected to ion exchange chromatography (DEAE-Sepharose column, 100 ml volume) for purification. Ion exchange chromatography was connected with AKTA-FPLC system to purify the

Secondary culture preparation *(E. coli)*

↓

Induction with IPTG

↓ **Centrifuge at 6000 rpm for 10 minutes at 4°C**

Resuspend pellet in 50 mM Tris- HCl + 1 mM PMSF (pH adjusted to 7.0) (Total- 40 mL)

↓

Homogenize at 8000 rpm for 3-4 minutes (for pellet resuspension) and sonicate (10 cycles)

↓ **Centrifuge at 12000 rpm for 20 minutes at 4°C**

Resuspend pellet in 50 mM Tris-HCl + 1 mM PMSF (pH 7.0) (40ml), sonicate (10 cycles)

↓ **Centrifuge at 12000 rpm for 20 minutes at 4°C**

Resuspend pellet in Tris- HCl (50 mM), pH- 8.5

↓ **Centrifuge at 12000 rpm for 20 minutes at 4°C**

Resuspend pellet in Tris- HCl (50 mM), pH- 8.5

↓ **Centrifuge at 12000 rpm for 20 minutes at 4°C**

Pure Inclusion Bodies of L-Asparaginase

↓

(Resuspend IB in 2 mL Milli-Q water)

Figure 4.4: Isolation of Pure Inclusion Bodies from *E. coli* Cells.

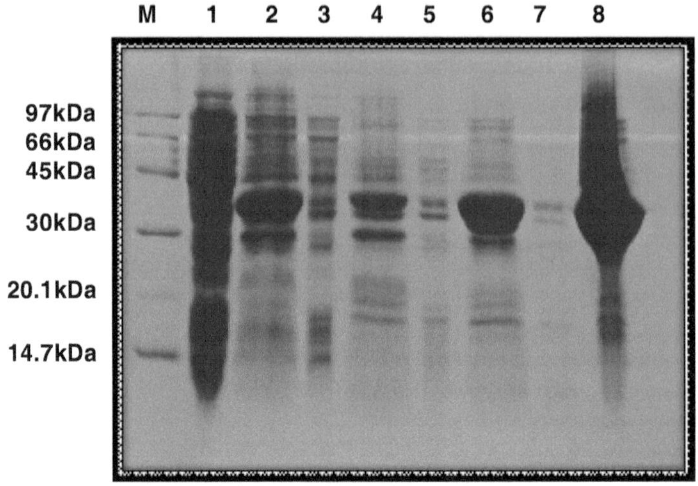

Figure 4.5: SDS-PAGE Analysis of Recombinant L-Asparaginase Expression in *E. coli.*

Lane 1: 1st sonication supernatant; Lane 2: 1st sonication pellet; Lane 3: 2nd sonication supernatant; Lane 4: 2nd sonication pellet; Lane 5: 1st wash supernatant; Lane 6: 1st wash pellet; Lane 7: 2nd wash supernatant; Lane 8: 2nd wash pellet or IB respectively.

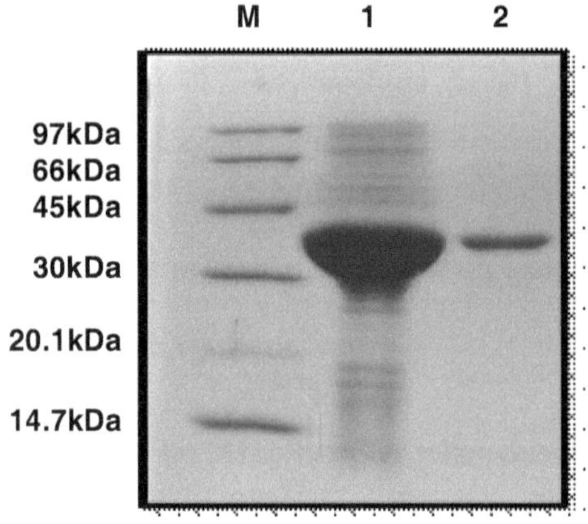

Figure 4.6: SDS-PAGE Analysis of Solubilized and Refolded Protein Samples.
M: Low molecular weight marker; LANE 1: Solubilized IB; LANE2: Refolded protein.

L-asparaginase. Initially DEAE-Sepharose column was washed with four-column volumes of Milli-Q water. The column was equilibrated at a flow rate of 1 ml/min with equilibration buffer (50 mM Tris-HCl, 5 per cent glycerol, at pH 8.5). The refolded L-asparaginase was loaded on to the pre-equilibrated DEAE-Sepharose column at a flow rate of 1 ml/min. The column was washed using four-column volumes of equilibration buffer at a flow rate of 1 ml/min to remove nonspecific contaminants. The bound L-asparaginase was eluted at a flow rate of 1 ml/min using a linear

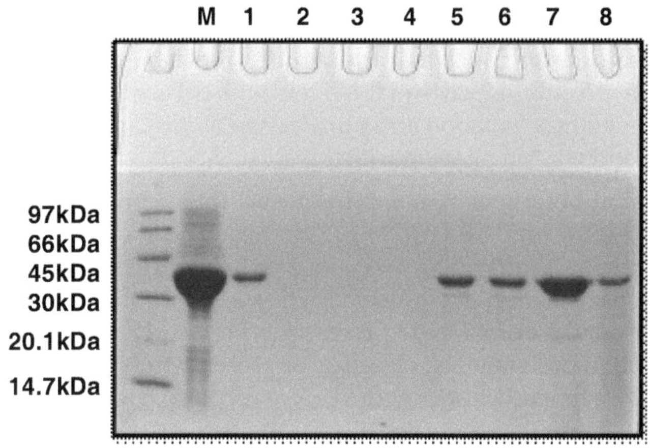

Figure 4.7: SDS-PAGE Analysis of Purification of L-Asparaginase by DEAE-Anion Exchange Chromatography.

M: Low molecular weight marker; LANE 1: Solubilized IB, LANE 2: Refolded protein; LANE 3: Flowthrough, LANE 4: Wash, LANE 5: Elute; LANE 6, 7, 8, 9: Elutes 1, 3, 5, 7.

continuous gradient of NaCl in equilibration buffer ranging from 0-0.5 N. Fractions (2 ml each) were collected and analysed on 12 per cent SDS polyacrylamide gel electrophoresis (Figure 4.7)

The protein was further dialysed (Tris HCL 25mM) for the removal of excess denaturants. The dialyzed protein was further concentrated in a centricon and observed by SDS PAGE as shown in Figure 4.8.

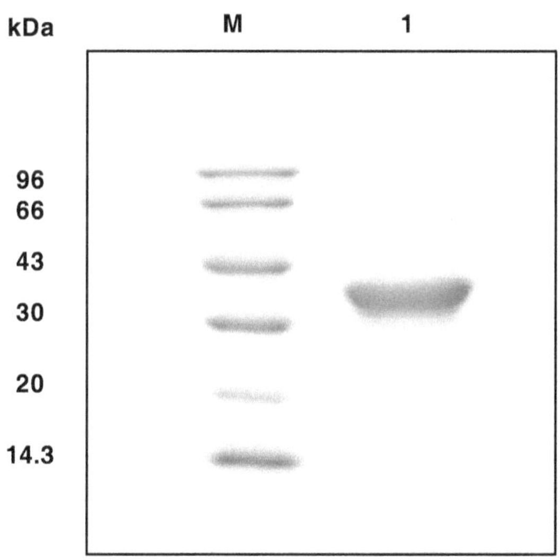

Figure 4.8: Concentrated Asparaginase in LANE 1.

LANE M: Low molecular weight marker; LANE 1: Concentrated asparaginase.

5. SUMMARY AND CONCLUSION

In the present work, an attempt was made to purify recombinant L-asparaginase from inclusion bodies of *E. coli.* Induction of *E. coli* cells with IPTG resulted in expression of r-Asp as inclusion bodies. Isolation and purification of inclusion bodies of r-asp through sonication and washing gave purified inclusion bodies.

Purified inclusion bodies were solubilized and then refolded by pulsatile renaturation method at the rate of 0.1 ml/min. Refolded protein was purified by ion exchange chromatography. Purification of recombinant proteins from inclusion bodies involves various steps: isolation of inclusion bodies, solubilization, refolding and purification. Thus, optimization of these processes is very crucial for achieving the better yield of bioactive proteins. The objective of present study was divided into various sections (a) Kinetic studies of growth of *E. coli* (b) purification of asparaginase protein.

The expression of recombinant proteins in E.coli as inclusion bodies resulted in reduction in cell growth, which was very prominent when cells were induced at early log phase.

Purified inclusion bodies were solubilized efficiently under proper combination of ionic strength, pH and concentration of chaotropic agents.

It was noted that renaturation in presence of 5 per cent glycerol gave good results.

Purification of L-asparaginase was carried out using DEAE-sepharose ion-exchange chromatography resulting in high yield of purified protein.

ACKNOWLEDGEMENTS

I would like to thank Dr. A.K. Panda, Scientist VII, Product Development Cell, National Institute of Immunology, Delhi, for having permitted me to carry out this project in his laboratory. His wisdom, knowledge and positive attitude always motivated me to move ahead in life.

I wish to express my deep sense of gratitude to Mr. Anupam Singh, Research Scholar at National Institute of Immunology for his able guidance and useful suggestions, which helped me in completing the project work, in time.

REFERENCES

1. Bowden GA, Paredes AM, Georgiou G. 1991. Structure and morphology of protein inclusion bodies in *Escherichia coli*. Biotechnology (N. Y.) 9: 725-30
2. Burgess RR, 2008. Protein Purification p. 1.
3. Campbell HA, Mashburn LT, Boyse EA, Old LJ. 1967. Two L-asparaginases from *Escherichia coli* B. Their separation, purification, and antitumor activity. *Biochemistry* 6: 721-30
4. Carrio M, Gonzalez-Montalban N, Vera A, Villaverde A, Ventura S. 2005. Amyloid-like properties of bacterial inclusion bodies. *J. Mol. Biol.* 347: 1025-37
5. Cedar H, Schwartz JH. 1967. Localization of the two-L-asparaginases in anaerobically grown *Escherichia coli. J. Biol. Chem.* 242: 3753-5

6. Clare E. Sansom, Mariusz Jaskolski. 2012. Center for Biocrystallographic Research, Polish Academy of Sciences, Poznan, Poland.
7. Georgiou G, Valax P. 1999. Isolating inclusion bodies from bacteria. Methods Enzymol. 309: 48-58
8. Hartley DL, Kane JF. 1988. Properties of inclusion bodies from recombinant *Escherichia coli. Biochem. Soc. Trans.* 16: 101-2
9. Maita T, Matsuda G. 1980. The primary structure of L-asparaginase from *Escherichia coli. Hoppe Seylers. Z. Physiol Chem.* 361: 105-17
10. Marston FA. 1986. The purification of eukaryotic polypeptides synthesized in *Escherichia coli. Biochem. J.* 240: 1-12
11. Mashburn LT, Wriston JC, Jr. 1964. Tumor Inhibitory Effect of L-asparaginase from *Escherichia coli. Arch. Biochem. Biophys.* 105: 450-2
12. Mitraki A, King J. 1989. Protein folding intermediates and inclusion body formation. *Bio/Technology* 7: 690-7
13. Mukhopadhyay A. 1997. Inclusion bodies and purification of proteins in biologically active forms. *Adv. Biochem. Eng Biotechnol.* 56: 61-109
14. Roberts, J., Prager, M., and Bachynsky 1966, N.: The Antitumor Activity of *Escherichia coli* Asparaginase, *Cancer Res 26,* 2213.
15. Rudolph R, Lilie H. 1996. In vitro folding of inclusion body proteins. *FASEB J.* 10: 49-56.
16. Schwartz, J., Reeves, J., and Broome, J. 1966: Two Asparaginases from *E. coli* and Their Action Against Tumors, *Proc Natl Acad Sci U S A 56.*
17. Swain AL, Jaskolski M, Housset D, Rao JK, Wlodawer A. 1993. Crystal structure of *Escherichia coli* L-asparaginase, an enzyme used in cancer therapy. *Proc. Natl. Acad. Sci. U. S. A* 90: 1474-8
18. Taylor G, Hoare M, Gray DR, Marston FAO. 1986. Size and density of protein inclusion bodies. Bio/Technology 4: 553-7
19. Verma N, Kumar K, Kaur G, Anand S. 2007. L-asparaginase: a promising chemotherapeutic agent. *Crit Rev. Biotechnol.* 27: 45-62
20. Wang L, Maji SK, Sawaya MR, Eisenberg D, Riek R. 2008. Bacterial inclusion bodies contain amyloid-like structure. *PLoS. Biol.* 6: e195

Chapter 5

Measurement and Control of Cultivation Parameters during Mammalian Cell Cultivation and Their Impact on Bioprocess Performance

*Hesham A. El Enshasy**

Institute of Bioproduct Development (IBD),
UniversitiTeknologi Malaysia (UTM)
Johor Bahru, Johor, Malaysia

ABSTRACT

Good measurement and control system became one of the main key factors for proper bioprocess design and development. Nowadays, different types of on-line, off-line and in-line sensors are widely used to measure and control many bioprocess parameters. Beside the traditional measures like temperature, pH and DO, many new sensors are currently used for efficient bioprocess measurement and control and required for efficient scaling-up and optimized economic operation. Measurement and control of different parameters became more important during the cultivation of bioprocessing sensitive cells such as mammalian and human cells. In this mini review, different measurement and control parameters for mammalian cell cultivation will be presented in more details to give complete overview on cultivation condition and measurement and control system during cultivation of mammalian and human cells in bioreactor.

Keywords: *Bioprocess, Measurement and control, Mammalian cells, Bioreactor.*

---

* E-mail: henshasy@ibd.utm.my

1. CELL CULTIVATION: THE UNIVERSAL MODEL (INPUT AND OUTPUT MODEL)

Bioprocess optimization is based on the real-time monitoring of different physical, chemical and biological parameters. Therefore, increasing interest have been given for many new techniques for online/inline process analysis. In parallel, further requirements will arise by regulatory affairs like the process analytical technology (PAT) initiative issued by the Food and Drug Administration (FDA). The major goal of this regulation issue is to improve the understanding and control of the manufacturing process. PAT is a system for designing, analyzing and controlling manufacturing through timely measurements (*i.e.* during processing) of critical quality and performance attributes of raw and in-process materials and processes with the goal of ensuring final product quality (Clementschitsch and Bayer, 2006). Thus, measurement and control of the cultivation conditions are very important for bioprocess control and they provide knowledge for better understanding of the process toward further optimization and complete bioprocess validation. Therefore, it is important to define the key parameters which are significant for cell cultivation and bioactive metabolites production. The growth of living system in the bioreactor is regulated by complex interactions between physical, chemical and biological conditions of the living environment surrounding the cells as well as biochemical processes inside the biosystem (Figure 5.1). The total effect of the interactions between all physical, chemical and biological parameters will govern the overall cell metabolic pathway and thus they will determine not only growth but also cell performance in different biochemical processes related to different metabolites production.

The most important physical parameters include: temperature, pressure, agitation rate, and power input and flow rate. The chemical factors for the process include pH, dissolved oxygen, out gas analysis, dissolved carbon dioxide and medium composition. The biological factors have very wide range of analytical data which indicate cell viability and growth parameters such as cell mass, cell viability, cell morphology, oxygen/carbon dioxide uptake rates and many other parameters. However, Table 5.1 summarizes most of known physical, chemical and biological parameters used for measurement and control of mammalian cell cultivation in bioreactor level.

2. MEASUREMENT AND CONTROL PARAMETERS OF MAMMALIAN CELL BIOREACTOR

Mammalian cell cultures show specific characteristics that differ from microbial cells. The main differences between both cultivation systems could be summarized in the following points:

1. Mammalian cells grow in slower rate compared to microbial cells. The specific growth rates of most of cells are, in general, 10-20 times lower than microbial cells.
2. Some types of cells require solid support for growth (anchrogenous dependent cells) and are not able to grow in free suspension culture.

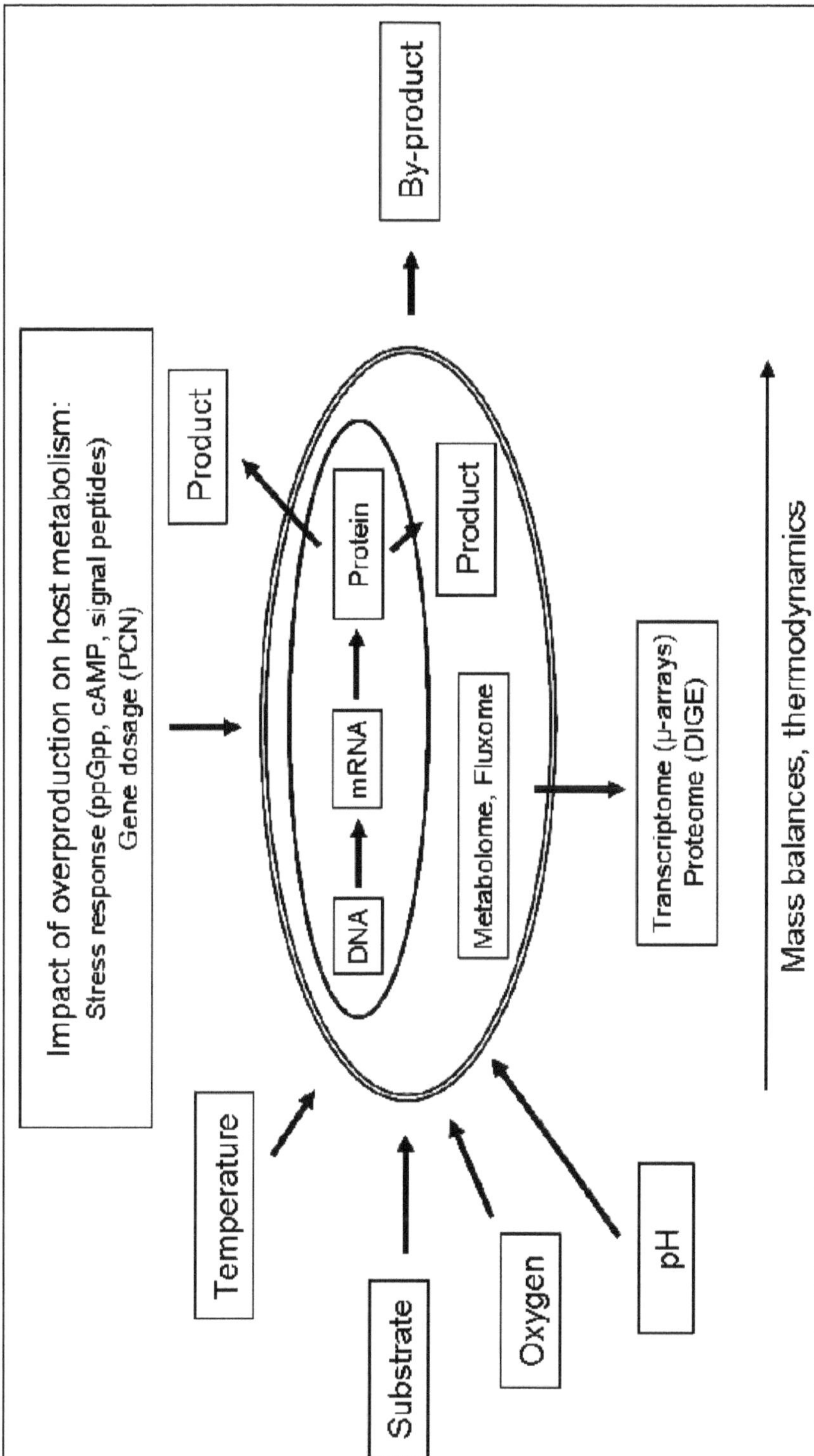

Figure 5.1: General Input/Output Model for Living Cells in Bioprocess Industries.
Cell growth and productivity is govern by multifunction factors (1ry. Factors: substrate and cultivation conditions) which reflect on overall cell metabolism in genomic, proteomic and metabolomics levels. (Clementschitsch and Bayer, 2006).

Table 5.1: Main Physical, Chemical and Biological Parameters for Mammalian Cell Cultivation. The upper part of table shows those basic parameters needed in any cultivation process. The lower part is those parameters needed to obtain complete knowledge/information about the bioprocess under study and required for metabolic engineering and modeling studies.

Physical	*Chemical*	*Biological*
☆ Temperature	☆ pH	☆ Cell viability
☆ Bioreactor Pressure (St. St. Bioreactors)	☆ Dissolved oxygen	☆ Optical Density
	☆ Dissolved carbon dioxide	☆ Cellular composition
☆ Agitation Speed		☆ Specific growth rate
☆ Gas Flow rate		☆ Specific substrate (s) consumption rates
☆ Total volume		
		☆ Specific production rate
☆ Feeding rate		
☆ Power Input		
☆ Foam		
☆ Reactor weight	☆ Redox potential	☆ Oxygen uptake rate
☆ Feeding tank weight	☆ Out gas analysis	☆ Carbon dioxide production rate
☆ Culture Viscosity	☆ (O_2, CO_2, N_2)	
☆ Gas Hold up	☆ Substrate (s)	☆ RQ
☆ Gas Mixing pattern	☆ Product (s)	☆ Growth inhibitors
	☆ Enzyme activities	☆ Protein
	☆ Conductivity	☆ DNA/RNA
	☆ Cell composition (C, H, O, N, P, S)	☆ ATP/ADP/AMP
	☆ Metabolite profiling	
	☆ Mineral Ions	

3. Mammalian and human cells are highly sensitive to shear stress because of the absence of cell wall.
4. Specific gas system is required for pH control (bicarbonate/CO_2 system).

Thus, real time measurement and control of mammalian cells is very crucial. However, in practice, not all above mentioned parameters (Table 5.1) are measured during running all processes but there are standard/basic measurement and control of bioreactor in routine cultivations of mammalian and human cells (Figure 5.2).

A bioprocess involving mammalian cell culture is different from a standard synthetic chemical reaction in many ways. Biological reactions tend to be stable compared to many chemical processes and most major variations in a biological reaction occur over long time scales (hours or days). However, if the cultivated cells have been subjected to an acute stress, they may not be able to recover and the desired product yield may not be obtained. Among differences sensors for a chemical process compared to those for a biological process lies in the complex milieu in which cells grow. The culture media contains proteins, amino acids, sugars, cell debris and salts. Together these compounds tend to coat or foul surfaces of sensing elements. However, significant fundamental differences exist between the use of monitoring and control methodologies applied in an academic setting (where capital costs dominate decisions)

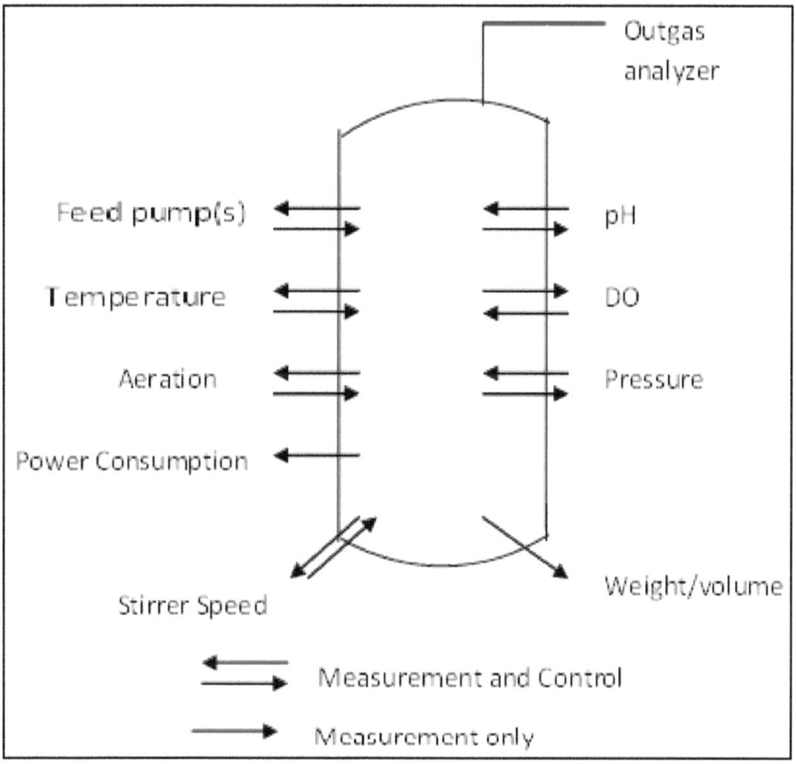

Figure 5.2: Common Measurement and Control of Bioreactors as Generally Accepted as Routine Equipment. The components of the figure have been grouped together.

and those in an industrial environment (where time and productivity can be more critical issues) as discussed by many authors (Olsson *et al.*, 1998).

3. BASIC CULTIVATION PARAMETERS AND THEIR IMPACT ON MAMMALIAN CELL CULTIVATION

3.1. Temperature

Temperature is one of the most critical variables to be monitored for the maintenance of healthy cell culture. In general, for all mammalian cells temperature should kept at 37°C. An accuracy of ±0.5°C or less is typically considered adequate for cell culture monitoring, while variation on temperature of more than 1°C can in many cases lead to an significant loss in cell viability and productivity. For some processes, a temperature shift batch culture may be desirable in which there are two controlled temperature values, one for the growth phase and another for the production phase (Fox *et al.*, 2004). It has been reported that a decrease in cultivation temperatures, less than the optimum of cellular growth (37°C), leads to reduced cell growth but prolonged culture viability. Therefore, a concept of two stages is proposed: a growth phase with high cell proliferation (*e.g.* 37°C) to obtain high cell density followed by temperature reduction to decrease cell death rate (Ducommun *et al.*, 2001). After the growth phase, the temperature is decreased to values ranged between 28°C and 32°C. Other study of Nam *et al.* (2008) showed also that when the cultivation temperature reduced from 37°C and 33°C during the beginning of stationary phase in culture of CHO cell producing human placental alkaline phosphatase, the viable cell density was increased by 62 per cent concomitant with an increase of 133 per cent in specific productivity. These together lead to more than threefolds increase in volumetric protein production. However, the cultivation strategy of temperature shift is dependent on the type of cell line used and type of product as well.

3.2. pH

Next to temperature, pH is considered the most critical parameter to monitor in a biological process based on the degree of damage that may occur as a result of losing the control. Variation of pH as low as ±0.1 away from optimal can have substantial impact on cell growth and productivity for certain cell types. While most cell culture media provide substantial buffering of pH, cellular metabolism invariably decreases pH due to lactate and CO_2 production as metabolic byproducts. In general, the pH can have a substantial impact on cell metabolism and growth by altering rates of substrate uptake and product release. In animal cell cultures, even a mimic change in pH value can affect cell growth, metabolism and protein synthesis significantly. For example, the pH 7.2 was found to be optimum for cell growth in most of cell lines applied in industrial level. When this pH value is shifted down to pH 6.9, a two folds decrease in specific glucose consumption rate, lactate production rate and cell growth rate could be occurred (Ozturk and Palsson, 1991). The culture pH is not only affecting the protein expression but also it can affect the final product quality since it effect is also on the protein glycosylation process (Zanghi*et al.*, 1999). Beside the traditional on-line pH measurement electrode, there has also been an increase in the ability to measure the intracellular pH, by flow cytometry and pH-dependent fluorescence indicator (Ozkan and Mutharasan, 2002) and nuclear magnetic resonance. There are several reports that relate the intracellular pH value to cell behavior, including metabolism, apoptosis and specific growth rate (Charlet and Marc, 1998).

3.3. Dissolved Oxygen (DO)

Probably the most important state variable for the process control is the dissolved oxygen concentration (DO) in contact with cells. Because of the very low solubility of oxygen in water and in culture medium, of about 6-8 mg/L at 37°C, air or air-mix with pure oxygen is supplied continuously to eliminate any oxygen limitation throughout cultivation. Mammalian cell culture requires oxygen for the production of energy from glucose and sometimes can be a limiting substrate in high cell density culture. The specific oxygen consumption rate is cell line dependent. For example, at standard cultivation temperature, these rates are 0.3 pmol/cell h^{-1} for CHO cells, 0.30 for BHK and 0.22 for hybridoma (Jorjani and Ozturk, 1999). In many cell cultivation systems, gas mixture is added to prevent oxygen limitation especially when the number of cells in culture exceeding 10^7 ml^{-1}. The value of DO in culture is also considered as important parameter to estimate cell activity and viability in culture. In general, when DO decreased in high rate in culture, this indicate the high cell growth rate and good viability.

3.4. Dissolved Carbon Dioxide (DCO_2)

Like dissolved oxygen, dissolved carbon dioxide in culture can give indirect indication for cell growth, viability and activity. During the cell active growth phase, the dissolved carbon dioxide in culture is usually high. This is because of its higher solubility in water compared to oxygen. At high viable cell concentration in large scale mammalian cell culture processes, dissolved carbon dioxide can accumulate due to low removal rates of reduced surface to volume ratio (Pattison *et al.*, 2000). High concentration of dissolved CO_2 can inhibit cell growth and metabolism and can impact the glycosylation of some desired protein products.

3.5. Foam Control Sensor

Foam occurs in bioreactor cultures during cell cultivation due to the high aeration/agitation and the presence of surface active substances in the cultivation medium or produced in metabolic process. This is usually undesirable and causes many problems in cultivation such as: reduction in working volume, increase chance of contamination, suppression of oxygen transfer, loss of active biomass and fouling of sensors (Alder *et al.*, 1980; Deshpande and Barigou, 1999). In case of many mammalian cell cultures, because of high cell sensitivity, a special type of silicon antifoam is usually applied. Foaming is also one of the main factors which can cause cell rupture during cultivation process.

3.6. Vessel Pressure Sensor

Bioreactors are usually run under low positive pressure to minimize the contamination risk. For most of bioreactor vessels made of stainless steel, they can stand with pressure range from -1 up to 3 bars. During cultivation, the pressure is usually higher than the surrounding environment. The pressure in bioreactor vessel is built continuously by sparged gas. In some process, working under relatively high pressure (not exceeding 0.5 bars) is desirable to increase the metabolites excretion. Working under higher pressure is generally not safe. Pressure gauge is usually installed on the bioreactor lid for pressure measurement. Beside the traditional pressure gauge, pressure sensor is installed in modern versions of bioreactors and submits a continuous signal to the main control panel to measure the pressure and make corrective action in case of high pressure to prevent the possible vessel explosion.

4. ON-LINE AND OFF-LINE SUBSTRATES/METABOLITES SENSORS

Metabolites can be measured in real time, using specific electrodes such as on-line glucose electrode or through techniques such as Flow Injection Analysis (FIA) that allow online measurement of many substrates and products. In FIA system, a small flow of culture medium is continuously pumped in a unit composed of tangential filter (for cell separation), injection pump, and detector (Reinecke and Stephanopoulos, 2000). Another possibility is to connect offline equipment to automated sampling systems to provide information on the metabolite concentration for a control system.

This is very helpful for controlling flow of fresh medium in a fed-batch culture (Konstantinov*et al.*, 1996; Ozturk*et al.*, 1997) and for chemostat culture as well. However, it is also possible to estimate cell concentration, including those immobilized in microcarriers based on measurements of real-time substrate consumption (Ducommun *et al.*, 2001). Advantages of FIA include a reduced risk of contamination, ease of recalibration or replacement of sensing elements, small sample requirements, and short response time.

5. IN-LINE OUTGAS ANALYSIS (OXYGEN CONSUMPTION, CARBON DIOXIDE PRODUCTION AND RESPIRATORY QUOTIENT)

Oxygen is a key substrate in animal cell metabolism and its consumption and the production of CO_2 are thus parameters of great interest for bioprocess monitoring and control. For determination of both of oxygen and carbon dioxide in out gases, gas analyzer is usually attached in-line with the exhaust gas line of the bioreactor. Out-gas analyzers are relatively expensive but is important for monitoring the cell physiological status and possible feed-back control during cultivation. The respiratory quotient (RQ) for a culture is defined as the molar ratio of CO_2 formed to O_2 consumed. This parameter is often used to describe the relative efficiency of the cellular metabolism for a given set of process conditions. Until recent year, RQ had infrequently been used to evaluate animal cell metabolism primarily due to difficulties in measuring the CO_2 evolution rate (Bonarius*et al.*, 1995). On the other hand, the oxygen uptake rate has traditionally been more readily quantified accurately. The complication of measuring CO_2 production rate comes from using bicarbonate as buffering agent in the cultivation media, and thus the RQ cannot directly be calculated from gas-phase measurements (Neelman*et al.*, 2000). The introduction or loss of CO_2 from culture medium during preparation and sterilization must be taken into account. However, RQ values for mammalian cells grown under near optimal conditions are generally 1.0±0.05. In general, an increase in RQ has been shown to correlate with an increase in cellular productivity and therefore RQ could serve as a means for estimating the physiological status of the cells.

6. CONCLUSION

Good measurement and control practice is a critical issue in the development of proper cultivation strategy especially in sensitive processes like mammalian and human cell culture systems. When process scaled up from small scale (Microplate well or T-flask) up to bioreactor level, a new set of cultivation variables should be monitored and controlled during the cultivation process to increase the cell viability, productivity and consequently the cell performance for high volumetric and specific metabolite production.

REFERENCES

1. Alder, I., Diekmann, J., Hartke, W., Hecht, V., Rohn, F. and Schügerl, K., 1980. Bubble coalescence behavior in biological media II: effect of antifoam additives. European J. Applied Microbiology and Biotechnology, 10, pp. 171-186.

2. Bonarius, H.P.J., Degooider, C.D., Tramper, J., and Schmid, G., 1995. Determination of the respiration quotient in mammalian cell culture in bicarbonate buffered media. Biotechnology and Bioengineering, 45, pp. 524-535.

3. Charlet, M., and Marc, A., 1998. Intracellular pH monitoring as a tool for the staudy of hybridoma cell behaviour in batch and continuous bioreactor cultures.Biotechnology Progress, 14, pp. 626-638.

4. Clementschitsch, F., and Bayer, K., 2006. Improvement of bioprocess monitoring: development of novel concepts. Microbial Cell Factories, 5, pp. 19-29.

5. Deshpande, N.S., and Barigou, M., 1999. Performance characteristics of novel mechanical foam breakers in stirred tank reactor. J. Chemical Technology and Biotechnology, 74, pp. 979-987.

6. Ducommun, P., Bolzonella, I., Rhiel, M., Pugeaud, P., van Stockar, U., and Marison, I.W., 2001. On-line determination of animal cell concentration. Biotechnology and Bioengineering, 72, pp. 515-522.

7. Fox, S.R., Patel, U.A., Yap, M.G., and Wang, D.I., 2004. Maximizing interferon-gamma production by Chinese hamster ovary cells through temperature shift optimization experimental and modeling. Biotechnology and Bioengineering, 85, pp. 177-184.

8. Jorjani, P., and Ozturk, S.S., 1999. Effects of cell density and temperature on oxygen consumption rate for different mammalian cell lines. Biotechnology and Bioengineering, 64, pp. 349-356.

9. Spier, R.E.; Griffiths, J.B. and Meignier, B., 1991. Production of biologicals from animal cells in culture. Butterworth-Heinemann Press, Oxford. pp 390-393.

10. Nam, J.H., Zhang, F., Ermoval, M., Linhardt, R.J., and Sharfstein, S.T., 2008. The effect of culture conditions on the glycosylation and secreted human placental alkaline phosphatase produced in Chinese hamster ovary cells. Biotechnology and Bioengineering, 100, pp. 1178-1192.

11. Neeleman, R., van den End, E.J., and van Boxtel, A.J.B., 2000. Estimation of the respiration quotient in a bicarbonate buffered batch cell culture. J. Biotechnology, 80, pp. 85-94.

12. Ozkan, P., and Mutharasan, R., 2002. A rapid method for measuring intracellular pH using BCECF-AM. Biochem. Biophys. Acta., 1572, pp. 143-148.

13. Ozturk, S.S., and Palsson, B.O., 1991. Effect of serum concentration, dissolved oxygen concentration, and medium pH in a batch reactor. Biotechnology progress, 7, pp. 481-494.

14. Ozturk, S.S., Thrift, J.C., Blackie, J.D., and Naveh, D., 1997. Real-time monitoring and control of glucose and lactate concentrations in mammalian cell perfusion reactor. Biotechnology and Bioengineering, 53, pp. 372-378.

15. Olsson, L., Schulze, U., and Nielsen, J., 1998. On-line bioprocess monitoring-an academic discipline or an industrial tools? Trends in Analytical Chemistry, 17, pp. 88-95.

16. Pattison, R.N., Swamy, J., Mendenhall, B., Hwang, C., and Frohlich, B.T., 2000. Measurement and control of dissolved carbon dioxide in mammalian cell culture processes using an in situ fiber optic chemical sensor. Biotechnology Progress, 16, pp. 769-774.
17. Reinecke, M. and Stepahnopoulos, G. (2000). Flow injection analysis for simultaneous quantification of protein concentration and glycosylation macroheterogeneity in cell culture samples. Cytotechnology.**34,** 237-242.
18. Zanghi, J.A.; Schmelzer, A.E.; Mendoza, T.P.; Knop, R.H. and Miller, W.M. (1999).Bicarbonate concentration and osmolalityare key determinants in the inhibition of CHO cell poly-sialylation under elevated pCO (2) or pH Biotechnology and Bioengineering. **65,** 182-191.

Chapter 6

Antinociceptive Activity of Haruan (*Channa striatus*) Traditional Extract

Zuleen Delina Fasya Binti Abdul Ghani[1]* *and Abdul Manan Bin Mat Jais*[2]

[1]*Industrial Biotechnology Research Centre (IBRC), SIRIM Berhad, Shah Alam, Selangor D.E.*
[2]*Faculty of Medicine and Health Sciences, University Putra Malaysia, Serdang, Selangor D.E.*

ABSTRACT

The objectives of this study were to determine the amino acid and fatty acid composition of Haruan Traditional Extract (HTE), to elucidate the mechanism responsible for its antinociceptive activity and to clarify the relationship between the presence of amino acids and fatty acids with the expected activity. The HTE was obtained by steaming fresh fillet of *Channa striatus* with a pressure cooker at 100°C, for 3 hours after 1 hour of the seasoning process. For the antinociceptive activities of HTE at different concentration, the extracts were purified, filtered and prepared in concentrations of 100 (stock solution), 50 and 10 per cent dilution in distilled water and subjected to the antinociceptive studies. For the elucidation of the involvement of opioid receptor in HTE antinociceptive activities, the antinociceptive action of the extract with the highest antinociceptive activity resulted from the prior study were tested against naloxone in all antinociceptive assays in a bid to further elucidate probable mechanisms of antinociception. In all of the above-mentioned studies were involved the use of 0.6 per cent acetic acid-induced abdominal constriction, 5 per cent formalin-induced paw-licking, and 50°C hot plate test in rodent to evaluate the HTE antinociceptive activities. For the determination of amino acid and fatty acid, the stock solution HTE was run into the High

* E-mail: zuleen@sirim.my

Performance Liquid Chromatography (HPLC) and Gas Chromatography (GC), respectively. All data obtained were analyzed using the One-Way Analysis of Variance (ANOVA) followed by a Dunnet test with $P<0.05$ as the limit of significance. From the data obtained, the HTE was found to contain major amino acid cysteine, histidine, glutamic acid, glycine and aspartic acid. In addition, the HTE was found to have a high myristic acid followed by palmitic, arachidonic, linolenic and oleic acid. The HTE exhibited concentration/dosage-dependent manner significant antinociceptive activity ($P<0.05$). HTE also were shown to have an involvement of central antinociceptive mechanism when tested against the naloxone. As a conclusion, the HTE contains all the important amino acids and fatty acids and possesses the antinociceptive activities. In this respect, it supports the traditional claims that it reduces pain, inflammation and promote wound healing.

Keywords: *Antinociceptive activity, Channa striatus, Haruan traditional extract (HTE), Amino acid, Fatty acid, Naloxone.*

1. INTRODUCTION

For thousands of years, natural products have been used in treating or preventing human diseases (Chin *et al.*, 2006). Natural products have been used as a medicinal source (Linblad, 2008). Natural product medicine comes from various sources and materials including plants, microorganism, marine, vertebrates and invertebrates (Newman *et al.*, 2000). Many of drugs preparation were derived from natural sources including a diverse array of plants, animal product and minerals. Many traditional medicine treatments today are traceable to ancient descriptions of similar preparation, although the uses of a preparation may have deviated (Linblad, 2008). Natural products have a potential to be a new drug and lately more of the research focus on the isolation of the bioactive compound (Dholwani *et al.*, 2008).

Channa striatus belongs to *Channidae* family; locally known as "haruan" which is one of the snakehead fresh water fish species (Figure 6.1) (Rajen, 2002). This fish has long been used by patients during the post-operative period to promote wound healing and alleviates post-operative pain and discomfort. One of the reported benefits in those taking *C. striatus* fish was based on traditional remedies for treatment of skin

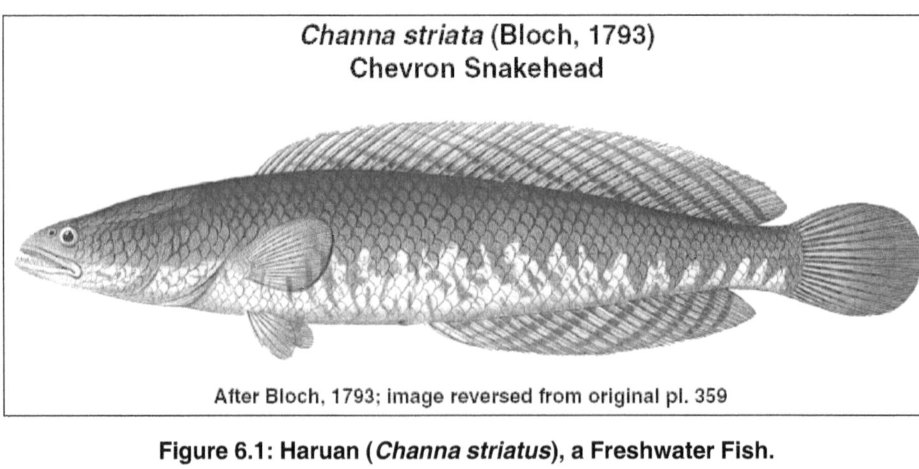

Figure 6.1: Haruan (*Channa striatus*), a Freshwater Fish.

conditions and to relief pain and irritation. The *C. striatus* is consumed after dry-frying, grilling or boiling in porridge as a dietary medicine for wound healing (Mat Jais *et al.*, 1997).

The potential of *C. striatus* induction of wound healing and promotion of tissue growth (Mat Jais *et al.*, 1994; 1998) and antinociceptive activity (Mat Jais *et al.*, 1997) have also been reported. It is also suggested as a good source of amino acid and fatty acid also have a potential as an alternative health food product (Mat Jais *et al.*, 1998; Zuraini *et al.*, 2006). Thus for further studies, it is interesting and important to investigate and to isolate the bioactive compounds that are responsible for the antinociceptive activities.

The current study was carried out to use the Haruan Traditional Extract (HTE) and identify the bioactive compound compositions such as amino acids and fatty acids. The HTE will also be evaluated for its antinociceptive activities using different concentrations and pre-treatment with opioid receptor, naloxone. All the results were compared, discussed and considered as a final conclusion to establish the HTE product.

2. MATERIAL AND METHODS

2.1. Preparation of Fresh Fillet of *C. striatus*

In this study, 6 month old *C. striatus* fish having a weight ranging from 200g and 400g were used. They were caught in Bagan Dato, Perak, Malaysia. The samples were kept in a tank and transferred to the Physiology Laboratory at Universiti Putra Malaysia. Preparation of fresh *C. striatus* fillet was carried out using the method described by Mat Jais *et al.* (1997). Briefly, pre-cleaned live fish was weighed and slaughtered. The fish fillets were obtained by carefully cutting the fish lengthwise along the backbone to gain the maximum amount of flesh without any backbone.

2.2. Preparation of Haruan Traditional Extract (HTE)

The whole fish fillet extract was prepared through cooking under pressure (1 atm) set at 100°C for 3 hours after 1 hour of the seasoning process. Fresh boneless fillet was weighed and placed on a stainless steel wire mesh mounted on a stainless steel tripod in cooker. Distilled water was then added to fish fillet at volume ratios of 1: 1 (w/v). At the end of the extraction procedure the fillets were discarded, while the liquid extracts were collected, filtered, centrifuged and stored at 4°C until further use.

2.3. Preparation of Different Concentration of HTE

The stock solution of HTE, considered as a 100 per cent concentration, together with the other two concentrations/strength (10 and 50 per cent concentration/ strength) prepared by serial dilution with dH_2O, was chosen for antinociceptive profile determination.

2.4. Determination of Protein Composition of HTE

The protein composition was analyzed using Kjedahl method by the Association of Official Analytical Chemist (1984), techniques where 1.5g of HTE sample was dissolved in 2.5 ml non-nitrogen concentrated H_2SO_4 in the fume hood in a digestive flask. The solution was heated-up for 4-5 hour at 400°C until the colorless solution was obtained and upon cooling to room temperature is often considered to be 40°C, minimum quantity of dH_2O was carefully poured into the flask. A distillation of the solution was performed inside a condenser and 10 ml of 45 per cent NaOH was added to the digested solution and placed in a 10 ml 2 per cent boric acid plus 3 drops of indicator (0.3 bromocresol green plus 0.2 g methyl red) the color has changed from violet to blue after 4 min indicate total distillation of ammonia (NH_4) into boric acid. Subsequently, a titration using 0.1 N H_2SO_4 for boric acid containing NH_4 (as blank) and the distilled solution, with color changed from blue to pink was performed and the percentage of nitroneous compound is calculated as follows:

Percentage Nitrogen

$$\frac{(\text{Volume of } H_2SO_4 - \text{Blank}) \times 0.1 \ (\text{Normality of } H_2SO_4) \times 14 \times 100}{\text{Weight of sample} \times 1000}$$

Percentage Protein = per cent of N x 6.25.

2.5. Determination of Amino Acid Composition of HTE

Amino acid analysis of HTE was carried out using the PICO-TAG method (Millipore Corporation, Waters Chromatography Division, USA). The HTE's amino acid extracts were hydrolyzed with 6N hydrochloric acid for 24 hours at 110°C followed sequentially by the addition of re-drying solution (methanol: water: triethylamine) in the ratio of 2: 2: 1 (v: v: v) and derivatization reagent (methanol: triethylamine: water: phenylisocynate) in the ratio of 7: 1: 1: 1 (v: v: v: v). An internal standard of α-aminobutyric acid (AABA) was added to each sample prior to the re-drying solution and derivatization reagent.

The hydrolyzed sample obtained after filtration was kept for 4 weeks at -20°C until used. The hydrolyzed sample was filtered again in nylon type 0.2 µm cellulose nitrate membrane filter. About 10 µl of solution was put into a vial and then added to the same volume of internal standard before being dried under vacuum for 30 min. About 20 µl of solution was then added to the dried sample and shaken vigorously for 15 min. The sample was dried again under vacuum for 30 min followed by the addition of 20 µl of derivation reagent. The mixture was shaken vigorously for 15 min and then left at room temperature for 20 min before being dried again under vacuum for 30 min and kept at -20°C until analysis by HPLC.

Prior to injection into HPLC, the sample and standard were mixed with 100 µl sample diluents and shaken for 15 min and injected into the Water HPLC in the volume of 20 µl and 8 µl, respectively. The free amino acids were separated using the Water PICO-TAG column for hydrolyzate amino acids (3.9 x 300 mm; Millipore Corporation, Waters Chromatography Division, USA) by reversed phase HPLC, with a flow rate of 1.0 ml/min, detected using a UV detector at 254 nm. Eluant A (50mM sodium acetate trihydrate buffer (pH 5.7)) and eluant B (60 per cent acetonitrile in water) were used as mobile phase. Gradient conditions were (1) 0.5 min, 100 per cent (A): 0 per cent (B), (2) 5 min, 75 per cent (A): 25 per cent (B), (3) 6 min, 52 per cent (A):

48 per cent (B), (4) 0.5 min, 0 per cent (A): 100 per cent (B), (5) 14 min, constant 100 per cent (A): 0 per cent (B).

2.6. Determination of Fatty Acid Composition of HTE

Total lipid extraction of the HTE was carried out according to the method of Folch *et al.* (1957) as described by Rajion (1985) but with slight modification. The HTE's in the volume 2 ml, were added to 40 ml of Chloroform: Methanol (CM) (2: 1, v/v) in a 50 ml stopper tube. After flushing with nitrogen, the mixture was allowed to stand for at least 12 hours, with occasional shaking. The mixture was filtered through a No.1 filter Whatman filter paper into a 250 ml separating flask and the residue on the paper was washed with 10 ml of CM. One-fifth of the final volume of saline solution was added, the mixture was shaken vigorously for one minute and was let stand for at least 4 h. This procedure removed non-lipid contaminants, which would be retained in the aqueous upper phase. After complete separation, the lower phase was collected and evaporated by rotary evaporation (water bath (WB 2001) and fractional distiller (VV2011)) (Heidolph, USA). The total lipid extract was transferred and made up to 5 ml with CM in a 7 ml capacity vial, which was flushed with nitrogen and stopperd.

The HTE's lipid extracts were saponified using the methanolic potassium hydroxide followed by trans-esterification with methanolic boron trifluoride. An internal standard of heneicosanoic acid (C21: 0) was added to each sample prior to methylation, which proceeded as described in the following: The HTE was dried under liquid nitrogen. 2 ml of 0.66N potassium hydroxide in methanol was added, and after flushing with nitrogen was heated in a boiling water (Memmert, Germany) bath for 10 min, with occasional shaking. After cooling, 2 ml of 14 per cent boron trifluoride (Sigma, U.S.A) in methanol (BDH, Germany) was added, as esterifying agent, and the mixture reheated for 10 min. After cooling, 4 ml of distilled deionized water and 4 ml of petroleum ether (BDH, Germany) were added and the mixture was shaken vigorously for a minute and then centrifuged. The top layer of petroleum ether phase was transferred to another test tube and about 0.5 g of anhydrous sodium sulphate added to remove any water present.

The petroleum ether containing the fatty acid methyl esters (FAME) was transferred to a 7 ml screw cap vial (Kimble, Opticlear, Mexico), flushed with nitrogen and stored at 4°C until analysis by gas-liquid chromatography. The derived FAME were then separated on a supelco series bonded phase fused silica capillary column (Supelco Co., USA) (30m x 0.25mm ID, 0.2 µm film thickness, SP™-2330) in a 5890 Hewlett Packard Gas-Liquid chromatography (Hewlett-Packard Co., USA). High purity nitrogen (Malaysian Oxygen Bhd., Malaysia) was the carrier gas at 40 ml/min. High purity hydrogen and compressed air (Malaysian Oxygen Bhd., Malaysia) were used for the flame ionization detector in the gas-liquid chromatography and was channeled at two bars and three bars, respectively. The injector temperature was programmed at 220°C and the detector temperature was 220°C. The column temperature was set in the range of 100-190°C with temperature programming at the rate of 5°C/min increment to facilitate optimal separation. The identification of the peaks was made by comparison of equivalent chain lengths with those of authentic fatty acid methyl esters (Sigma, USA). Peak areas were determined using a HP-3393A Integrator (Hewlett-Packard, Avondale, PA). The concentration of the various fatty acids was expressed in normalized percentage of the total fatty content of the sample.

2.7. Preparation of the Dosage Drugs

About 100 mg/kg Acetylsalicylic acid (ASA) (Bayer Singapore), 5 mg/kg of Morphine (Delta West, USA) and 5 mg/kg Naloxone were used for the purpose of comparison against the HTE, was prepared by dissolving them in dH_2O.

2.8. Experimental Animals

Male Swiss albino mice (25-30g: 5-7 weeks) and *Sprague-Dawley* rats (180-200g; 8-10 weeks old) were used in this study. All animals were kept at room temperature (27±2°C; 70-80 per cent humidity; 12 h light/darkness cycle) in the Animal Holding Unit, Faculty of Medicine and Health Sciences, UPM for at least 48 hours before use. Food and water were supplied *ad libitum* up to the beginning of the experiments. At all times the mice and rats were cared for in accordance with current UPM principles and guidelines for the care of laboratory animals and the UPM ethical guidelines for investigations of experimental pain in conscious animals as adopted from Zimmermann (1983). All experiments were conducted between 09.30 and 12.30 hours to minimize the effects of environmental changes.

2.9. Establishment of the Antinociceptive Profile of HTE

All mice and rats were equally divided into 6-8 groups, which consist of 7seven mice per group for treatment with SC-administered dH_2O, ASA (100 mg/kg), Morphine (5mg/kg), Naloxone (5mg/kg) or HTE (10 per cent, 50 per cent and 100 per cent concentration/strength), respectively. The mice were then left to rest for 30 min before being administered intraperitoneally with acetic acid (0.6 per cent), Intraplantar-administration of formalin (5 per cent) or introduced to hotplate test. All the solutions were administered in the volume of 10 ml/kg.

2.10. Abdominal Constriction Test

The abdominal constriction test (Dambisya and Lee, 1995) was used to evaluate the chemical induced peripheral antinociceptive activity. Briefly, the acetic acid (J.T. Baker, U.S.A.), prepared as 0.6 per cent (v/v) solution in dH_2O and use to induce pain in mice peritoneal cavity, was administered intraperitoneally (IP) in the volume of 10 ml/kg of mice, 30 min after the subcutaneous (SC) administering respective drugs, dH_2O or extracts. The abdominal constriction or writhing response resulted from the injection of acetic acid were observed as the abdominal region together with a stretching of the hind limbs. The numbers of abdominal constrictions were counted cumulatively over the period of 25 min, 5 min following the acetic acid administration. Antinociceptive activity was indicated by the reduction in the mean of the number of abdominal constrictions in the test groups compared to the control group.

$$\frac{(dH_2O\text{ control group mean}) - (\text{Test group means})}{dH_2O\text{ control group means}} \times 100$$

2.11. Formalin Test

The formalin test described by Hunskaar and Hole (1987) was used but with slight modification. The extract was administered into rats subcutaneously (SC) in the volume of 10 ml/kg. After 30 minutes, 50 µl of 5 per cent formalin was injected into the subplantar region of the left hind paw on rats for antinociceptive studies. The rats were individually placed in transparent Plexiglass cage observation chamber. Immediately following the formalin injection, the amount of time the animal spent to lick the injected hind paw were recorded at the interval time of 0-5 min for the first phase and 10-30 min for the second phase.

2.12. Hotplate Test

The 50°C hot plate test described by Wilson *et al.* (2003) with slight modification was used to assess the thermal-induced central antinociceptive activity of the extract. This assay is a modification of a classic hot plate test in which the lower intensity is designed to increase the sensitivity of the test to weak analgesic (Ankier, 1974). The temperature of the metal plate (model 7280, Ugo Basile, Italy) was maintained at 50 ± 0.2°C. Mice were placed on the Plexiglas walls on the heated surface to constrain their locomotion on the plates and latency to a discomfort reaction (licking of the paws or jumping) was recorded in 30, 60, 120, 180, 240 and 300 min following subcutaneous (SC) administration of the test agents. The cut off time of 20 s was chosen to indicate complete analgesia and to avoid tissue injury.

2.13. Antinociceptive Test Pre-Treated With Naloxone

The naloxone was administered subcutaneously (SC) with the volume of 10ml/kg to the animals 10 min before administering respective drugs, dH_2O and extracts. All the antinociceptive assays (abdominal constriction, formalin, and hotplate test) were followed as previously described.

2.14. Statistical Analysis

The results of antinociceptive studies were presented as Mean ± Standard Error of Mean (S.E.M). The One-way analysis of Variance (ANOVA) test with Post-Hoc Dunnet test was used to analyze and compare the data, with $P<0.05$ as the limit of significance.

3. RESULTS

3.1. Amino Acid and Fatty Acid Composition of HTE

The 100 per cent concentration/strength of HTE was found to have 5.37 ± 0.31 mg/g of total protein. The compositions of the amino acids as a percentage of total protein in the HTE are shown in Table 6. 1. The HTE was found to contain all amino acids with the major amino acid found being cystine, histidine, glutamic acid, glycine and aspartic acid (13.145 ± 0.395, 9.760 ± 0.110, 8.760 ± 0.840, 6.075 ± 0.285, 5.925 ± 0.035 per cent of the total protein respectively).

Table 6.1: The Amino Acid Composition of HTE.

Amino Acid	*Per cent of Total Amino Acid ± S.E.M*
Aspartic Acid	5.925 ± 0.035
Glutamic Acid	8.760 ± 0.840
Serine	1.945 ± 0.005
Glycine	6.075 ± 0.285
Histidine	9.760 ± 0.110
Arginine	2.070 ± 1.040
Threonine	1.605 ± 0.195
Alanine	2.720 ± 1.010
Proline	3.520 ± 1.620
Tyrosine	0.670 ± 0.010
Valine	1.105 ± 0.025
Methionine	0.255 ± 0.050
Cystine	13.145 ± 0.395
Isoleucine	0.550 ± 0.010
Leucine	1.945 ± 0.650
Phenylalanine	2.000 ± 0.130
Lysine	3.270 ± 0.190

The composition of the fatty acids present in the HTE as a percentage of total fatty acids is given in Table 6.2. The most abundant fatty acid present in the HTE was myristic acid (C14: 0), which accounted for approximately 42.96 ± 6.08 per cent of total fatty acids. The other major fatty acids included palmitic acid (C16: 0), arachidonic acid (C20: 4), linolenic acid (C18: 3) and oleic acid (C18: 1), which accounted for the 15.52 ± 2.43, 14.02 ± 1.14, 12.12 ± 1.02 and 11.95 ± 1.54 per cent of the total fatty acids, respectively. HTE was also found to have the ratios of ω-3: ω-6 and polyunsaturated fatty acid: saturated fatty acid (PUFA/SFA) lower than 1 as shown in Table 6.3.

Table 6.2: The Fatty Acid Composition.

Fatty Acid	*per cent of Total Fatty Acid ± S.E.M*
Lauric Acid (C12: 0)	3.29 ± 0.44
Myristic Acid (C14: 0)	42.96 ± 6.08
Palmitic Acid (C16: 0)	15.52 ± 2.43
Palmitoleic Acid (C16: 1)	3.58 ± 0.01
Stearic Acid (C18: 0)	6.21 ± 3.26
Oleic Acid (C18: 1)	11.95 ± 1.54
Linoleic Acid (C18: 2)	8.48 ± 1.39
Linolenic Acid (C18: 3)	12.12 ± 1.02
Eicosadienoic Acid (C20: 2)	10.71 ± 0.27
Arachidonic Acid (C20: 4)	14.02 ± 1.14
Ligoceric Acid (C24: 0)	6.80 ± 2.265

Table 6.3: The Total Fatty Acid of HTE.

Total Fatty Acid	*Composition (µg/g)*
Total Saturated	70.07 ± 2.93
Total Unsaturated	59.30 ± 3.58
Total Monoamines	13.98 ± 3.08
Total PUFA ω-3	12.12 ± 1.02
Total PUFA ω-6	33.20 ± 0.53
Overall Total	129.36 ± 0.65
ω-6: ω-3 Ratio	0.28 ± 0.03
Unsat: Sat	0.09 ± 0.01
Poly: Sat Ratio	0.34 ± 0.27

3.2. Antinociceptive Activities of HTE at Different Concentration

Figure 6.2 shows the antinociceptive profile of HTE assessed using the acetic acid–induced abdominal constriction test in mice. The extracts, at all concentration used, exhibited a significant ($p<0.05$) antinociceptive activity in a concentration–dependent manner. Interestingly, increasing the concentration of the extracts to 50 and 100 per cent was found to enhance the HTE antinociceptive activity with the percentage of analgesia recorded were 72 and 88 per cent, respectively compared to dH_2O.

The antinociceptive profile of HTE assessed using the formalin test in rats is shown in Figure 6.3. HTE exhibited significant ($p<0.05$) activity in 50 and 100 per cent of the concentrations in both phases used in a concentration-dependent manner. The antinociceptive activity can be seen in the early and late phases of the formalin-induced nociception. In the early phase, by increasing the concentration of the extracts to 50 and 100 per cent was found to cause analgesia at about 68 and 85 per cent, respectively. While in the late phase at 100 per cent concentration HTE exhibited its antinociceptive activities with 73.5 per cent inhibition compared to control group.

The antinociceptive profile of HTE assessed by using the hot plate test in mice was shown in Figure 6.4. The HTE at all concentrations used, also exhibited a significant ($p<0.05$) antinociceptive activity in a concentration-dependent manner. The 10 per cent concentration HTE was found to show an equally effective activity when compared with 100 mg/kg ASA after 240 min. Interestingly, the activity of 50 and 100 per cent concentration of HTE was found to increase significantly ($p<0.001$) after 30 minutes and maintained until the end of the experiment.

3.3. Elucidation of the Involvement of Opioid Receptor in HTE Antinociceptive Activities

Figures 6.5 shows the antinociceptive activities of HTE in 100 per cent concentration compared with extract pre-treated with naloxone, assessed using the abdominal constriction test in mice. All the test shown to exhibit a significant ($p<0.05$) antinociceptive activity. Naloxone shows partially reversed the antinociceptive activity of the extracts.

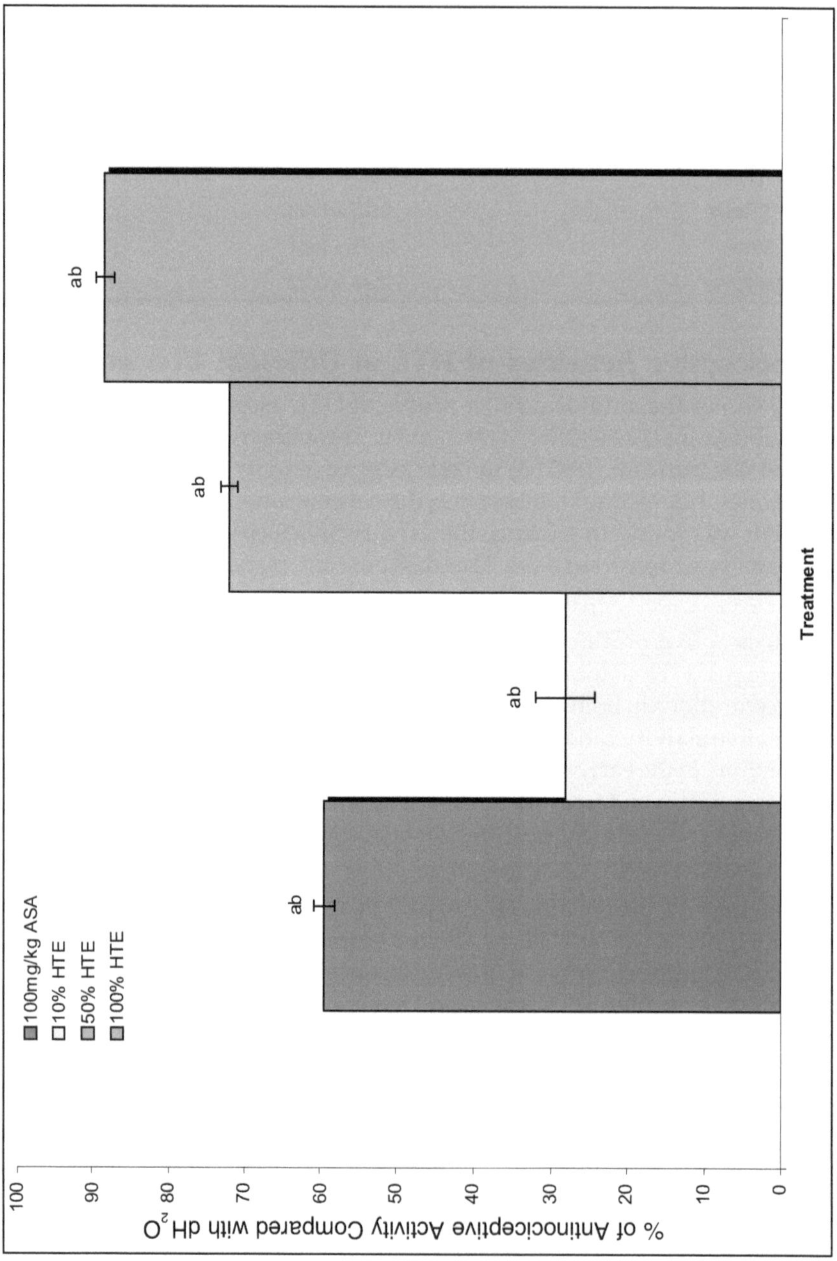

Figure 6.2: The Antinociceptive Profile of HTE Assessed by the Abdominal Constriction Test in Mice. Data were present as mean ± S.E. (n=7). [a]Significant ($p<0.05$) when compared to dH_2O-treated group. [b]Significant ($p<0.05$) when compared to 100mg/kg ASA-treated group.

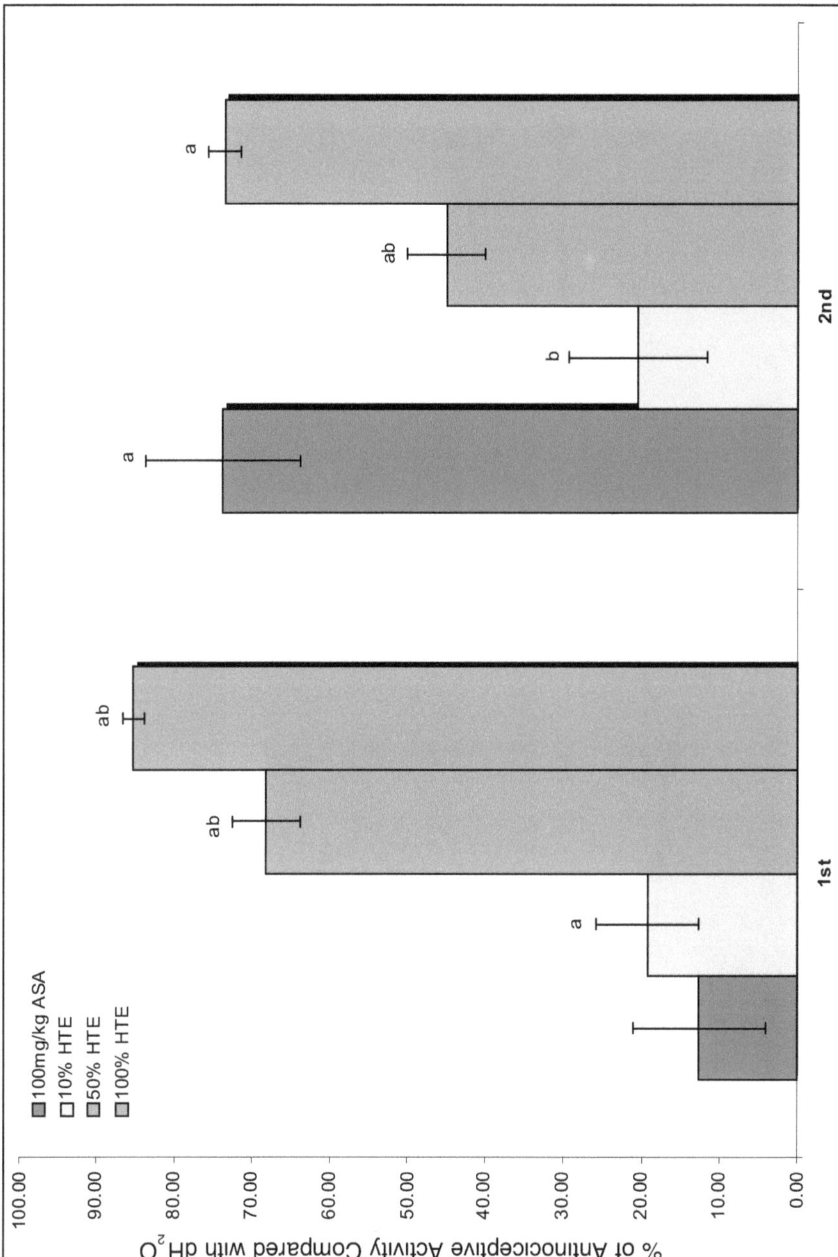

Figure 6.3: The Antinociceptive Profile of HTE Assessed by the Formalin Test in Rats.
Data were present as mean ± S.E. (n=7). [a]Significant ($p<0.05$) when compared to dH_2O-treated group.
[b]Significant ($p<0.05$) when compared to 100mg/kg ASA-treated group.

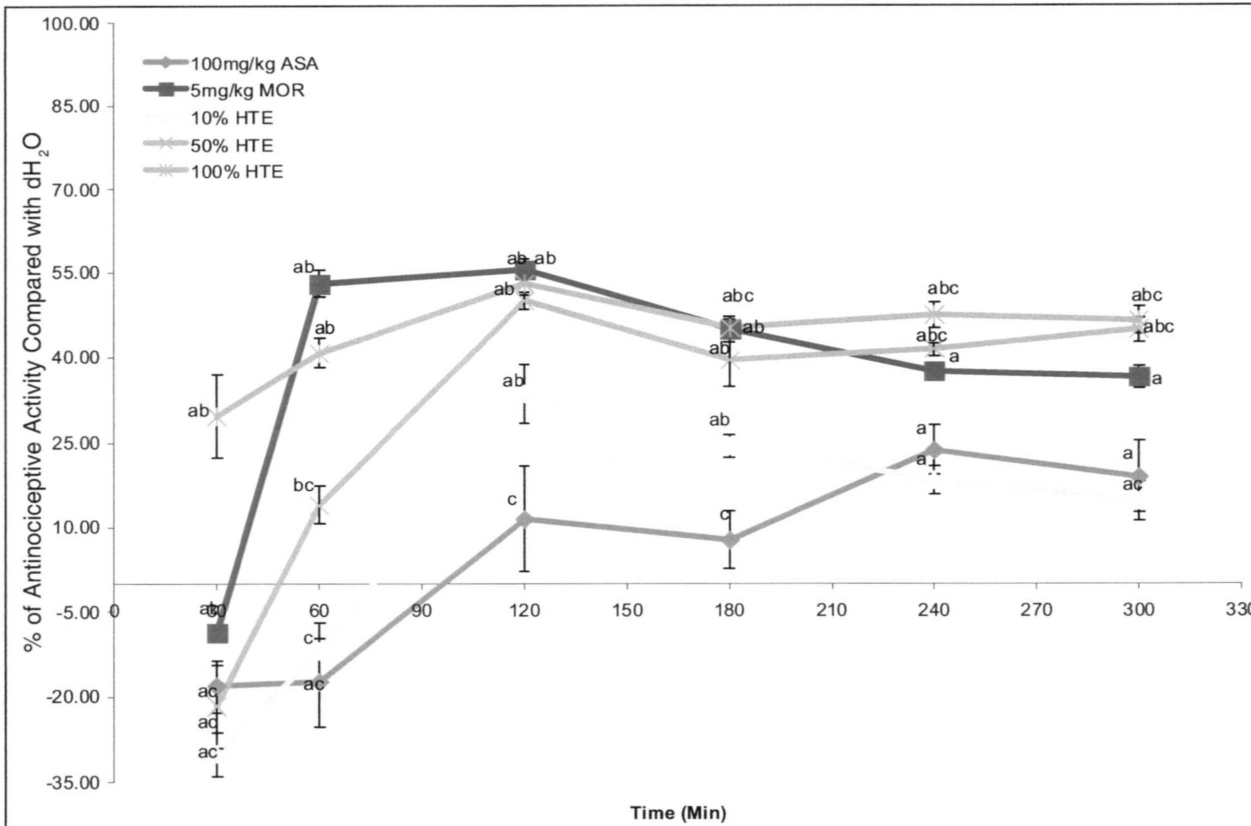

Figure 6.4: The Antinociceptive Profile of HTE Assessed by the Hot Plate Test in Mice.
Data were present as mean ± S.E. (n=7). [a]Significant ($p<0.05$) when compared to dH_2O-treated group. [b]Significant ($p<0.05$) when compared to 100mg/kg ASA-treated group. [c]Significant ($p<0.05$) when compared to 5mg/kg MOR-treated group.

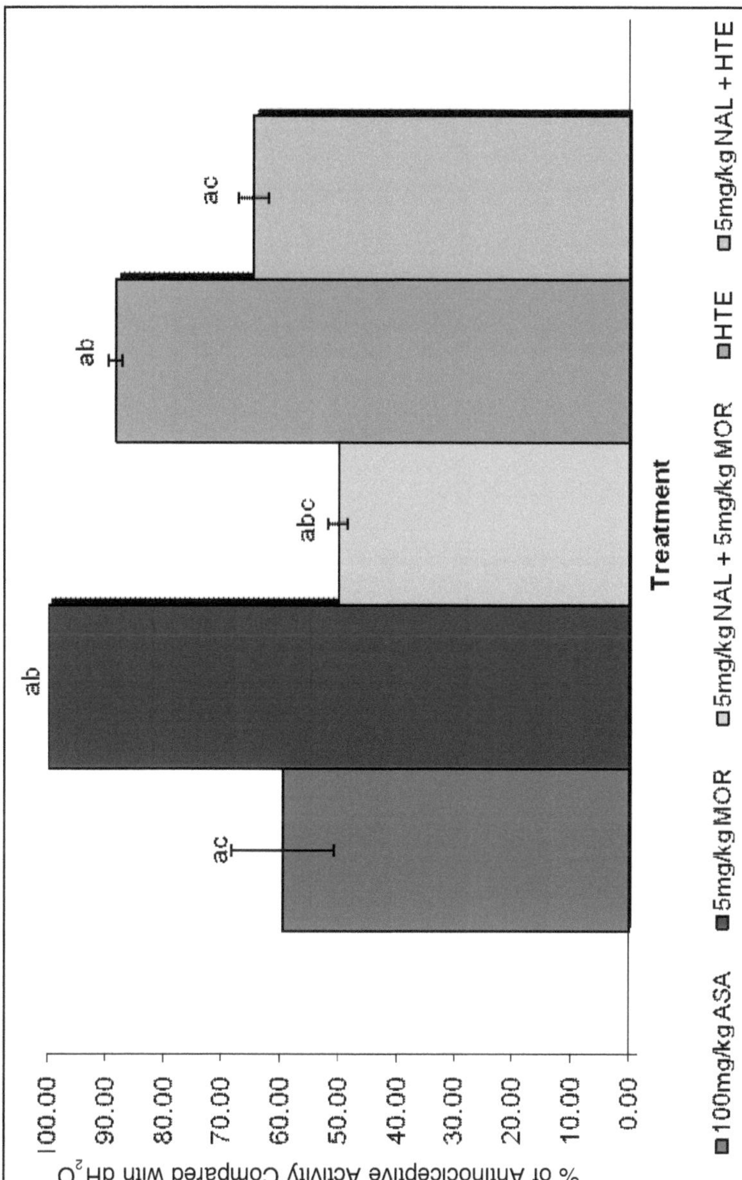

Figure 6.5: The Antinociceptive Profile of HTE with Naloxone Assessed by the Abdominal Constriction Test in Mice. Data were present as mean ± S.E. (n=7). [a] Significant ($p<0.05$) when compared to dH_2O-treated group. [b] Significant ($p<0.05$) when compared to 100mg/kg ASA-treated group. [c] Significant ($p<0.05$) when compared to 5mg/kg MOR-treated group.

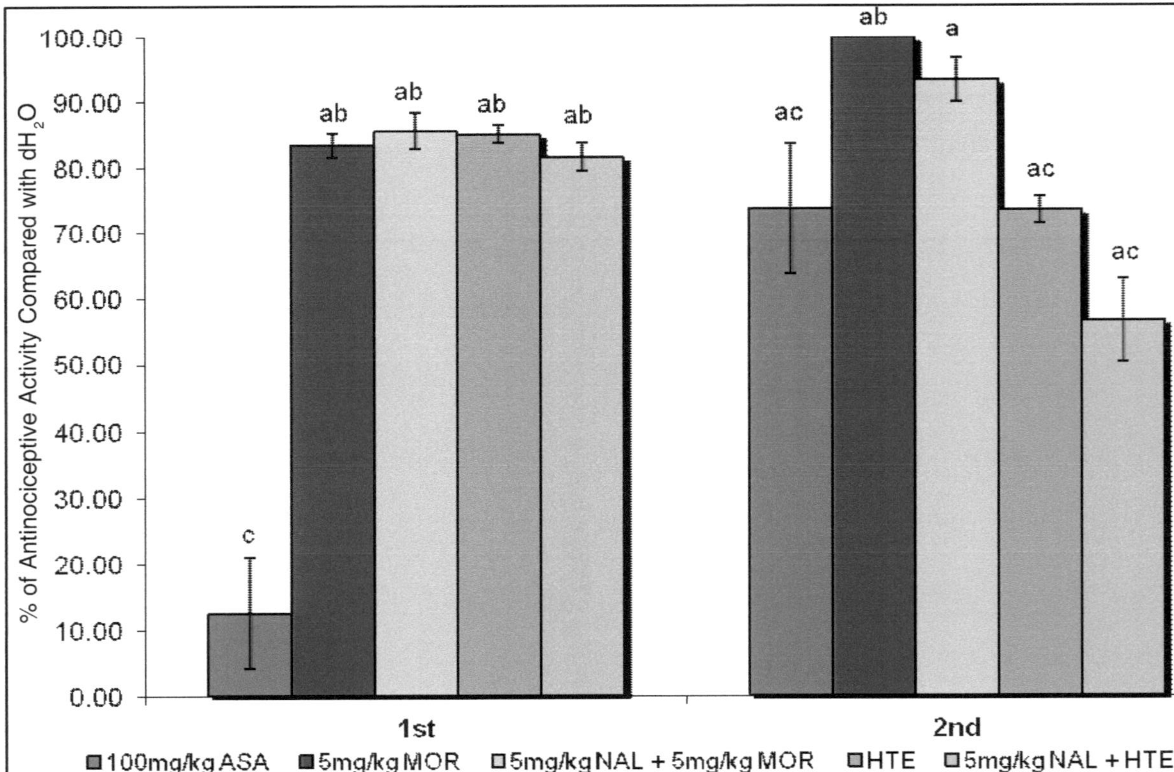

Figure 6.6: The Antinociceptive Profile of HTE Compared with Naloxone Assessed by the Formalin Test in Rats. Data were present as mean ± S.E. (n=7). [a] Significant ($p<0.05$) when compared to dH_2O-treated group. [b] Significant ($p<0.05$) when compared to 100mg/kg ASA-treated group. [c] Significant ($p<0.05$) when compared to 5mg/kg MOR-treated group.

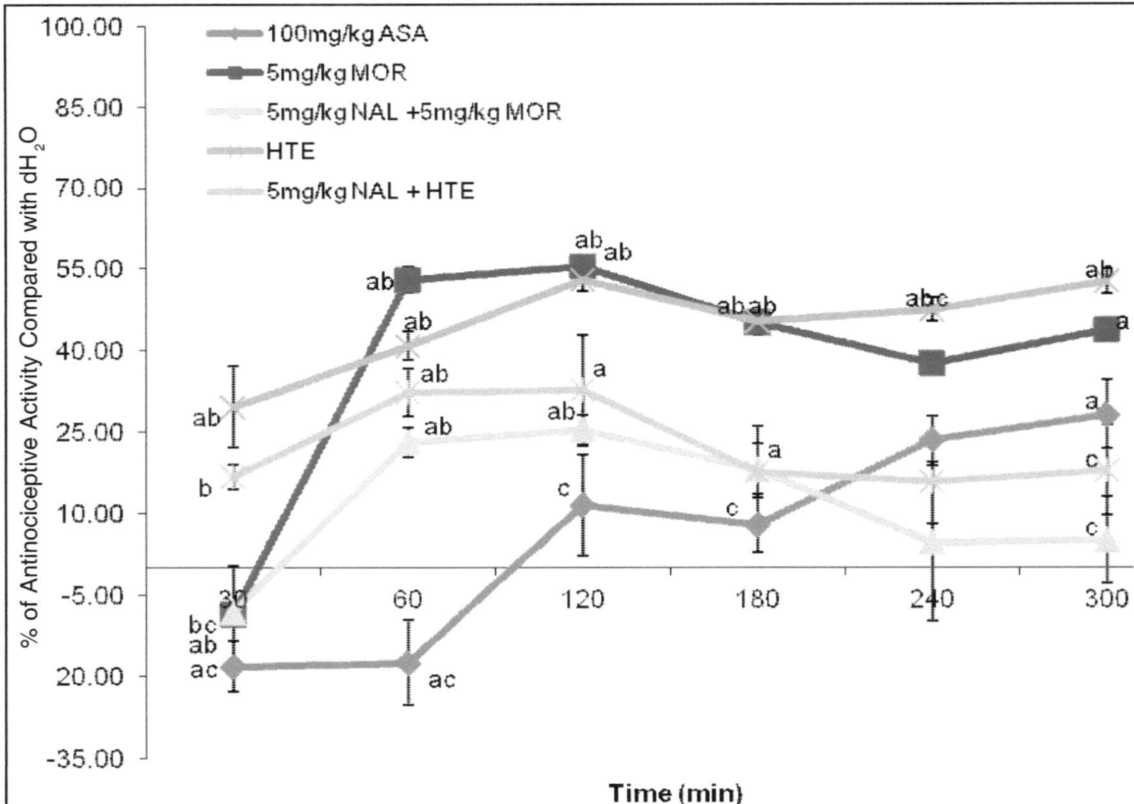

Figure 6.7: The Antinociceptive Profile of HTE Compared with Naloxone Assessed by the Hot Plate Test in Mice. Data were present as mean ± S.E. (n=7). [a]Significant ($p<0.05$) when compared to dH_2O-treated group. [b]Significant ($p<0.05$) when compared to 100mg/kg ASA-treated group. [c]Significant ($p<0.05$) when compared to 5mg/kg MOR-treated group.

The antinociceptive profile of HTE in 100 per cent concentration compared with extract pre-treated with naloxone, assessed using the formalin test in rats was shown in Figures 6.6. The HTE exhibited significant ($p<0.05$) activity in both phases of the extracts.

Figure 6.7 show the antinociceptive profile of HTE in 100 per cent concentration compared with extract pre-treated with naloxone, assessed by the hot plate test in mice. The HTE exhibited significant ($p<0.05$) antinociceptive activity. The pre-treated with naloxone shows partially reversed the antinociceptive activity of the extracts but it gave the antinociceptive effect when compared with the dH_2O-negative control.

4. DISCUSSION

Haruan Traditional Extract is believed to be a polypeptide/conjugated compounds with hydrophilic/polar characteristics. Previous studies have reported that *C. striatus* contains a good profile of amino acid and fatty acids (Mat Jais *et al.*, 1998). The amino acids and fatty acids detected in the of HTE are believed to directly contribute to the observed antinociception (Mat Jais *et al.*, 1997; 1998) with the former ability as the building blocks of various types of polypeptides (Livett *et al.*, 2004) and precursor for the synthesis of several compounds such as cyclo-pentanone prostaglandins which possess the antinociceptive activity (Hosoi *et al.*, 1999)

High content of arachidonic acid in *C. striatus* fillet was claimed to be acting as a precursor for prostaglandin and thromboxane biosynthesis (Pompeia *et al.*, 2002) which interfering with the normal blood clotting process and its ability to attach to endothelial cells within a wound (Bowman and Rand 1980; Crawford 1983; Mat Jais *et al.*, 1994). Oleic acid C18: 1 is the most abundant fatty acid in living organisms (Christie, 1982) and it is one of the major components of fatty acid in all parts of *C. striatus*. The ω-3: ω-6 ratio was suggested to become a useful indicator for comparing relative nutritional values of fish oil. It was suggested that ratio 1: 1-1: 5 would constitute in healthy human diet (Osman *et al.*, 2001). Proportion of fatty acid incorporated into membrane phospholipids influence cell function by changing the membrane fluidity. This is because the membrane fluidity depends on the chain length and saturation of phospholipids fatty acids (Crocker *et al.*, 2001). Higher content of unsaturated and monounsaturated fatty acid in *C. striatus* will undoubtedly influence membrane fluidity and will affect many cell functions, including Polymorphonuclear Leukocytes (PMN) activation (Zakaria *et al.*, 2007).

Glycine is one of the major compounds of human collagen together with other essential amino acids such as alanine, proline, arginine, serine, leucine, isoleucine, and phenyl alanine combined with aspartic acid and glutamic acid to form a polypeptide that will promote regrowth and tissue healing (Heiman 1982; Witte *et al.*, 2002). In recent studies, the presence of potential antinociceptive and anti-inflammatory cyclo-pentanone prostaglandin and conjugates of lipid and amino acids, called as lipo-amino acid (Fan and Chapkin, 1998; Stock *et al.*, 2001; Huang *et al.*, 2001). Prostaglandin such as PGE1 and PGE2 exhibited antinociceptive activity which derived from the breakdown of fatty acid (arachidonic acid) (Fan and Chapkin, 1998; Hosoi *et al.*, 1999). These activities also induced platelet aggregation and initiated blood clotting (Baie *et al.*, 2000). Glutamate and aspartate were grouped as excitatory

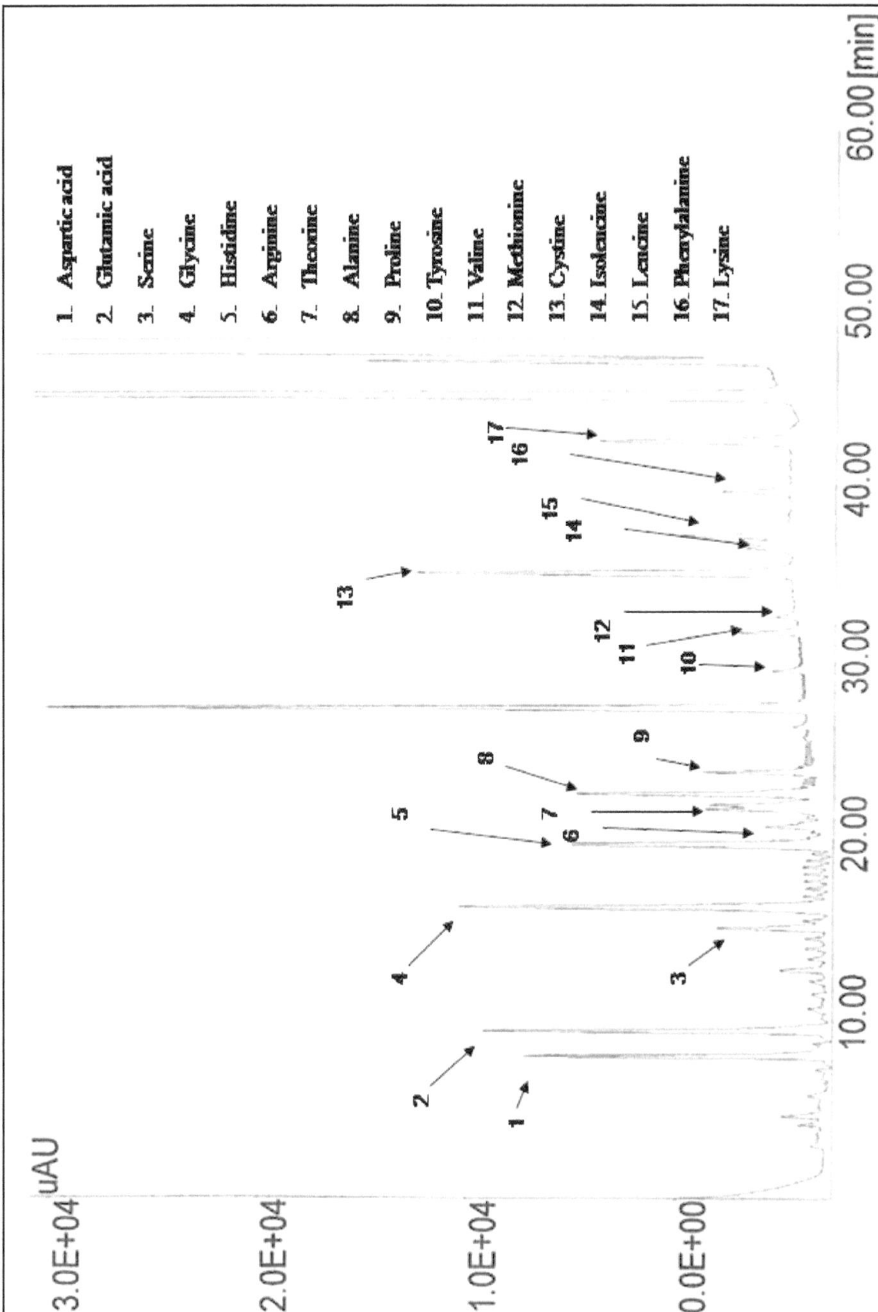

Figure 6.8: The Amino Acid Profiling of HTE.

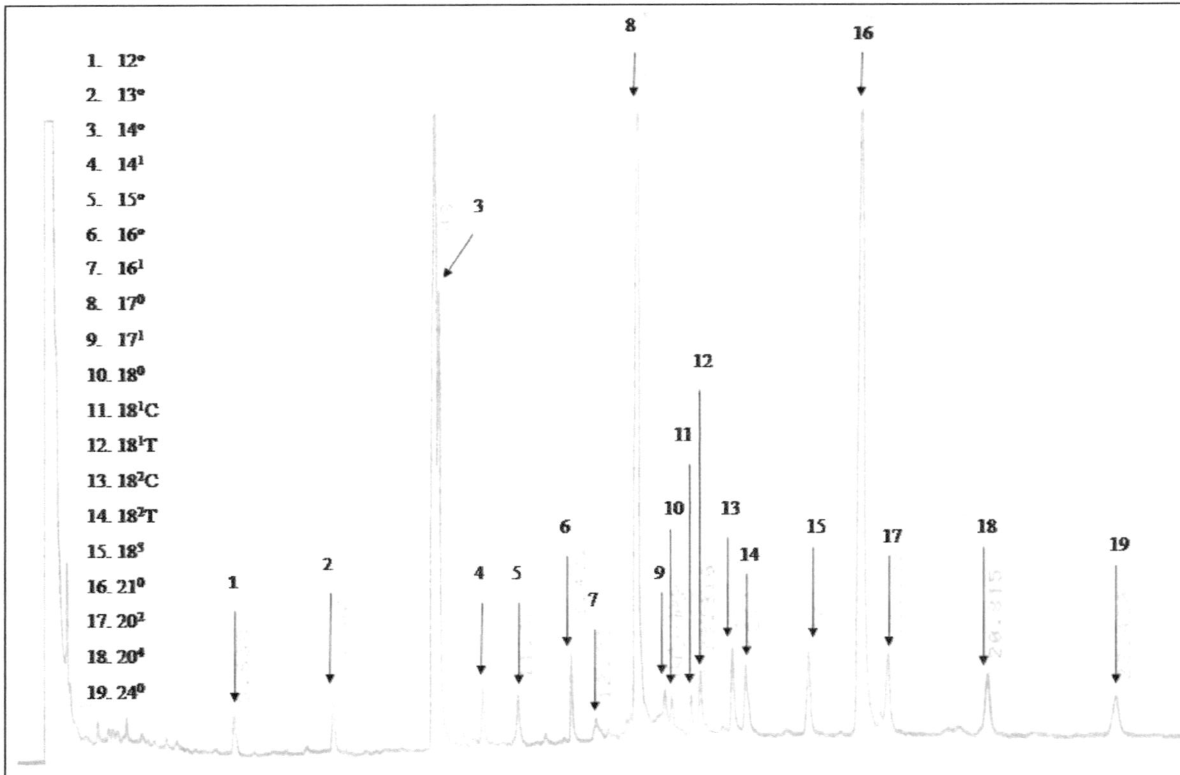

Figure 6.9: The Fatty Acid Profiling of HTE.

12^0: Lauric Acid; 13^0: Tridecanoic Acid; 14^0: Myristic Acid; 14^1: Myristoleic Acid; 15^0: Pentadecaneic Acid; 16^0: Palmitic Acid; 16^1: Palmitoleic Acid; 17^0: Heptadecanoic Acid; 17^1: Cis-10-Heptadecanoic Acid; 18^0: Stearic Acid; 18^1: Cis-Aleic Acid; 18^1: Trans-Elaidic Acid; 18^2: Cis-Linoleic Acid; 18^2: Trans-Linoielaidic Acid; 18^3: Linolenic Acid; 21^0: Henecosanoic Acid; 20^2: Cis-11-14-Eicasadienoic Acid; 20^4: Arachidonic Acid; 24^0: Lignoceric Acid.

amino acids and one of the major amino acid found in *C. striatus* demonstrated to be involved in endogenous pain inhibition (Aimone, 1986; Jacquet, 1988).

As we know *C. striatus* has a potential to possess anti-inflammatory and analgesic activities. This has been proved by Huang *et al.* (2001) who had shown that one type of lipoamino acid called arachidonylglycine suppressed edema and pain. Lipo-amino acids N-arachidonylglycine found in bovine, rat brain and other tissue were capable of suppressing tonic inflammatory pain (Huang *et al.*, 2001). Glycine and arachidonic acid were one of the major amino and fatty acid content in *C. striatus*. While cysteine, has been classified as non-essential amino acid and sulfur-containing amino acid that occurs naturally in foods and can also be manufactured by the body from the amino acid methionine (Mateljah, 2001). To produce the cysteine, methionine is converted to s-adenosyl methionine (SAM), and then will convert to homocysteine. Homocysteine will react with serine to form cysteine (Rudiger, 1997). Cysteine can be found in most high-protein foods and also is taken as supplement medication such as N-acetyl cysteine which is used to prevent the development of tolerance to nitroglycerin in treatment of chest pain.

Silberring *et al.* (1993) and Tan-No *et al.* (2008), reported that cysteine protease will degrade endogenous agonist receptor such as dynorphins that convert to the shorter opioid peptide and significantly prolong the antinociceptive activities. Tan-No *et al.* (2008) also reported possibilities that cysteine protease inhibitors can suppress the development of antinociceptive tolerance to morphine and also produced antinociceptive effect. Development of tolerance to morphine antinociception was not only suppressed by ê-opioid receptor agonist but also by cysteine protease inhibitors, which could block the degradation of endogenous agonist of these receptors such as dynorphine (Tan-No *et al.*, 2008). This will lead the explanation of HTE that is found to have analgesic effect without the side effects that are famous for morphine long term usage.

Content of amino acid and fatty acid in *C. striatus* (Mat Jais *et al.*, 1994; Zuraini *et al.*, 2006 and Zakaria *et al.*, 2007) explain its traditional and clinical uses as the dietary medicine for wound healing. Furthermore, it was suggested that the amino acid and fatty acid profiling would give different results from the previous studies because HTE was obtained from pressure cooking and seasoning process, which differs from previous approaches done by Zakaria *et al.* (2007) or (Mat Jais *et al.*, 1994; Zuraini *et al.*, 2006). In antinociceptive studies, three different assays were used which are the abdominal constriction test, formalin test and hotplate test to analyze the different mechanisms of pain in HTE. Each of these assays has its own specificity in analyzing the antinociceptive activities as described below.

The abdominal constrictions observed in this assay are due to irritation to the peritoneal cavity caused by acetic acid administration (Deraedt *et al.*, 1980). The increased levels of peritoneal fluid prostaglandin lead to prolonged irritation by the abdominal constriction. The increased prostaglandins level in the peritoneal cavity enhance the inflammatory pain by increasing its capillary permeability (Vogel and Vogel, 1997). This assay was also very sensitive and able to detect the pain relieving effect of compounds which are inactive in other tests (Bentley *et al.*, 1981). However the activity observed with this assay did not indicate whether the activity was due to peripheral and/or central activity (Chan *et al.*, 1995). In order to confirm the antinociceptive activity, it is necessary to carry out the hot plate and formalin tests before finally determining the possible mechanism involved.

The formalin test was used to study the non-inflammatory, antinociceptive properties of drugs (Hunskar *et al.*, 1985) and has been known to produce a biphasic nociceptive response. Early and late phases have different properties, which could be used for assessing the potency of analgesic agents and for elucidating the mechanism of analgesia. The early phase is caused by a direct effect of formalin on nociceptors, while the late phase is a tonic response in which inflammatory processes are involved and neurons in the dorsal horns of the spinal cord are activated (Tjølsen *et al.*, 1992). Centrally acting drugs (like morphine) have been proven to inhibit both phases while peripherally acting drugs (like ASA) inhibit only at the late phase of the test (Chan *et al.*, 1995). The formalin test can also be used to indicate the potential of analgesic agents for chronic pain due to inflammatory process (Cowan, 1990). From the results, HTE have shown inhibition in both phases when induced with formalin suggesting that the antinociceptive activity of HTE mediated via a central pathway, thus may also have the potential in the treatment of chronic pain.

It is well known that centrally acting drugs, like morphine, exhibited in the abdominal constriction and hotplate assays (Hosseinzedah and Younesi, 2002), while peripherally acting drugs (like ASA) exhibited analgesic activity only in the abdominal constriction test (Amanlou *et al.*, 2005). The hot plate test is used to indicate the involvement of the central antinociceptive mechanism and thought to involve the spinal reflex (Pini *et al.*, 1997). This assay was usually used to measure the complex response to a non-inflammatory, acute nociceptive input. From the current results, the significant activity observed using the hot plate test did clarify the involvement of central antinociceptive mechanism. In this experiment the HTE were prepared in 10, 50 and 100 per cent concentration/strength and subjected to the antinociceptive studies, were found to demonstrate the significant and concentration-dependent manner antinociceptive activity. Thus in line with the previous studies by Mat Jais *et al.*, 1997 and Zakaria *et al.*, 2005.

In the previous studies by Dambisya *et al.* (1999), Mat Jais *et al.* (1997) and Zakaria *et al.* (2005), they reported that the naloxone, and non-selective opioid receptor antagonist failed to block the mucus, fillet and ASH extract. While in this study it shows that the naloxone reversed the antinociceptive effect of HTE in all antinociceptive studies. It is important to mention that one of the main strategies in nociception studies is to search for opioid analgesics acting on opioid receptors outside the central nervous system, with the prospect of avoiding centrally mediated side effects such as tolerance and dependence (Stein *et al.*, 2000).

These results indicated that the HTE act on opioid receptors, which is contradicted with the previous finding by Zakaria *et al.* (2007). According to Zakaria *et al.* (2007), ASH extract was found to work as centrally acting analgesic when tested in formalin assays. The negative results obtained from the fillet and mucus extract reported by Mat Jais *et al.* (1997), however seems to contradict the result reported by

Zakaria *et al.*, 2007. It is suggested that the extract is more effective in treating nociception induced by a chemical stimulus rather than thermal stimulus (Vaz *et al.*, 1996). Whist in this study, HTE have been proven to inhibit both phases of the formalin test and shows the significant activities when observed with the hot plate test and thus clarify its involvement of central antinociceptive mechanism.

Finally, this new finding was better than previous studies of *C. striatus* due to the improvement of the extraction process which is involved with the seasoning process. The seasoning process might have given the synergistic effects with HTE which can produce the central and peripheral antinociceptive results. This recent study also proved that HTE possesses the antinociceptive effect.

5. CONCLUSION

Based on the results obtained in the present studies, the HTE was found to have all important amino acids and fatty acids composition which might be associated with the concentration-dependent antinociception activities. The HTE was demonstrated to contain the major amino acids like cysteine, histidine, glutamic acid, glycine and aspartic acid, while the major fatty acids found are myristic acid, arachidonic acid, palmitic acid, linolenic acid and eicosadienoic acid. These amino acids and fatty acids were believed to produce antinociceptive activities especially the amino acid (glycine) and fatty acid (ARA) which are believed to act directly and indirectly in forming N-arachidonylglycine or by forming fatty acid (palmitic acid) derivatives like palmitotlethanomide. The 100 per cent concentration/strength HTE were found to exhibit the nociceptive pain when pre-treated with naloxone. Thus suggesting that the HTE were bound to the opioid receptors.

In conclusion, the HTE was found to have a potential to exhibit an antinociceptive activity when assessed using the abdominal constriction, hot plate and formalin tests. The activities, which occur in a concentration-dependent manner, indicate the involvement of the peripheral and central antinociceptive mechanisms. HTE also proved to enhance the antinociceptive activities to possess the peripheral and central mediated pathway in antinociceptive activities and proved the traditional uses of *C. striatus* for relieving pain in the post-operative period.

ACKNOWLEDGEMENTS

This study was supported by a research grant of Ministry of Science Technology and Innovation (MOSTI) and Government State of Pahang. The authors would like to thank University Putra Malaysia for providing the facilities for this work.

REFERENCES

1. Aimone LD, Gebhart GF. Stimulation-produced spinal inhibition from the midbrain is mediated by an excitatory amino acid neurotransmitter in the medial medulla. J. Neurosci. 6: 1803-13 (1986).
2. Amanlou M, Dadkhah F, Salehnia A, Farsam H, Dehpour AR. An anti-inflammatory and antinociceptive effect of hydrochloric extract of *Satureja khuzistanica* Jamsad extract. J. Pharm, Pharmaceut. Sci. 8 (1): 102-6 (2005).

3. Association of Official Analytical Chemists. Official method of analysis. 14th ed (Williams S, ed.), AOAC, Virginia. 1984.
4. Baie SH, Sheikh KA. The wound healing properties of *Channa striatus*- cetrimide cream-wound contraction and glycosaminoglycan measurement. J. Ethnopharm. 73: 15-30 (2000).
5. Bentley GA, Newton SH, Starr J. Evidence for an action of morphine and the enkephalins on sensory nerve endings in the mouse peritoneum. Br. J. Pharmacol. 73: 325-32 (1981).
6. Bowman WC Rand MJ. Textbook of pharmacology. 2nd ed. Blackwell Scientific Publications, London, Great Britain; 1980.
7. Chan TF, Tsai HY, Tian-Shang W. Anti-inflammatory and analgesic activities of Spilanthes acmelle in experimental animal models. Indian J. Pharmacol. 36 (3): 148-50 (1995).
8. Chin YW, Balunas MJ, Chai HB, Kinghorn AD. Drug discovery from natural product. J. The AAPS. 8 (2) article 28 (2006).
9. Christie WW. Lipid analysis: Isolation, separation, identification and structural analysis of lipids.2nd ed. Pergamon Press, Oxford. 1982.
10. Cowan A. Recent approaches in the testing of analgesics in animals. In: Modern methods in pharmacology: Testing and evaluation of drugs abuse. (Vol. 6) Wiley Liss Inc., New York. 1990. p.33-42.
11. Crawford MA. Essential fatty acids and their postanoid derivatives. Br. Med. Bull. 114: 1705-15 (1983).
12. Crocker IP, Lawson N, Baker PN, Fletcher J. The anti-inflammatory effects of circulating fatty acid in obstructive jaundice: Similarities with pregnancy-induced immunosuppression. Quart. J. Med. 94: 475-484 (2001).
13. Dambisya YM, Lee TL, Sathivulu V, Mat Jais AM. Influence of temperature ph and naloxone on the antinociceptive activity of *Channa striatus* (haruan) extracts in mice. J. Ethnopharmacol. 66: 181-86 (1999).
14. Dambisya YM, TL Lee. Effects of l-name, l-nmma and l-arginine on the antinociceptive effects of morphine in mice. Methods Find. Exp. Clin. Pharmacol. 17: 577-82 (1995).
15. Deraedt R, Jougney S, Delevalcee F, Falhout M. Release of prostaglandins E and F in algogenic reaction and its inhibition. Eur. J. Pharmacol. 51: 17-24 (1980).
16. Dholwani KK, Saluja AK. Gupta AR, Shah DR. A review plant-derived natural products and their analogs with anti tumor activity. Indian J. Pharmacol. 40 (2): 49-58 (2008).
17. Fan YY, Chapkin RS. Importance of Dietary g-Linolenic Acid in human health and nutrition. J. Nutr. 128 (9): 1411-14 (1998).

18. Folch J, Lees M, Sloan–Stanley GH. A simple method for the isolation and purification of total lipids from animal tissues. J. Bio. Chem. 226: 497-509 (1957).
19. Heimann W. Fundamentals of food chemistry. AVI Publishing Company, Connecticut, 1982. p. 227-33.
20. Hosoi M, Oka T, Abe M, Hori T, Yamamoto H, Mine K, Kubo C. Prostaglandin E (2) has antinociceptive effects through EP (1) receptor in the ventromedical Hypothalamus in rats. Pain. 83: 221-7 (1999).
21. Hosseinzedah H, Younesi HM. Antinociceptive and anti-inflammatory effects of *Crocus sativus* L. stigma and petal extracts in mice. BMC Pharmacol. 2: 7 (2002).
22. Huang SM, Bisogno T, Petros TJ, Chang SY, Zavitsanos PA, Zipkin RE, Sivakumar R, Coop A, Maeda DY, De Petrocellis L, Burstein S, Di Marzo V, Walker JM. Identification of a new class of molecules, the Arachidonyl amino acids and characterization of one member that inhibits pain. J. Bio. Chem. 276 (46): 42639-44 (2001).
23. Hunskar S, Farmer OB, Hole K. Formalin test in mice: A useful technique for evaluating mild analgesics. J. Neurosci. (14): 69-76 (1985).
24. Hunskar S, Hole K. The formalin test in mice: Dissociation between inflammatory and non-inflammatory pain. Pain. 0: 103-04 (1987).
25. Jacquet YF. The NMDA receptor: Central role in pain inhibition in rat periqueductal gray. Eur. J. Pharmacol. 154: 271-6 (1988).
26. Lindblad WJ. Consideration for determining if a natural product is an effective wound-healing Agent. The Int. J. Low. Extrem. Wounds 7 (2): 75-81 (2008).
27. Livett BG, KR Grayler, Khalil Z. Drugs from the sea: Conopeptides as potential therapeutics. Curr. Med. Chem. 11: 1715-23 (2004).
28. Mat Jais AM, Dambisya YM, Lee TL. Antinociceptive activity of *Channa striatus* (haruan) extracts in mice. J. Ethnopharm. 57: 125-30 (1997).
29. Mat Jais AM, Matori MF, Kittakoop P, Suwanborirux K. Fatty Acid composition in mucus and roe of Haruan, *Channa striatus,* for wound healing. Gen. Pharmacol. 30: 561-3 (1998).
30. Mat Jais AM, Mc Cullock R, Croft K. Fatty acid and amino acid composition in haruan as a potential role in wound healing. Gen. Pharm. 25: 947-50 (1994).
31. Mateljah G. The world's healthiest food. Mateljeh George Foundation 2001. http: //www.whfoods.com/genpage.php?tname=nutrient and dbid=54# drug nutrient interactions. Accessed 2010 January 16.
32. Osman H, Suriah AR, Law EC. Fatty acid composition and cholesterol content of selected marine fish in Malaysian waters. Food Chem. 73: 55-60 (2001).
33. Pini LA, Vitale G, Ottani A, Sandrini M. Naloxone-reversible antinociception by Paracetamol in the rat. J. Pharmacol. Exp. Ther. 280 (2): 934-40 (1997).

34. Pompeia C, Freitas JS, Skim J, Zyngier SB, Curi R. Arachidonic acid cytotoxicity in leukocytes: Implication of oxidative stress and eicosanoid synthesis. Bio. Cell. 94: 251-265 (2002).

35. Rajen M. Fish speed up healing of wounds posted by omarlee. The Star. 2002. Http: //www.malaysiancuisine.net/cgiin/editor/print.pl?Article=18. Accessed 2006 Jun 31.

36. Rajion MA. Essential fatty acid metabolism in the fetal and neonatal lamb. The University of Melbourne, Australia, 1985.

37. Rudiger H. Molecular physiology of plant sulfur metabolism. Planta. 202 (2): 138-48 (1997).

38. Silberring J, Demuth HU, Brostedt P and Nyberg F. Inhibition of dynorphin converting enzymes from human spinal chord by N-peptidyl-O-acyl hydrolamines. J. Biochem. 114: 648-51 (1993).

39. Stein C, Schafer M, Machelska H. Why is morphine not the ultimate analgesic and what can be done to improve it. J. Pain 3 (1): 51–6 (2000).

40. Stock JL, Shinto K, Burkhardt B, Roach M, Taniguchi K, Ishikawa T, Kim HS, Flannery PJ, Coffman TM, McNeish JD, Audoly LP. The prostaglandin E2 EPI receptor mediates pain perception and regulates blood pressure. J. Clin. Invest. 107 (3): 325-31 (2001).

41. Tan-No K, Shimoda M, Sugawara M, Nakagawasai O, Niijima F, Watanabe H, Furata S, Sato T, Satoh S, Arai Y, Kotlinska J, Silberring J, Terenius L and Tadano T. Cysteine protease inhibitors suppress the development of tolerance to morphine antinociception. Neuropeptides. 42: 239-44 (2008).

42. Tjølsen A, Berge OG, Hunskaar S, Rosland JH and Hole K. The formalin test: an evaluation of the method. Pain 51: 5-17 (1992).

43. Vaz ZR, Cechinel Filho V, Yunes RA, Calixto JB. Antinociceptive action of 2- (-4-bromobenzoyl)-3-methyl-4,6-dimethoxy benzofuran, a novel xanthoxyline derivative, on chemical and thermal models of nociception in mice. J. Pharmacol. Exp. Ther. 278: 304-12 (1996).

44. Vogel HG and Vogel WH. Analgesic, anti-inflammatory and antipyretic activity. In: Drug discovery and evaluation: Pharmacological assays. J.A. Majors Company, Leswisville, USA. 1997. p. 360-418.

45. Wilson SG, Bryant CD, Lariviere WR, Olsen MS, Giles BE, Chesler EJ and Mogil JS. The heritability of antinociception II: Pharmacogenetic mediation of three over-the-counter analgesics in mice. J. Pharmacol. Exp. Ther. 305; 755-64 (2003).

46. Witte MB, Thronton FJ, Tantry U, Barbul A. L-Arginine supplementation enhances diabetic wound healing: involvement of the nitric oxide synthase and arginase pathway. Metabolism 51 (10): 1269-73 (2002).

47. Zakaria ZA, Mat Jais AM, Goh YM, Sulaiman MR, Somchit MN. Amino acid and fatty acid composition of an aqueous extract of *Channa striatus* (Haruan) that exhibits antinociceptive activity. Clin. Exp. Pharm and Phy. 34; 198-204 (2007).

48. Zakaria ZA, Sulaiman MR, Somchit MN, Mat Jais AM. Effects of various antagonists on Haruan *(Channa striatus*) fillet extract antinociception in mice. Can J.Phy. Pharm. 83: 635-42 (2005).

49. Zimmermann M. Ethical guidelines for investigation of experimental pain in conscious animals. Pain. 16: 109-10 (1983).

50. Zuraini MN, Somchit MH, Solihah, Goh YM. Fatty acid and amino acid composition of three local Malaysia *Channa* spp. Fish. Food Chem. 97; 674-78 (2006).

Chapter 7

The Pathogenicity of *Beauveria bassiana* on *Spodoptera litura* in Cotton Field

Kyi Pyar Win, Weine Nway Nway Oo** and Mya Mya Oo*

Department of Biotechnology,
Mandalay Technological University, Myanmar

ABSTRACT

Cotton leafworm, *Spodoptera litura,* is a common spring pest that occasionally causes catastrophic losses in small grains. *Beauveria bassiana* is one of several natural agents for controlling a broad range of insects by direct penetration of the host cuticle. In this research, one strain of *B. bassiana* was isolated and compared with *Beauveria bassiana* (BCC strain No. 2655) from Thailand BIOTEC culture collection based on cultural and microscopic morphologies. The pathogenicity of isolated and BCC strains were tested against *Spodoptera litura* by leaf-disc assay and direct method. The percentage mortality of cotton leafworm larvae was investigated in terms of the concentration of spore suspension (10^5, 10^6, 10^7 and 10^8 spores/ml) against the 1st, 2nd, 3rd and 4th instars stages of *S. litura*. The toxic activity of two strains were evaluated by probit analysis and expressed in terms of median lethal concentration (LC_{50}). It has been observed that the LC_{50} values for isolated *B. bassiana* were found at 6.55×10^5, 5.78×10^5, 6.03×10^5 and 3.59×10^6 spores/ml respectively and for *B. bassiana* (BCC strain No. 2655); they were found at 3.72×10^5, 5.4×10^5, 1.31×10^6 and 2.43×10^7 spores/ml respectively on the 1st, 2nd, 3rd and 4th instars of *S. litura* by leaf-disc assay method. In *S. litura's* natural niche, the cotton field, the direct method was used to control 2nd instar of *S. litura* and the estimated LC_{50} values for isolated strain and BCC strain were 4×10^5 spores/ml and 7.55×10^6 spores/ml respectively.

Keywords: *Pathogenicity, Beauveria bassiana, Spodoptera litura, Leaf-disc assay.*

E-mail: *kyipyarpyar@gmail.com, **weinenno@gmail.com

1. INTRODUCTION

Agriculture is one of the building stones of Myanmar. Crops are host to several insect pests. These insects inflict heavy damage to crops leading to reduced productivity. Therefore, protection of plants from insects is an important role in agricultural sector.

Spodoptera litura (Fabricius) (Lepidoptera: Noctuidae) is a polyphagous sporadic pest with high mobility and reproductive capacity (Holloway, 1989). *Spodoptera litura* devastates a large host range of more than 120 host plants (Ramana, *et al.*, 1988). The major ones include tobacco, cotton, groundnut, jute, lucerne, maize, rice, soybeans, tea, cauliflower, cabbage, capsicum, potato and castor (Sharma and Bisht, 2008). The early larval stages remain together at first, later radiating out from the egg mass, stripping the interveinal leaf surface and skeletonising the leaves as they advance. Later stages, now solitary, the larvae eat all the parts of the leaf, including the petioles. The larvae are widely dispersed in Asia and the Pacific (Monobrullah and Shankar, 2008). *Spodoptera litura* has a wide host range. Hence the search for biocontrol agents for incorporation into Integrated Pest Management (IPM) programmes against this insect is in dire need.

Entomogenous fungi are potentially the most versatile biological control agents, due to their wide host range that often results in natural epizootics. An attractive feature of these fungi is infectivity by contact through penetration. Entomopathogens are microorganisms that cause diseases in arthropods particularly insects and mites. Entomopathogens are naturally widespread in the environment and include bacteria, fungus, viruses, nematodes and protozoa. Some entomopathogens can be applied against pests in a way that is similar to a pesticide and are called microbial biopesticides. Fungal species such as *Metarhizium anisopliae* and *B. bassiana* are well characterized in respect to pathogenicity to several insects and they have been used as agents for the biological control of agriculture pests' worldwide (Lingappa *et al.*, 2005). *Beauveria* species are entomopathogenic fungi, in the subdivision of Deuteromycotina which occurs worldwide. They form unicellular conidia that are typically hydrophobic and very small. *Beauveria* species are commonly found associated with insects or habitats supporting insects, including soil and private dwellings. *Beauveria bassiana*, the most widely known member of this genus, has been developed as a biological pesticide for various insect pests. *B. bassiana* is a fungus which causes a disease known as the white muscardine disease in insects. In culture, *B. bassiana* grows as a white mold. On most common cultural media, it produces many dry, powdery conidia in distinctive white spore balls. It is being used as a biological insecticide to control a number of pests such as termites, thrips, whiteflies, aphids and different beetles. Its use in the control of malaria-transmitting mosquitos is under investigation (McNeil Jr, 2005). The fungus rarely infects humans or other animals, so it is generally considered safe as an insecticide.

The aim of the study was to evaluate the efficiency of the *B. bassiana* strain isolated from soil samples from the Lonkyaw cotton plantation in Kyaukse District, as a biopesticide against *S. litura*.

2. MATERIAL AND METHODS

2.1. Fungal Strains

The indigenous strain of *B. bassiana* was isolated from soil collected from the Lonkyaw cotton plantation. *B. bassiana* (BCC strain No. 2655) was obtained from Thailand Biotech culture collection. The indigenous strain of *B. bassiana* was compared with BCC strain based on cultural and microscopic morphologies.

2.2. Rearing of Insects

Second instars *Spodoptera litura* were placed in containers and fed with pesticide free fresh castor leaves until they had pupated and the pupae were starved. Several pairs of male and female pupae were placed in a rearing box for laying egg. Adults were fed with diluted honey (10 per cent) on cotton wool. The diet of the moths was changed every day to avoid fungal contamination (Santharam, 1985). The castor leaves were inserted in the plastic boxes on which the female could lay eggs. After hatching, each first instar larvae were placed separately on castor leaves and were then ready to use in the analysis.

2.3. Insecticidal Potency of *Spodoptera litura*

Two *B. bassiana* cultures, isolated and BCC strain were used to control *S. litura* using leaf discs or also known as leaf-disc bioassay (Rowland *et al.*, 1991). In this study, the leaf-disc bioassay was conducted with first, second, third and fourth instars of cotton leafworm, *S. litura* by using the isolated and BCC strains at concentration of 10^5, 10^6, 10^7 and 10^8 spores/ml. Ten larvae were used per replication and eight replications were carried out for one treatment.

2.4. Preparation of Inoculum

The conidia of the isolated strain and BCC strain were produced by growing the fungus on PDA plates. The plates were then incubated at room temperature for 7 days. The spore count was estimated using haemocytometer and Rose bengal (Feng, *et al.*, 1994). Serial dilution was done to prepare the suspensions at the concentration of 10^5, 10^6, $10^7$and 10^8 spores/ml.

2.5. Bioassay Experiment under Laboratory Condition

One millilitre of different concentrations of each of the two *B. bassiana* strains were sprayed onto freshly prepared castor leaf disc (6 cm in diameter) and allowed to air-dry. Sterile distilled water containing 1 per cent Tween 80 as a wetting agent (Rombach *et al.*, 1986) that was also prepared to use as the control. After the prepared discs had air-dried, 10 larvae of the target insects were placed on each the castor leaf disc (Malarvannan, 2010) which had been put up in an appropriate container covered by a thin layer of well ventilated cloth.

The experiment was conducted using 10 insects per treatment and eight replications were carried out for one treatment. The bioassay experiment was maintained at 25±2 C and 75±2 per cent RH. New freshly prepared leaf discs without any toxic materials were fed to the larvae every 24 hrs. The number of dead insect larvae was counted daily.

2.6. Pathogenicity of *Beauveria bassiana* on *Spodoptera litura* in Cotton Field

Two *B. bassiana* strains were used to control *S.litura* in the cotton field by direct field trial method (Navon and Ascher, 2000). In this experiment, the direct method was conducted with second instar of *S.litura.*

2.7. Plantation of Cotton Plants

BT toxin gene free of cotton seeds was obtained from the fields of Lonkyaw cotton plantation. The seeds were planted and watered daily. Chemical pesticides and biofertilizer were not used. After 45 days, the cotton seeds were planted.

2.8. Biossay Experiment

The conidia of the isolated strain and *B. bassiana* (BCC strain No. 2655) were produced by growing the fungus on PDA plates. After incubation, 0.1 gram of the two strains of conidia were harvested from many plates and diluted with 1 per cent Tween 80 and adjusted to four concentrations (10^5, 10^6, 10^7 and 10^8 spores/ml) and, were used as treatments. Sterilized distilled water containing 1 per cent Tween 80 was used as negative control and Shwemidar, a commercial insecticide was used as positive control.

Ten millilitre of each of the above concentrations was sprayed on each plant respectively for treatment and 10 millilitre of water with 1 per cent Tween 80 was sprayed on four plants for negative control. Positive control, Shwemidar was used according to its instructions. Second instar of 10 target insects were placed on each plant for treatments and controls. All of the plants were covered with cotton cages. One plant per cotton cage and four cages per one treatment were used.

3. RESULTS AND DISCUSSIONS

3.1. Insecticidal Potency of *Spodoptera litura*

Determination on the insecticidal activity of two entomopathogenic fungal spores against 1st, 2nd, 3rd and 4th instars of *S. litura* were studied by spraying various concentration of diluted solutions onto their diets (castor leaves) using the leaf–disc assay method. Each treatment was performed in the plastic container covered with thin layer of well ventilated cloth sheath and shown in Figure 7.1. After testing with both strains of *B. bassiana* for 7 days on 1st, 2nd, 3rd and 4th instars larvae, the ratio of mortality to survival of the insect larvae were recorded.

Results obtained from the leaf – discs bioassay experiment indicated that the isolated fungus has insecticidal activity. The insecticidal activity of *B. bassiana* is usually expressed in terms of median lethal concentration (LC_{50}). The insecticidal activities of two strains were studied and the values of LC_{50} were estimated by profit analysis. The LC_{50} values for the isolated strain on 1st, 2nd, 3rd and 4th instars of *S.litura* were at 6.55×10^5, 5.78×10^5, 6.03×10^5 and 3.59×10^6 spores/ml respectively. For BCC strain, the LC_{50} values were found at 3.72×10^5, 5.4×10^5, 1.31×10^6 and 2.43×10^7 spores/ml respectively on 1st, 2nd, 3rd and 4th instars of *S.litura* as shown in the Table 7.1. Therefore, the fungal concentration of 10^5 spores/ml is effective against 1st, 2nd and 3rd

Figure 7.1: Bioassay Experiment for the Pathogenicity of Two Strains on 1st, 2nd, 3rd and 4th Instars of *S. litura.*

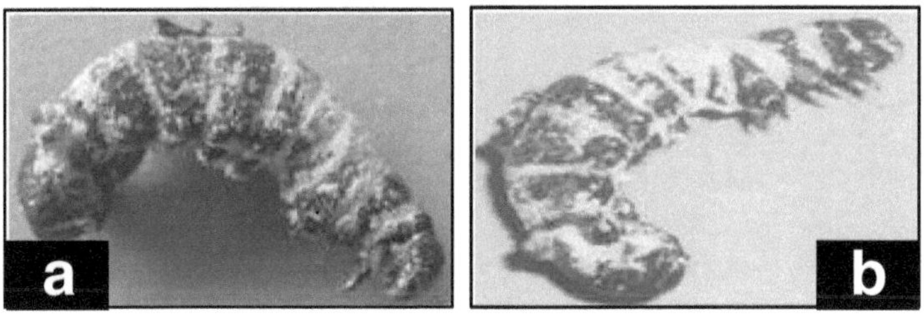

Figure 7.2: Appearance of Dead *S. litura* Infected by (a) Isolated Strain (b) BCC Strain.

instars of *S.litura* for isolated strain but for BCC strain, 10^6 spores/ml is effective against 3rd instar of *S.litura*. The LC_{50} of isolated strain and BCC strain was found to be 10^6 spores/ml and 10^7 spores/ml respectively for the 4th instar.

Table 7.1: Summary of LC_{50} Values for Pathogenicities of Two *B. bassiana* on Four Instars of *S.litura.*

	LC_{50} Values (spore/ml)	
Instar of Insects	*Indigenous Strain*	*BCC Strain*
1st Instar	$6.55x10^5$	$3.72x10^5$
2nd Instar	$5.78x10^5$	$5.4x10^5$
3rd Instar	$6.03x10^5$	$1.31x10^6$
4th Instar	$3.59x10^6$	$2.43x10^7$

3.2. Pathogenicity of *Beauveria bassiana* on *Spodoptera litura* in Cotton Field

Two *Beauveria* strains were used to control *S. litura* in cotton field by spraying various concentrations of diluted solutions onto the cotton plants and larvae by using the direct method. The experiment in cotton field is described in the Figure 7.3. In this experiment, the direct method was conducted with second instar of *S.litura*. After this experiment was carried out, the mortality and survival larvae were recorded after day by day and the suitable result was found at 7 days after treatment for two strains. The appearances of dead insects infected by both strains are shown in Figure 7.2. The LC_{50} values for both strains are calculated by profit analysis. The LC_{50} value for isolated strain was $4x10^5$ spores/ml and $7.55x10^6$ spores/ml for BCC strain against 2nd of *S. litura*. It was found that, the concentration of 10^5spores/ml is reliable for isolated strain and 10^6spores/ml for BCC strain in field trial experiment.

Figure 7.3: Experiment for Pathogenicity of Two *B. bassiana* Strains on *S. litura* in Cotton Field.

The *Beauveria* species have the potential to control over 70 insect pests of various crops, and appears to be innocuous to most non-target organisms (Feng, *et al.*, 1994). (Purwar and Sachan, 2005) reported that in general, *B. bassiana* was more virulent than *Metarhizium anisopliae* to *Spodoptera* spp. (Tanada and Kaya, 1993) argue that infection and sporulation of several entomopathogenic fungi are influenced by environmental factors, especially temperature and humidity, and to a lesser extent photoperiod. The speed of mortality depends on the number of spores contacting the insect, insect ages, susceptibility and environmental conditions. In this study, the most popularized entomopathogenic fungus (*B. bassiana*) was isolated and this isolated local strain had pathogenicity on four instars of *S. litura*. The results indicate the potential for utilization of the entomopathogenic fungus (*B. bassiana*) to control insect, *S. litura*.

4. CONCLUSION

In this research, the main concern was to isolate and identify the entomopathogenic fungus; *B. bassiana* which was confirmed as *B. bassiana* (BCC 2655) based on cultural and microscopic morphologies and their insecticidal activity.

The pathogenicity of the isolated strain was evaluated against four instars of *S.litura* compared with BCC 2655 by leaf-disc assay method and these two *B. bassiana* strains were pathogenic to cotton leafworm larvae at different concentrations. In the field trial experiment, the two *Beauveria* strains were used to control 2nd instar of *S. litura* by direct method. According to overall data obtained from both experiments, the two strains showed insecticidal activity on *S. litura*. This study shows that *Beauveria* strains are suitable to infect *S. litura* and have the potential for utilization of entomopathogenic fungi to control insect, *S. litura*.

ACKNOWLEDGEMENTS

I would like to express deepest gratitude to Rector, Mandalay Technological University, for the far-sighted guidance and encouragement, throughout the research. Sincerest thanks are to my beloved family for their constant encouragement.

REFERENCES

1. Donald G. McNeil Jr., Fungus Fatal to Mosquito May Aid Global War on Malaria, The New York Times, 10 June 2005.
2. Feng, M. G., Poprawski, T. J., Khachatourians, G. G. 1994. Production, formulation and application of the entomopathogenic fungus *Beauveria bassiana* for insect control: current status. Bioscience Control Technology, 4: 3-34.
3. Holloway, J. D. 1989. The moths of Borneo: Family Noctuidae, trifine subfamilies: Noctuinae, Heliothinae, Hadeninae, Acronictinae, Amphipyrinae, Agaristinae. *Malayan Nature Journal* 42: 57-226.
4. Lingappa, S., Saxena, H. and Devi Vimala, P. S. 2005. Role of biocontrol agents in management of *Helicoverpa armigera* (Hubner). In: Recent advances in *Helicoverpa armigera* Management (Hem Saxena, A. B. Rai, R. Ahmad and Sanjeev Gupta eds.). *Indian* Society of Pulses Research and development, IIPR, Kanpur. 159-184 PP.
5. S. Malarvannan, P. D. Murali, S. P. Shanthakumar, V. R. Prabavathy and Sudha Nair, 2010. Entomopathogenic fungi on *Spodoptera litura*. Biopesticides, 126–131 (2010).
6. Mohammad Monobrullah and Uma Shankar. 2008. Sublethal effects of SpltNPV infection on developmental stages of *Spodoptera litura* (Lepidoptera: Noctuidae). *Bio-control Science and Technology*, 18: 431-437.
7. A.Navon and K.R.S. Ascher, 2000, "Bioassay of Entomopathogenic microbes and nematodes" ISBN 0-85199-422-9.
8. Purwar, P. and Sachan, G. C. 2005. Biotoxicity of *Beauveria bassiana* and *Metarhizium anisopliae* against *Spodoptera litura* and *Spilarctia oblique*. Annals of Plant Protection Sciences, 13: (2).
9. Ramana, V. V., Reddy, G. P. V. and Krishnamurthy, M. M. 1988. Synthetic pyrethroids and other bait formulation in the control of *Spodoptera litura* (Fab.) attacking rabi groundnut. *Pesticides*, 1: 522 524.

10. Rombach, M. C., Aguda, R. M., Shepard, B. M. And Roberts, D. W. 1986. Infection of rice brown plant hopper, *Nilaparvata lugens* (Homoptera: Delphacidae), by field application of entomopatho genic Hyphomycetes (Deuteromycotina). *Environmental Entomology*, 15: 1070-1073.

11. Rowland, M., B. Hackett and M. Stribley. 1991. Evaluation of insecticides in field -control simulators and standard laboratory bioassays against resistant and susceptible *Bemisia tabaci* (Homoptera: Aleyrodidae) from Sudan. Bull. of Entomol. Res. 81: 189 -199.

12. Sharma, R. K. and Bisht, R. S. 2008. Antifeedant activity of indigenous plant extracts against *Spodoptera litura* Fabricius. *Journal of Insect Science*, 21: 56-60.

13. Santharam, G. 1985. Studies on the nuclear polyhedrosis virus of the tobacco cutworm, *Spodoptera litura* (Fabricius) (Noctuidae: Lepidoptera), Ph.D Thesis, Tamil Nadu Agricultural University, Coimbatore.

14. Tanada, Y., and Kaya, H. K. 1993. *Insect Pathology*. San Diego, CA, USA: Academic Press, 666 PP.

Chapter 8

Status of Biotechnology and Prospects of Biotechnology Related Small and Medium Size Enterprises in Nepal

*Chiranjivi Regmi**

Nepal Academy of Science and Technology, Khumaltar, Lalitpur, P.O. Box 3323, Nepal

ABSTRACT

Nepal is a late starter in research and development of modern biotechnology. Plant tissue culture laboratory established in 1975 under Department of Plant Resources is the pioneer of modern biotechnology in Nepal. This laboratory has already developed protocols of tissue culture of 75 plant species. Although science education at university level started in 1960s, higher education technical field started in 1980s. Biotechnology education at the university started very late actually in the beginning of 20th century: At Kathmandu University in 2007 and at Tribhuwan University in 2010. At present there are as many as 14 institutions and colleges affiliated to four universities (Tribhuvan, Kathmandu, Purbanchal and Bokhara) providing higher education in Biotechnology. Out of these only two are teaching at MSc level and the rest only at Bachelor level. According to the status of S&T in Nepal, 2010). 70 scientists and technologists are in the field of biotechnology and it is a good asset for the development of biotechnology.

Considering the importance of biotechnology, the Government of Nepal has formulated "Biotechnology Policy" in 2006. This document has set some priority action plans on Biotechnology in six broad areas; Forestry and Agriculture, Human/Plant and Animal Health Care, Environment and Biodiversity; Biotechnology based Industry, DNA Technology and

* E-mail: info@nast.org.np; planning@nast.org.np

Human resources Development. It also facilitated the establishment of SMEs. Several research organisations are engaged in research and development activities in different fields of biotechnology. There are very few institutions that are involved in industrial biotechnology. Although Nepal has great potential for developing biotechnology based industries, it requires sufficient investment, skilled manpower and technological packages. Hence, priority areas to begin with Small and Medium scale enterprises have been identified as, Diagnosis services for plant diseases, Bio fertilizers, Production of biological control agents and preparations, Plant nurseries to produce disease free plantlets of horticultural crops, Production of spawn of mushrooms locally.

Keywords: *Nepal industrial biotechnology, Biotechnology policy, Small and medium size enterprises,*

1. INTRODUCTION

Nepal has been utilising the tools and products of biotechnology like many countries since a very long time. But the history of modern biotechnology in Nepal goes to mid 1970s when the plant tissue laboratory was established at Godawari in 1975 under the Department of Forestry with the objective to develop protocols of important floricultural, medicinal and forest tree plants for mass propagation. It developed protocols of about 75 plants including orchids, banana, potato and several others. Production of rabies vaccine in Nepal started at the Central Veterinary Laboratory by the same time in 1980. National Potato Research Programme (NPRP) was established as a well equipped Tissue Culture Laboratory in 1989 with technical and financial cooperation of the Swiss Development Cooperation. Nepal Academy of science and Technology initiated biotechnological research activities beginning with Shoot Tip Grafting in vitro of citrus in 1989. However, formal courses on biotechnology at the university level started at Kathmandu University in 2007 and at Tribhuwan University in 2010. At present, as many as 14 institutions and colleges affiliated to four universities (Tribhuvan, Kathmandu, Purbanchal and Pokhara Universities) are providing higher education in Biotechnology. Considering its importance, the Government of Nepal has given due priority to Biotechnology and formulated Biotechnology Policy in 2006.

2. BIOTECHNOLOGY POLICY, 2006

The overall objective of this policy is to make contribution to the reduction of poverty by developing and expanding biotechnology and its uses in the sectors of comparative benefits and its application for the development of the country as well as environment protection and public welfare. Other objectives of this policy are as follows:

- ✰ To fulfill the minimum need of food for growing population, thereby assisting poverty reduction
- ✰ To encourage research and development of biotechnology contributing for the development forest, agriculture and food sector in an internationally competitive and environmentally sustainable manner.
- ✰ To promote managerial skill in the field of biotechnology, attract the competent researchers and experts, promote entrepreneurship and maintain a balance between demand and supply for the expert skill.

- ☆ To reduce environmental degradation and protect natural resources and means.
- ☆ To develop simple and new programmes for ensuring the transformation of the results of research into professional use subject to making contribution to making rural and national economic system.

To meet the above mentioned objectives, some strategies have been mentioned in the Biotechnology Policy, 2006. Strategies relevant to Industrial biotechnology are as follows:

- ☆ To establish biotechnology –based industries on the basis of national requirement, market demands and regional characteristics, and encourage as well as provide concession to such industries.
- ☆ To facilitate a venture capital fund and flow of bank loan to be provided for the biotechnology- based industries.
- ☆ To promote private sector investment in high priority research, development and expansion of biotechnology.

In order to provide an effective foundation for intergovernmental cooperation, promote partnership amongst stakeholders, establish open and transparent processes, increase awareness and public understanding, some policies have been adopted relevant to the industrial biotechnology as follows:

- ☆ To exchange facility and technology amongst neighbouring and other developing countries and striving to maximize a cordial relationship with development partners of Nepal for the development and expansion of biotechnology.
- ☆ To provide financial support to the feasible biotechnology based programmes.
- ☆ To encourage domestic and foreign investment for the development of biotechnology.

As implementation strategy, the policy document setup action plans in following sectors:

2.1. Forest, Agriculture and Food Grains

- ☆ Tissue culture
- ☆ Biopestcides, biofertilizers and other related aspects
- ☆ Animal feeds/supplements for agriculture products
- ☆ Aquaculture
- ☆ Plant animal improvement
- ☆ Ornamental flowers, medicinal plants and mushrooms

2.2. Human/Plant and Animal Health Care

- ☆ Diagnostic
- ☆ Vaccines

- ☆ Immunology and therapeutics
- ☆ Embryo transfer
- ☆ Gene therapy

2.3. Environment and Biodiversity

- ☆ Development of microbial culture for waste management
- ☆ *In situ* conservation and utilization of plant resources
- ☆ Monitoring tools and biosensors
- ☆ Pest management through natural bioagents and botanics

2.4. Industry

- ☆ Food and industrial products
- ☆ Fermentation products
- ☆ Bioenergy

2.5. DNA Technology

- ☆ Identification and isolation of genes to use in molecular hybridization
- ☆ Studies on polymorphism molecular mapping of endangered and commercial species
- ☆ Selection of gene for breeding programme and development of diagnostic kits
- ☆ DNA profiling for forensic applications
- ☆ Diagnosis of genetic diseases
- ☆ Paternity analysis, immigration and citizenship records

In addition to these objectives, special emphasis has been given to the development of human resources in biotechnology and updating their skills and creating conducive environment for their work.

3. EDUCATION IN BIOTECHNOLOGY

Higher level education in biotechnology is most important for the research and development activities including establishment of small and medium scale biotechnology related industries in the country. At present, there are14 constituent institutions/campuses of different universities (Tribhuvan University, Kathmandu, University and Pokhara University) including their affiliated private colleges providing higher education in the biotechnology and related fields leading to BSc and MSc degrees. Some of them are producing PhDs also. Total intake capacity of these institutions is 350 and 500 students at MSc and BSc level respectively. It seems that the number of biotechnologists will increase to a critical mass within few years. Out of these institutions, only two are teaching at MSc level and the rest only Bachelor level.

Table 8.1: List of Educational Institutions Providing Higher Education in Biotechnology

Sl.No.	Name and Address of the Institution	Level Taught
1.	Central Department of Biotechnology, TU, Kirtipur	M.Sc. Ph.D
2.	Central Department of Botany, TU, Kirtipur	M.Sc.
3.	Central Department of Microbiology, TU, Kirtipur	M.Sc.
4.	Central Campus of Technology, TU, Dharan	M.Sc., B.Sc.
5.	Department of Microbiology, Trichandra Campus, TU	B.Sc.
6.	Institute of Agriculture and Animal Science, Rampur	B.Sc.
7.	Department of Biotechnology, Kathmandu University, Dhulikhel	B.Sc.
8.	Himalayan College of Agricultural Science and Technology, Bhaktapur	B.Sc.
9.	Universal Science College, Kathmandu	B.Sc.
10.	National College, Kathmandu	M.Sc., B.Sc.
11 .	White House College, Lalitpur	B.Sc.
12.	Lord Buddha Education Foundation, Kathmandu	B.Sc.
13.	SAAN International College, Kathmandu	B.Sc.
14.	St. Xavier's College, Kathmandu	B.Sc.

The total number of scientists and technologists in all disciplines of science and technology in the country with PhD degree is slightly more than 1200 (Status of S&T in Nepal 2010). Out of them, 70 scientists and technologists are in the field of biotechnology. According to a study (NAST and MoEST 2009), 70 PhDs, 156 MScs and only about 80 BScs are working in different biotechnology related research laboratories and institutions. However, the fresh graduates are facing acute problems of getting job in the country. Hence, many of them are going abroad for further studies and work. Therefore, there is an urgent need of new avenues such as promotion of biotechnology related SMEs to absorb them within the country streamlining to national development.

4. RESEARCH LABORATORIES

Main institutions with biotechnology laboratory facilities are described below.

4.1. Nepal Academy of Science and Technology

It has separate Biotechnology laboratory in which well qualified researchers (5 PhDs and 10 MScs) are conducting research in following areas:

- ☆ Molecular characterization of medicinal plants
- ☆ Microbial biotechnology
- ☆ Plant disease diagnosis
- ☆ Biofertilizers

4.2. Nepal Agriculture Research Council

Biotechnology related research activities are carried out in 4 different laboratories; Biotechnology unit, Plant Pathology Division, National Potato Research Programme,

Entomology Division, Animal Breeding Division and Animal Health Research Division on following areas:

- ✰ Anther culture
- ✰ Embryo rescue from interspecific rice
- ✰ Isozyme studies
- ✰ RAPD and SSR fingerprinting for the assessment of genetic variation
- ✰ Survey and surveillance of diseases of agricultural crops
- ✰ Research on development of biological control measures of crop pests
- ✰ Production of pre-basic seed potato through tissue culture
- ✰ Production and testing of nuclear poly-hydrosis virus and *Bacillus thuringiensis* for pest management
- ✰ Semen production and artificial insemination in cattle
- ✰ Characterization of buffalo
- ✰ *Salmonella* antigen production

4.3. Department of Plant Resources

Tissue culture Laboratory of this Department is the pioneer of starting tissue culture in the country that has already developed tissue culture protocols of more than 75 five plant species. At present its two laboratories are engaged in research and development activities on following areas:

- ✰ Micro propagation of medicinal, ornamental, and endangered plants
- ✰ *In vitro* conservation of endangered and important plant species
- ✰ Develop protocols of tissue culture of plants

4.4. Department of Live Stock and Animal Health

It has two laboratories *viz.* Central Veterinary Laboratory and Rabies Vaccine production Laboratory and following activities are carried in these laboratories:

- ✰ Animal disease investigation including bird flu, Japanese encephalitis and PPR
- ✰ TCARV production for animals and human use

4.5. Department of Food Technology and Quality Control

This is the reference laboratory for bio safety of food with very good facilities to carry out following activities:

- ✰ Provide services of food quality analysis
- ✰ Research on detection of GMOs-GM FFP
- ✰ Screening of yeast and evaluation of fermented foods and beverages

4.6. National Public Health Laboratory

This Laboratory belongs to the Ministry of Health and provides diagnosis services of special diseases such as AIDS, Japanese encephalitis, Polio, Measles, Cancer etc.

4.7. National Forensic Laboratory

This is a semiautonomous national laboratory. Its main function is to provide forensic services for crime investigation. It also does research on DNA data basing of Nepalese population.

In addition to the above centres, all the educational institutions providing higher education related biotechnology have their own laboratories. Laboratory of Central Department of Biotechnology and Laboratory at Central Food Technology Campus under Institute of Science and Technology, Tribhuvan University, Biotechnology laboratory of Kathmandu University. In addition to that, 17 medical colleges have very good laboratories where they provide diagnostic services and relevant research activities. Similarly, there are private laboratories that are also active in doing research and analytical services.

In Nepal, all the institutions are working in one another sectors; Plant Biotechnology, Animal Biotechnology Medical Biotechnology, Industrial Biotechnology, Environment Biotechnology, Biotechnology and Forensic Biotechnology.

5. INDUSTRIAL BIOTECHNOLOGY

Industrial biotechnology sector is gaining momentum in research and development in Nepal. Status of Human Resources, infrastructure and current major activities of institutions/organisations are given in the Table 8.2.

Table 8.2: Current Activities of Key Institutions in Food and Industrial Sector in Nepal.

Sl.No.	*Name of Institution*	*Activities*
1.	Department of Food	Screening of yeast strains for cider making
	Technology and	Development of lactic drink
	Quality Control	Laboratory preparation of pure murcha from local strain of yeast
		Preparation of Wine, Cider, Perry and other alcoholic beverages using pure and mixed culture
		Preparation and quality evaluation of indigenous fermented foods
		Studies on preparation of soy sauce
2.	Central Campus of	Improving traditional kinnema technology for commercialization
	Technology, Hattisar	Optimization of Jand (local alcoholic beverage)
		Fermented dairy products
		Fruit juice production
		Enzyme production
		Food bacterial and fungal detection
3.	Centre for Agriculture	Development of Shitake mushroom cultivation technology
	Technology (Private)	Spawn production for *Agaricus* and *Pleurotus* mushroom with capacity of 40,000 bottles of spawn/year

Contd...

Table 8.2–*Contd...*

Sl.No.	*Name of Institution*	*Activities*
4.	Nepal Dairy Private Limited	Production and marketing of different types of dairy products Conducting feasibility study for the expansion of industry in different hilly districts of Nepal with special emphasis on making Yak Cheese, buffalo milk cheese
5.	Nepal Biotech Nursery Private Limited	Conservation, production and commercialization of cut flowers, orchids through participatory approach with local community and women farmers *Ex situ* conservation of some high altitude medicinal plants (*Dactylorhiza hatagirea* and *Picrorhiza scrophulariiflora*)

Source: National State of the Art Report, 2008 on Biotechnology for Nepal.

5.1. Prospects of Biotechnology Related SMEs

The above table showed that there are very few institutions/private enterprises involved in industrial biotechnology.

Nepal is a land locked mountainous country; it is most desirable to establish industries producing low volume high value products. Industrial biotechnology is one of the technologies that enable such products. Biotechnology based industries can be established to produce antibiotics, vaccines, diagnostic kits and several other products in Nepal in future when critical mass of skilled human resources are produced and the national and foreign investors are attracted.

However, considering the fact that the majority of population of Nepal is facing the problems of food security and safety in many remote areas. The government policy has rightly given emphasis to agriculture. It is the duty of biotechnologists of Nepal to develop packages of biotechnology that could be used for the establishment of small and medium scale industries locally to produce products and services to be used locally for increasing the agricultural productivity.

Considering the favourable policy and implementation strategies set by government and availability of required human resources to establish SMEs, following fields seem to be more relevant to address the urgent need of food security, in Nepal:

1. Diagnostic services for plant diseases
2. Biofertilzers- *Rhizobium, Azolla*, etc
3. Production of biological control agents and preparations
4. Plant nurseries to produce disease free plantlets of horticultural crops
5. Production of spawn of mushrooms locally

Establishment of SMEs for the production and service providing has to be encouraged involving young biotechnologists by the government for at least 5-7 years. Once such enterprises become successful, avenues will be opened for establishment of Medium and Large scale industries in the country.

ACKNOWLEDGEMENT

I would like to express sincere thanks to Vice Chancellor of NAST, Prof. Dr. S.R. Kafle, Director, NAM S&T Center Prof. Dr. Arun Kulshreshtha and Prof. Dr. Mahmoud M. Sakr, Executive Director STDF, Egypt for providing me the opportunity to participate in the First Winter School on Industrial Biotechnology in Cairo, Egypt.

REFERENCES

1. Biotechnology Policy Document, 2006, Ministry of Environment, Science and Technology, Government of Nepal.
2. National State of the Art Report on Biotechnology for Nepal 2008, NAST and MoEST.
3. Status of Science Technology in Nepal, 2010. NAST and MoEST.
4. Joshi, S.D., 2009, Status and Prospects of Biotechnology education in Nepal, In Proceedings of National Seminar on Present Status and Future Prospects of Biotechnology in Nepal, pp.85-98.
5. Regmi, C., 2009. Status of Plant Virus and Virus like diseases in Nepal, In Proceedings of National Seminar on Present Status and Future Prospects of Biotechnology in Nepal, pp.36-41.

Chapter 9

Temporary Immersion Bioreactors in Nigeria for *In vitro* Propagation of Plants: Status and Prospects

M.T. Abdulkareem, A.A. Adekunle,*
O.A. Adetunji and J.M. Madu

National Biotechnology Development Agency,
Umaru Musa Yar'adua Expressway, Lugbe,
P.M.B. 5118, Wuse, Abuja, Nigeria

ABSTRACT

Temporary Immersion Bioreactor system (TIBs) is a relatively recent micropropagation technique that simplifies the whole tissue culture process, reducing production cost, and making micropropagation available to a larger number of species. TIBs is emerging as an alternative method of micropropagation, with advantages of culture on semi-solid and in submerged medium, without the disadvantages of a liquid environment. In order to boost agricultural productivity and meet the food demand of the nation, the Federal Government of Nigeria, through the Ministry of Science and Technology, in 2010 collaborated with the Cuban Government to promote the transfer of the technology to Nigeria. Several research Institutes in the country have since benefitted from this collaboration. These include: National Biotechnology Development Agency (NABDA), Sheda Science and Technology Complex (SHESTCO) and National Centre for Genetic Resources and Biotechnology (NACGRAB) among others. Some of these institutes have even fabricated the TIBs from locally available materials and are working towards the indigenous computerization of the technology.

* E-mail: taokarim2000@yahoo.com

Recent researches are directed towards using TIBs for micropropagation of pineapples and bananas. This will enable the country to meet raw material demand for the fruit juice industry, 95 per cent of which is presently imported, despite the fact that Nigeria has the capacity to produce adequate tropical fruits.

Keywords: *Micropropagation, Temporary immersion bioreactors, TIB, Tissue culture, Medium.*

1. INTRODUCTION

The term plant tissue culture or micropropagation encompasses a variety of *in vitro* manipulation of plant cells, tissues and organs that leads to the differentiation of the parental cells into meristematic or embryonic cells, which then multiply and differentiate into plant organs and/or whole plants (Watt, 2012). The explant, piece of the parent plant utilized to initiate the culture, is typically small, but the end result is the mass multiplication of the parent genotype. Micropropagation protocols are dependent upon the empirical manipulation of medium components (plant growth regulators, nutrients) and environmental conditions (light, temperature). These vary from plant to plant and with the type of explant. All plant cells, once isolated and cultured are capable of expressing totipotency (regenerating to form a whole plant). Plant cells regenerate to whole plants through two morphogenic routes: organogenesis (formation of shoots followed by rooting) and embryogenesis (formation of somatic embryos and their germination into complete plants). Both can occur via an intervening callus stage (Lyam *et al.*, 2012).

This paper reviews the status of Temporary Immersion Bioreactor systems (TIBs), a new micropropagation technique that is faster, more cost effective, and less labour intensive, in Nigeria. It also discusses its prospects in helping the fruit juice industry in Nigeria to meet its fruit demands.

1.1. Conventional Tissue Culture

Micropropagation is divided into five stages: selection and conditioning of explant donor plants for tissue culture; initiation of organogenesis or embryogenesis by placing the explant in culture media (induction); repeated multiplication of shoots, hence increase in biomass (multiplication); *in vitro* rooting; and transfer to soil and hardening (Murashige, 1974). Conventional micropropagation or tissue culture techniques are carried out in small culture vessels containing a solidified culture media, which serves as substrates on which the plant tissues are cultured. This method, however, has certain disadvantages which limits its usage across plant species. The semi-solid nature of the culture medium makes the culture heterogeneous and not all the tissues are in contact with the nutrients. Also, tissues need to be transferred into different culture vessels containing fresh media as each stage of the micropropagation process requires different media compositions and growth regulator concentrations. These make micropropagation labour intensive and increases the production cost of plants produced *in vitro* (Robert *et al.*, 2006).

Micropropagation in liquid medium addresses some of the challenges associated with semi-solid media. However, microbial contamination is more difficult to control, which is a major disadvantage. Also, plants may become vitrified (Robert *et al.*, 2006).

1.2. Temporary Immersion Bioreactors

Temporary immersion systems, designed by Teisson *et al.* (1995), combine the advantages of both semi-solid and liquid culture media. Temporary Immersion Bioreactor is a semi-automated bioreactor that allows plants to be propagated in liquid media. It is a simpler and cheaper method which decreases the amount of labour input. It also makes micropropagation available to a larger number of plant species (Robert *et al.*, 2006). It has also been shown to achieve a much higher yield compared to the conventional micropropagation technique (Table 9.1) (Escalona, 2003).

Table 9.1: Effects of Temporary Immersion Bioreactors on Biological Yield.

Crop	*Variety*	*Conventional Micropropagation*	*Temporary Immersion Systems*
Pineapple	Smooth cayenne	8.0	68.8
	MD2	5.8	26.8
Sugarcane	C91-301	3.7	34.1
	CP-5234	4.0	32.5
Banana	FHIA-18	3.8	7.4
	FHIA-01	3.4	10.4
	Grand Nane	4.0	16.6

Source: Escalona *et al.* (2003).

A typical TIB system (Figure 9.1) consists of two large and separate glass vessels, one for the plant tissue and the other for the liquid medium which is moved from one vessel to the other by pressurized air. The system allows alternate short periods of total immersion in liquid medium with longer ones of complete aeration (Escalona *et al.*, 2002). Electrovalves are connected to a programmable timer to regulate the frequency and duration of immersion by controlling air circulation as they open and close. Other variations to this temporary immersion system include: RITA system (Teisson and Alvard, 1995) and BioMINT system (Robert *et al.*, 2006). Temporary immersion systems have been successfully used for the propagation of various plant species (Alvard *et al.*, 1993; Escalosa *et al.*, 1999; Etienne *et al.*, 1997).

2. MATERIALS

To assemble the TIB system, the following materials are required: shelves of three floors illuminated with fluorescent lights, transparent polycarbonate flask with a cover of two holes to connect tubes, hydrophobic filters (0.22 μmol), PVC or silicone transparent tubing (10 mm of Ø), electrovalve (solenoid valve), timers and compressor (Figure 9.2). It is important that the flasks, their covers and the connecting tubes be autoclavable (Lyam *et al.*, 2012).

Each unit of the TIBs consist of two glass containers of equal sizes. The containers are of varying capacities, depending on the plants being cultured. However, they should be small and light enough to be easily autoclaved and transported from the

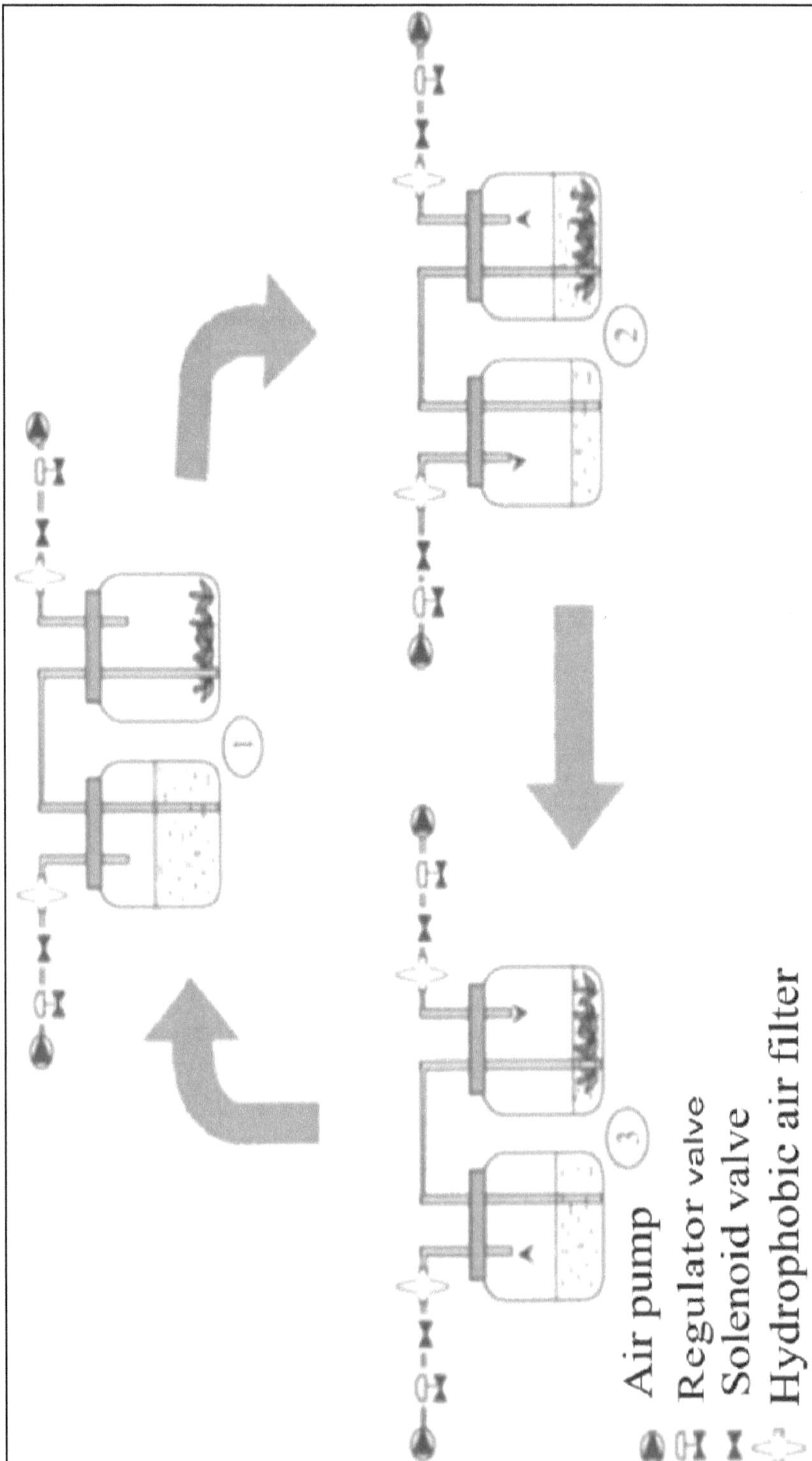

Figure 9.1: Schematic Representation of the Operational Procedure of TIBs.

Source: Escalona *et al.* (1999).

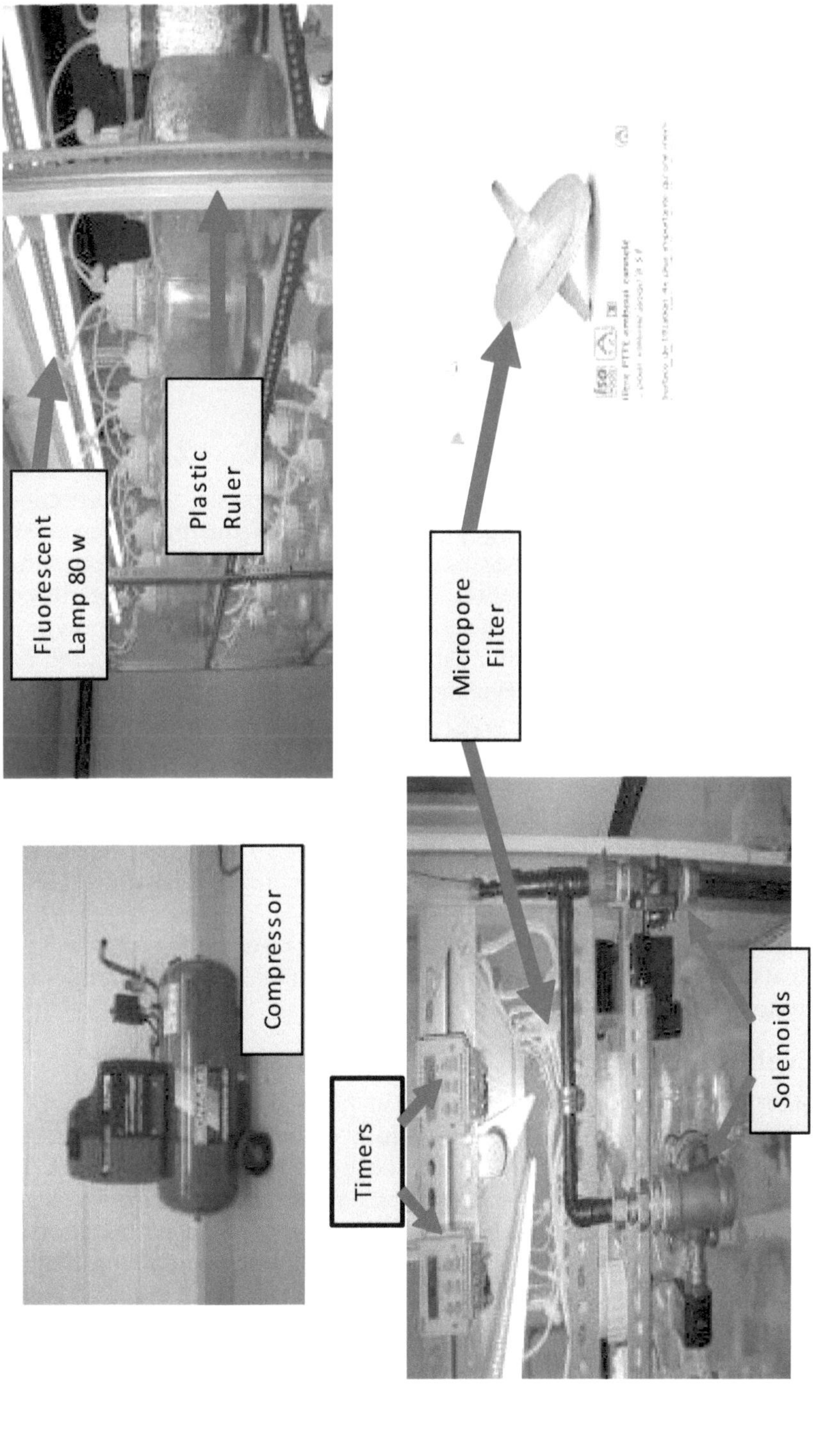

Figure 9.2: Various Components of a Typical Temporary Immersion Bioreactor System Setup. The plastic ruler serves to cover up the wiring of the system.

***Source*: Manual for mounting and setting up TIBs.**

airflow cabinet to the culture room. One of the two vessels contains the plant tissue, while the other contains the liquid medium. The two containers are connected by tubes that pass through holes in the covers and allows liquid medium to be transferred from one container to the other with the aid of pressurized air supplied by the compressor. The air is supplied through similar tubes which are connected to hydrophobic filters on the other end. The hydrophobic filter serves to guarantee the sterility of the air. Electrovalves are connected to a programmable timer to regulate the frequency and duration of immersion by controlling air circulation as they open and close (Figure 9.2) (Lyam *et al.*, 2012).

3. METHODS

Four important steps are required for plant micropropagation using the temporary immersion systems: establishment of the mother explants on agar gel medium, zero shelving of plants to liquid medium, cultivation in temporary immersion systems and acclimatization and *ex vitro* transfer (Lyam *et al.*, 2012)

3.1. Establishment of the Mother Explants on Agar Gel Medium

Mother explant establishment involves the pre-propagation steps of the selection of a healthy donor parent of the plant to be propagated and pre-treatment to ensure it is free of viral, bacterial and fungal diseases. This is followed by the initiation of the explants, the first step in micropropagation. Tiny plants pieces are cut and sterilized on their surface with chemicals such as sodium hypochlorite and then growth is initiated on appropriate growth media. Established explants are subcultured on agar-gelled media with specific auxin/cytokinins combination to induce proliferation.

3.2. Zero Shelving of Plants to Liquid Medium

Cultures to be propagated by temporary immersion system must be allowed to go through the zero phase, where there is a gradual reduction of agar concentration in the nutrient medium from semi solid to liquid medium. This helps prepare the explants for the adaption and survival desired for the next phase which utilizes only liquid medium. The explant in liquid media is allowed to stay on the shelf for a while to detect possible microbial contamination that may be present in the culture. This will ensure that only healthy propagules are selected for transfer into the temporary immersion systems.

3.3. Cultivation in Temporary Immersion System

Cultivation in temporary immersion system involves multiplication, elongation and rooting (and harvest) phases. This stage is fully automated and carried out in liquid media. Plantlet transfer must be done aseptically under laminar flow hood. To harvest the plantlets from the TIBs, the mouth of the bottle of the container must be disinfected with sodium hypochlorite before opening to prevent contamination of the explants. Finally, 50 per cent of the plants are placed in trays containing 10mg/l of indole-acetic acid to allow rooting. Another 50 per cent is placed in zero shelves to inoculate in new TIBs.

3.4. Acclimatization and *Ex-vitro* Transfer

At this stage, rooted plants are washed with tap water and placed in the nursery for *ex vitro* acclimatization on a medium composed of Coconut fibre, Top Soil and Stone dust mixed in the ratio 7: 2: 1. They can be left in shade for 3 to 6 days where diffused natural light helps them adapt to the new environment. The plants are then transferred to an appropriate substrate (sand, peat, compost, etc.), and gradually hardened.

4. TEMPORARY IMMERSION BIOREACTOR SYSTEMS IN NIGERIA

TIBs is a modern micropropagation tool that is designed for intensive and scaled-up cultures. It affords maximum opportunity for monitoring and control over the conditions such as temperature, aeration and illumination that are required for growth, development and survival (Watt, 2012). It also allows increase in multiplication and survival rate of plants being propagated. Recognising these facts, the Federal Government of Nigeria, through the Ministry of Science and Technology collaborated with the Cuban Government to transfer the technology to Nigeria. The technology has since then been transferred to Nigeria and replicated in several research institutes. Some of the benefitting research Institutes are National Biotechnology Development Agency (NABDA), Sheda Science and Technology Complex (SHESTCO) and National Centre for Genetic Resources and Biotechnology (NACGRAB).

NABDA was established on 23rd of April 2001 with the aim of promoting biotechnology activities that would positively meet national aspiration such as food security, job/wealth creation, affordable health care delivery and sustainable economic development. (http: //www.nabda.gov.ng). One of the numerous achievements of NABDA is the acquisition of TIBs technology for the rapid and mass production of elite (disease-free) plantlets (Figure 9.3). This technology is ready for commercialization as it is a critical production facility in desertification and erosion control, food security and germplasm conservation.

NACGRAB was established in 1987 to conduct research, gather data and disseminate technological matters relating to genetic resource conservation, utilization and biotechnology applications. One of the main activities of the its Biotechnology unit is the mass propagation of economic and agronomic crop species using Temporary Immersion Bioreactor (TIBs) based on demand (http: // www.nacgrab.gov.ng/biotechnology).

SHESTCO is a multidisciplinary research and development establishment in the Federal Capital Territory, Abuja. It was commissioned on 17th August 1995 and it consists of three main national laboratories, one each for biotechnology, chemistry and physics. The purpose of SHESTCO is to be a centre of excellence that enables institutions as well as individual scientists to undertake a wide range of research activities (http: //www.shestco.org/biotech).

These three and other similar research institutes can help spread the technology to private seed companies who can embrace it to achieve a substantial increase in propagation of plantlets with less labour and cost inputs.

Figure 9.3: A Locally Fabricated Temporary Immersion Bioreactor System at NABDA.

5. PROSPECTS

The increasing health-consciousness, coupled with the intensive marketing activities by fruit juice manufacturers in Nigeria has led to an increase in demand of fresh fruits. Also, a ban on importation of finished fruit juice products in Nigeria has opened up several opportunities and led to the growth of the fruit juice industry.

Having one of the best climatic and soil conditions in the world, Nigeria has a comparative advantage in production of tropical fruits. Some of the fruits produced in Nigeria include banana, orange, mango and pineapple. These fruits can also be packaged for exportation once local demand has been met.

Temporary immersion system has been used successfully to culture various fruit plantlets (Escalona *et al.*, 1999; Espinosa *et al.*, 2002) which are useful in the Nigerian fruit juice industry. Adoption of this technology will not only help meet the raw material demand, but also reduce production cost associated with importation of the fruits.

In 2009, the Raw Materials Research and Development Council (RMRDC) in collaboration with the Manufacturers Association of Nigeria (MAN) organised a stakeholder's forum on "sourcing of raw materials for the fruit juice industry". At that meeting, NABDA proposed the use of TIBs for the mass production of planting materials such as mango and oranges. Since then, RMRDC has partnered with

NABDA to put machinery in place to take care of the mass propagation of elite plantlets that would be used for the fruit juice project.

6. CONCLUSION

The commercial utilization of the conventional *in vitro* micropropagation techniques of plants in meeting fruit demands is limited due to the high production costs, as a result of high labour cost, low multiplication rate, long duration, and low survival rate due to contamination and during acclimatization. Temporary Immersion Bioreactor systems employ the automated gadgets to control the rapid multiplication of plant cultures. Plantlets propagated in TIBs perform better than those propagated by conventional methods. Hence, temporary immersion systems can be employed for rapid and efficient propagation system for many fruits and other plant species.

REFERENCES

1. Alvard, D., Cote, F. and Teisson, C. (1993). Comparison of methods of liquid medium culture for banana micropropagation.Plant Cell, Tissue Organ Culture.32, pp. 55–60.
2. Escalona, M., Lorenzo, J.C., Gonzales, B.L., Daquinta, M., Borroto, C.G., Gozales, J.I. and Desjardine, Y. 1999. Pineapple (*Ananas comosus* L. Merr) micropropagation in temporary immersion systems.Plant CellRep. 18, pp. 743–748.
3. Escalona, M., Samson, G., Borroto, C. and Desjardins, Y. (2003). Physiology of Effects of Temporary Immersion Bioreactors on Micropropagated Pineapple Plantlets. In *Vitro Cell Developmental Biology of Plant*, (39): 651-656.
4. Espinosa, P., Lorenzo, J.C., Iglesias, A., Yabor, L., Menéndez, E., Borroto, J., Hernández, L. and Arencibia, A.D. (2002). Production of pineapple transgenic plants assisted by temporary immersion bioreactors. Plant Cell Report.21,pp. 136–140.
5. Etienne, H., Lartaud, M., Michaux-Ferrie're, N., Carron, M.P., Berthouly, M. and Teisson, C. (1997). Improvement of somatic embryogenesis in *Hevea brasiliensis* (Mu¨ ll. Arg.) using the temporary immersion technique. *In vitro* Cellular and Developmental Biology of Plant. 33, pp. 81–87.
6. Lyam, P.T., Musa, M.L., Jamaleddine, Z.O, Okere, U.A. and Odofin, W.T. (2012). The Potential of Temporary Immersion Bioreactors (TIBs) in Meeting Crop Production demand in Nigeria. Journal of Biology and Life Science. 3 (1), pp. 66-86.
7. Manual for mounting and setting forth shelves for temporal immersion Bioreactor (TIBs). ZugarMinistery.Genetic and Biotechnology Department, National Institute for Sugarcane Research. Havanna City, Cuba.
8. Murashige, T., 1974. Plant propagation through tissue cultures. Annu. Rev. PlantPhysiol. 25, pp. 135–166.
9. Robert, M.L., Herrera-Herrera, J.L, Herrera-Herrera, G. Herrera-Alamillo, M.A. and Fuentes-Carrillo, P., 2006. Methods MolBiol 318: 121-9.

10. Teisson, C. and Alvard, D. 1995. A new concept of plant in vitro cultivationliquid medium: temporary immersion, in Current Issues in Plant Molecular and Cellular Biology (Terzi, M., Cella, R., and Falavigna, A., eds.) Kluwer Academic Publishers, Dordrecht, The Netherlands, pp. 105–110.
11. Watt, M.P. 2012.The status of temporary immersion system (TIS) technology for plant micropropagation.African Journal of Biotechnology 11 (76), pp. 14025-14035.

Chapter 10

Optimisation of Alpha-amylase Production by *Bacillus subtilis*: A Local Isolate Grown on Cassava Starch

O.A. Adetunji[1], B.O. Solomon[1], M.T. Abdulkareem, A.A. Adekunle, M. Madu Josephine, R.E. Okonji[2], T.F. Adepoju[3], O.A. Adesina[3] and S.K. Layokun[3]*

[1] National Biotechnology Development Agency, Umuaru Musa Yaradua Expressway, Lugbe Area, P.M.B 5118, Wuse, Abuja, Nigeria
[2] Department of Biochemistry, [3] Department of Chemical Engineering, Obafemi Awolowo University, Ile-Ife, Osun State, Nigeria

ABSTRACT

The Nigerian enzyme requirements and demands are currently solely dependent on importation with high cost implications. Local sources of substrate and microorganism for enzymes production have been found to be a cheaper option being emphasized in the deregulation policy of the country. Hence, the need to investigate the use of local substrate (Cassava) and microorganism (*Bacillus subtilis*) to ascertain their suitability for Alpha-Amylase production an enzyme of high economic importance. Therefore, this work was carried out to evaluate the efficacy of locally isolated *Bacillus subtilis* and suitability of cassava starch as a potential substrate for the production of alpha amylase enzyme. The results showed the potential and ability of *B.subtilis* in the production of alpha amylase enzyme using cassava starch (Growth Associated) while the Response Surface Methodology (RSM) predicted the

* E-mail: adetunjiolusegun44@gmail.com

optimal temperature, agitation rate and substrate concentration to be 40°C, 150 rpm and 15 per cent respectively for the production of the enzyme with coefficient of determination (R^2) of 0.9. The specific growth (μ) of 0.0086 h^{-1} and doubling time (t_d) of 5.44 h showed the efficiency of the microorganism in the bioreactor. Alpha amylase obtained from *B. subtilis* showed good affinity towards the cassava starch with K_m, and V_{max} values of 0.184 mg/ml and 4.149 Units/ml, respectively. The study concluded that *B. subtilis* and cassava starch could be used to produce alpha amylase of acceptable characteristics.

***Keywords**: Alpha-Amylase, Cassava, Response surface methodology and Bacillus subtilis.*

1. INTRODUCTION

Bello (2002; 2006) reported that local production of industrial enzymes in Nigeria such as *Bacillus protease, Amyloglucosidase, Isomerase,* Bacterial amylase, Pectinase, Microbial rennet, fungal amylase, fungal protease is highly imperative for the Nigerian Economy and would also break the current importation monopoly in the Country and therefore reduce the foreign exchange drain. In Nigeria, a growing demand for industrial enzymes have been rising with the increasing number of industries most of which are bio-based and require enzymes for their operation. Such industries include the food and beverages, detergent, textiles and pharmaceutical industries and recently the renewable energy sector comprising of Biofuel production. Considering the fact that the main potential feedstock for producing bio ethanol are composed of carbohydrates, the use of enzymes to break down these oligosaccharides into easily fermentable sugars being the precursor and the first step before conducting the fermentation (Kim *et al.*, 2004). The candidacy of Cassava as a feedstock for various Agro-allied based products such as starch, chips, flour and recently for enzyme production has been reported by several workers (Sani *et al.*, 1992; Grace, 1977; Mathew *et al.*, 1991; Radley *et al.*, 1976 and Queynh and Cecil, 1996). Sixty per cent of Alpha amylase production occurs in Europe, with fifteen per cent in the United State of America and fifteen percent in Japan and the rest goes to other parts of the World. Unfortunately, Nigeria the most populous black nation has a little or no participation in the production process. Furthermore, the indigenous substrate selection and other production parameters of most importance for the overproduction of these enzymes in large quantities to meet industrial demands have been given little or no research attention locally. Hence, the need to study the optimization of the various production parameters was the major focus of this research work.

Beside cellulose, starch is the most widespread carbohydrate that is globally acceptable for both animal and human consumption. It is a non-poisonous, relatively cheap and renewable resource and it is easily separable in fairly purified form from raw materials. In addition, the abundance of starch makes it an important economic and political feature (Calleja *et al.*, 1986). The current practice is the utilization of bacterial and fungal amylases to efficiently hydrolyze grain or tuber starch to glucose. According to the concepts of Reed (1975), and Takagi *et al.* (1971), the responsible enzymes for starch degradation are widely distributed in nature. Acid and enzyme hydrolysis have been the main methods used for starch saccharification. Various works done on acid hydrolysis of starch favour the use of dilute hydrochloric acid because it acts mildly on starch with lesser amount of side products (Swanson and Cori, 1948; Leman and Didry, 1950). Sulphuric and phosphoric acids produce many by-products, which ultimately inhibit the progress of hydrolysis and growth of microbes. Adversely, Aderibigbe (2005) and Aransiola (2005) reported that the enzyme-enzyme method gave the highest yield during the hydrolysis of cassava starch compared with acid-acid and acid-enzyme methods. Starch hydrolysing enzymes, analogous to catalysts used in petroleum industries, are manufactured in small amounts when compared to the amount of material produced by their reaction. Amylases are more common enzymes which can hydrolyse the glucosidic bonds in starch. Among them is alpha-amylase, which acts on starch, glycogen and polysaccharides cleaving glycosidic α-1, 4 bonds. The production of this starch degrading enzyme is now becoming a current pursuit central to the modern biotechnology industry. This is borne out of the recent global interest in finding an alternative energy source especially biofuels such as bioethanol, biodiesel and biogas (Johansson *et al.*, 1993; Rosillo and Cortez, 1998; Sree *et al.*, 2000; Kim and Dale, 2004; Monte Alegre *et al.*, 2003; MOE, 2003; Daishou, 2004; Licht, 2005 and Norimatsu, 2005). Many reports abound on the synthesis of bacterial (Hayashida *et al.*, 1988; Jin *et al.*, 1990 and Specka, *et al.*, 1991) and fungal amylases (Bhumibhamon 1986; Yamamoto, 1988; Ogundero and Osunlaja, 1986 and Odibo *et al.*, 1992).

Alpha-amylases are widely used for the liquefaction of the starch to allow the efficient production of dextrose by the saccharifying enzymes which are mainly beta-amylase and glucoamylases. The sources of amylases are very numerous. A number of amylases are produced by bacteria and moulds; an example is the heat stable alpha-amylase produced by *Bacillus subtilis* which was used in this work. Starch degrading enzymes like amylase have received great deal of attention because of their perceived technological significance and economic benefits. Cassava has the advantage over all other starch sources of being able to mature between six to twelve months, extensively cultivated in the Nigeria. The present increase in the price of processed food from cassava should not be a deterrent to continuing work on it. This is because the high cost of processed food from cassava is due to inadequate use of human resources whereby young men who are supposed to be engaged in farming to increase agricultural production of food crops are currently engaged in menial jobs for livelihood. This situation can be gradually discouraged by encouraging both the subsistence and large-scale farmers in providing them agricultural inputs at subsidized rates. Subsequently, the establishment of medium and small scale industries for producing enzymes and other industries that would depend on the enzymes to produce various other products would provide employment opportunity for young men and women in the country. This research work therefore investigated the optimization of α-amylase production by *B.subtilis* isolate grown on cassava starch using the Response Surface Methodology (RSM).

2. MATERIALS AND METHODS

The isolate of *Bacillus subtilis* maintained on Nutrient Agar at 30°C was obtained from the Department of Microbiology, Obafemi Awolowo University, Ile-Ife. The isolate was subcultured for multiplication of the microorganism. The medium for the propagation of the inoculums was developed using the method of El-Banna *et al.* (2008). Freshly harvested cassava tubers were obtained from Obafemi Awolowo University Teaching and Research farm in Osun State, Nigeria. The cassava was soaked in water for five days after which the water was decanted for further processing that involved mashing, sieving, sedimentation and decantation. The dry starch was sterilized before gelatinization in a hot air oven at 175°C for 40 min with the powder depth not exceeding 1 cm (El Tayeb *et al.*, 2007). The starch flour obtained from the extraction was weighed and apportioned into 10 per cent, 15 per cent and 20 per cent starch solutions using distilled water. These cassava starch solutions were subjected to heating at 80°C for 10 min for the process of gelatinization. The gelatinized starch was later cooled to the room temperature and kept for the shake flask experiment. The optimisation was carried out using the Design Expert Software. The Design expert was used to optimize the process variables such as substrate concentration, agitation rate and temperature being key parameters for the enzyme production (Tables 10.1 and 10.2). The optimal condition was scaled up in a New Brunswick Twin-ferm Fermentor. Samples were withdrawn at various time intervals to determine the enzyme activity using the Dinitrosalicylic acid (DNS) method of Millers. The microbial behavior and integrity with the substrate of choice was determined through the magnitude of the sustaining kinetic parameters embedded in the existing model equations such as K_m and V_{max} were obtained.

Table 10.1: Experimental Range and Levels of the Independent Variables.

Independent Variables	*Range and Levels*		
	-1	*0*	*+1*
Temperature (°C)	38	40	42
Substrate Conc. (per cent)	10	15	20
Agitation rate (rpm)	100	150	200

Table 10.2: Box Behnken Design of the Experiment Generated by Design Expert® 8.0.3 Trial Version Software.

Std	*Run*	*Factor 1 Temperature (°C)*	*Factor 2 Substrate Conc. (per cent)*	*Factor 3 Agitation Rate (rpm)*
13	1	40.00	15.00	150.00
8	2	42.00	15.00	200.00
3	3	38.00	20.00	150.00
7	4	38.00	15.00	200.00
14	5	40.00	15.00	150.00
10	6	40.00	20.00	100.00
1	7	38.00	10.00	150.00
4	8	42.00	20.00	150.00
2	9	42.00	10.00	150.00

Contd...

Table 10.2–*Contd...*

Std	*Run*	*Factor 1 Temperature (°C)*	*Factor 2 Substrate Conc. (per cent)*	*Factor 3 Agitation Rate (rpm)*
17	10	40.00	15.00	150.00
15	11	40.00	15.00	150.00
5	12	38.00	15.00	100.00
12	13	40.00	20.00	200.00
16	14	40.00	15.00	150.00
11	15	40.00	10.00	200.00
6	16	42.00	15.00	100.00
9	17	40.00	10.00	100.00

2.1. Enzyme Activity Assay

Alpha Amylase was assayed by the standard method described by Tarek *et al.* (2008) at the beginning of each run. The reaction mixture consisted of 0.4 ml of 1 per cent soluble starch gelatinized in 1.1 ml of 0.2 M citrate phosphate buffer (pH 6.0), and 0.5 ml of crude enzyme extract. After 20 min of incubation at 40°C, the mixture was centrifuged at 10,000 rpm for 10 min and the liberated reducing sugars (glucose equivalents) were estimated by the DNS method. The absorbance was read at 540 nm using a Cecil CE 3041, 3000 Series spectrophotometer. Glucose was used as standard. One unit (IU) of Alpha Amylase is defined as the amount of enzyme releasing one µmol of glucose equivalent per minute under the assay conditions. The enzyme activities used for representations are the average values of three independent experiments.

2.2. Kinetic Parameters

The following kinetic parameters were determined: (a) specific growth rate (µ) was determined as slope of a straight line between In X/X_o (X is the biomass, g L^{-1} and X_o is the biomass at the start of exponential growth phase) and fermentation time (h). (b) the K_m and V_{max} of alpha amylase were determined at pH 6 and 40°C by varying the substrate concentration between 0.1 per cent and 1.0 per cent of soluble starch in a 0.2 phosphate buffer solution with the enzyme aliquot. Data were plotted using Lineweaver and Burk model on Microsoft office Excel 2003.

2.3. Biomass Concentration

The optical density of the culture media was monitored by reading the absorbance of the samples taken at 12 hr intervals on the spectrophotometer at 600 nm. The biomass formation was determined by measuring the optical density at a wave length of 600 nm for tracking the growth of the organism. The filter paper assay method was employed to analyse for biomass concentration obtained in the course of sampling in the bioreactor at the 12 hr interval. The filter paper was pre-weighed before it was used to filter the broth. The residue was oven dried at 80°C for 24 hr to constant weight. After which it was allowed to cool and final weight was recorded. The weight of the biomass was determined by subtracting the weight of the filter paper from the weight of the paper plus cell.

3. RESULTS AND DISCUSSION

3.1. Growth Pattern of the Organism

Figure 10.1 illustrates the growth pattern for *Bacillus subtilis* over the 84 hr in starch medium. The increasing values of absorbance given by the samples showed that the organism was actively growing in the culture media which resulted in increasing values of the optical density with time. Growth and α-amylase production by *B. subtilis* increased reaching a maximum values after 48 hr, after which, the production of the enzyme decreased. The observed peak and through of the production of extra-cellular enzymes can be attributed to (1) The products of action of one component inducing the synthesis of another, (2) differential inhibition by products of substrate hydrolysis, and/or (3) decrease in growth observed after 48hr of *B. subtilis* This probably resulted from cellular lysis as reported by El Banna *et al.* (2007). These results indicate that production of extracellular alpha amylase production by *B. subtilis* was growth associated and this is in agreement with the reports of other investigators (Bajpai and Bajpai, 1989; Stephenson *et al.*, 1998; Raiz *et al.*, 2003).

The shake flask culture was set up in triplicates for each of the 17 experimental runs with varied agitation rate, temperature and substrate concentration to determine the optimal condition for the production of alpha amylase. Starch is known to induce the production of alpha amylase in different bacterial strains (Saito and Yamamoto, 1975; Forgaty and Bourke, 1983; Wind *et al.*, 1994; Aiyer, 2004 and Ryan *et al.*, 2006). Bacterial cells have various mechanisms that allow them strictly to control excretion

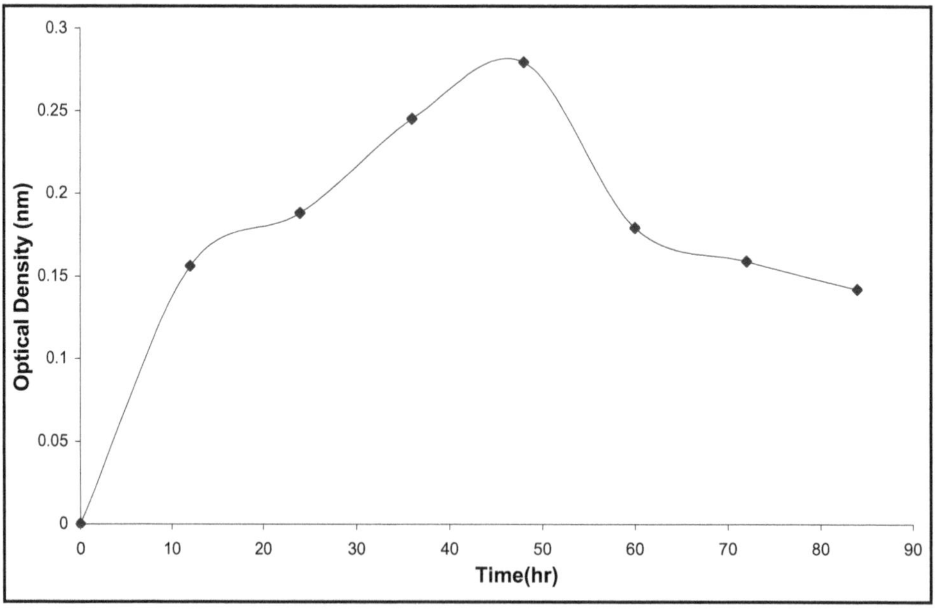

Figure 10.1: Growth Pattern of *Bacillus subtilis* in Starch Medium.

(Mamo and Gessesse, 1999). Change in the nature of cell envelope can affect the release of extracellular enzymes into the culture medium (Antranikian, 1990). Temperature is one of the factors that induce such changes on cell membranes and cell walls (de Vrij *et al.*, 1990; Nordstrom, 1993). It is also reported that in Bacillaceae, the surface protein layer (S-layer) is involved in the control of exoenzyme release (Egelseer *et al.*, 1996a and b). The resultant effect of agitation rate and substrate concentration on the enzyme secretion has been reported by El- Banna *et al.* (2008) and Haq *et al.* (2003). The optimal conditions selected by the Design Expert for the α-amylase production are 40°C, 15.00 per cent and 150 rpm. The regression equations obtained after Analysis of variance (ANOVA) gave the level of α-amylase production as a function of the initial values of substrate concentration, agitation rate and temperature. The final response equation (1) that represented a suitable model for α-amylase production is given below:

$$Y= 8.68-0.068X_1 - 0.000878X_2 - 0.23X_3 + 0.28X_1X_2 + 0.20X_1X_3 + 0.064X_2X_3 - 0.74X_1^2 - 0.47\, X_2^2 - 1.23X_3^2 \quad (1)$$

Where Y is response variable (enzyme activity) and $X_{1,}$ X_2 and X_3 are the factors. The ANOVA for α-amylase production is in Table 10.3. The predicted and observed responses are shown in Table 10.4. The coefficient of determination (R^2) was calculated as 0.897 for α-amylase production (Table 10.3), indicating that the statistical model can explain 95.64 per cent of variability in the response. The R^2 value is always between 0 and 1. The closer the R^2 is to 1.0, the stronger the model and better it predicts the response (Rao and Satyanarayana, 2003). The predicted R^2 (-1.961) implies that the overall mean is a better predictor of the response.

Table 10.3: ANOVA for α-amylase Production.

Source	*Sum of Square*	*Degree of Freedom*	*Mean Square*	*F-Value*	*p-value*
Model	11.74	9	1.30	6.80	0.0097
Pure error	0.86	5	0.17		
Total	12.60	14			

R^2= 0.8974, Adjusted R^2= 0.7654, Predicted R^2= -1.9612, Adequate precision = 6.941, Lack of fit F-value = 1.39 not significant

The model F-value of 6.80 and values of "prob>F" less than 0.05 indicated that the model terms are significant. For alpha amylase production A^2 and C^2 revealed a significant model. The "lack of fit F value" of 1.39 implied that the "lack of fit" is not significant. The response surface was generated by plotting the response (enzyme activity) on the z-axis against any two independent variables while keeping the other independent variables at zero level as shown in Figures 10.2-10.4.

Figure 10.2 depicts three dimensional diagram of response surface from the interaction between substrate concentration and temperature while keeping the agitation rate at zero level. An optimal α-amylase activity was observed when substrate concentration was increased up to 15 per cent and thereafter, it declined. However, in

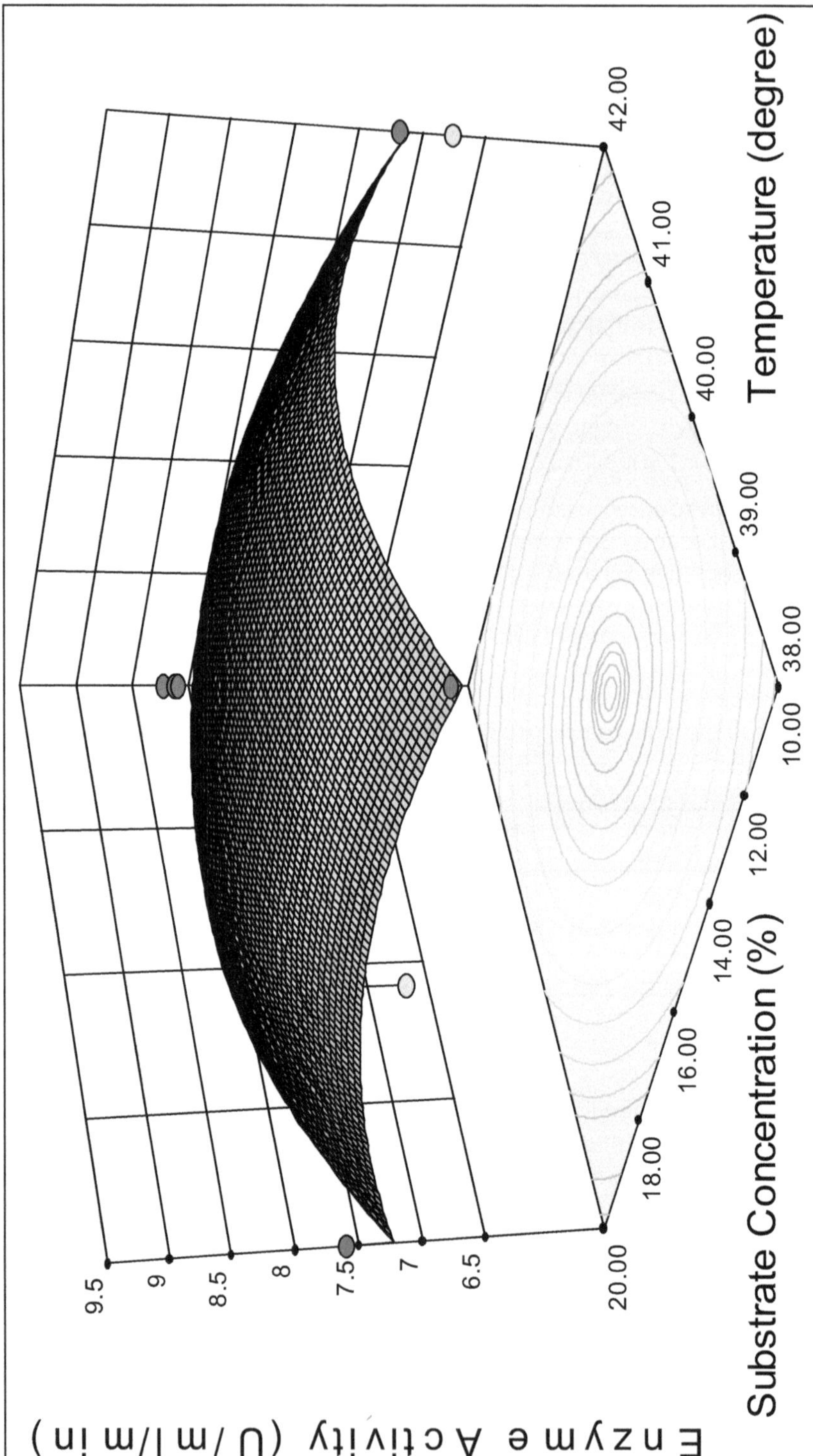

Figure 10.2: Response Surface Model for the Enzyme Activity versus Temperature and Substrate Concentration.

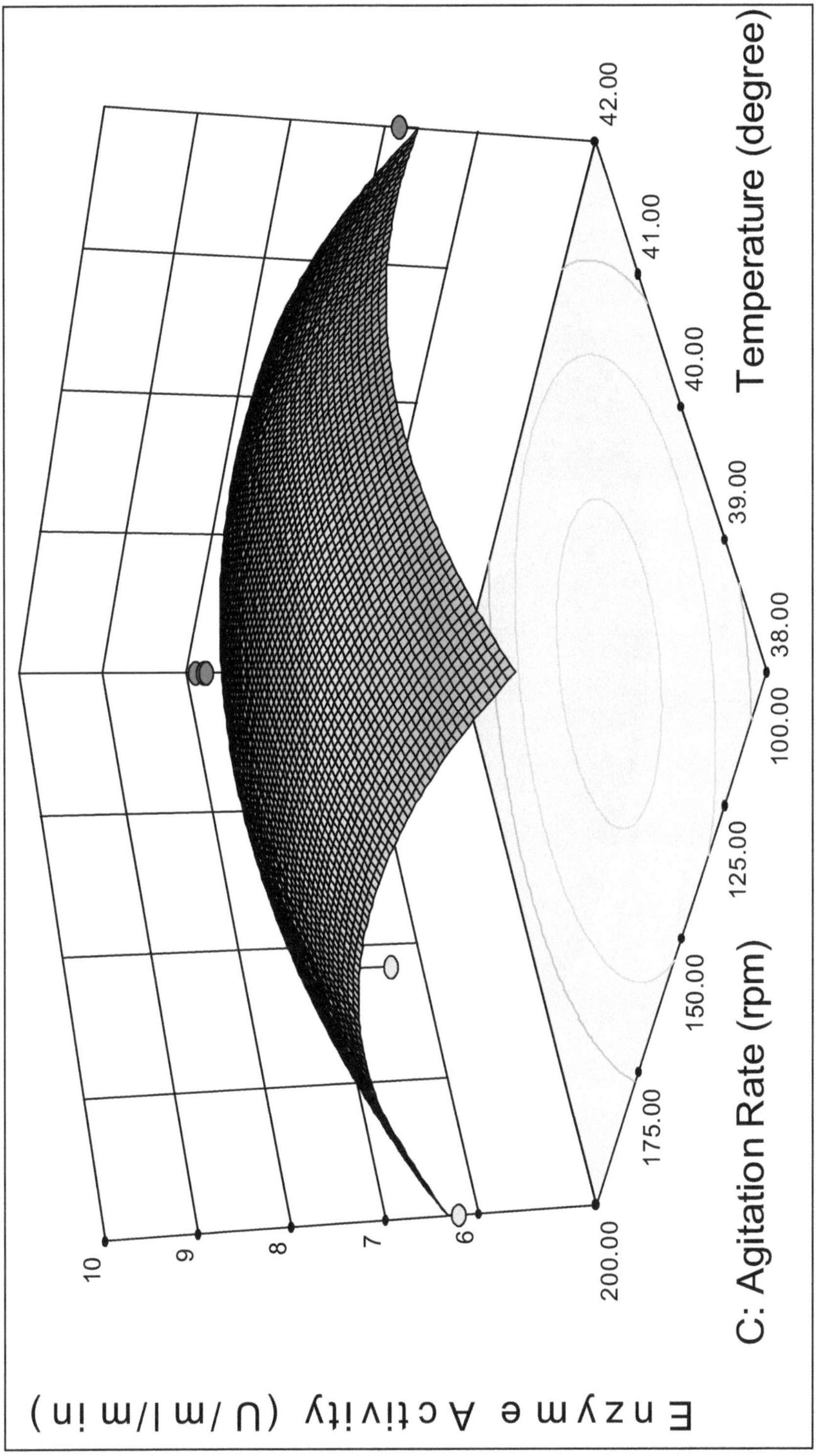

Figure 10.3: Response Surface Model for the Enzyme Activity versus Temperature and Agitation Rate.

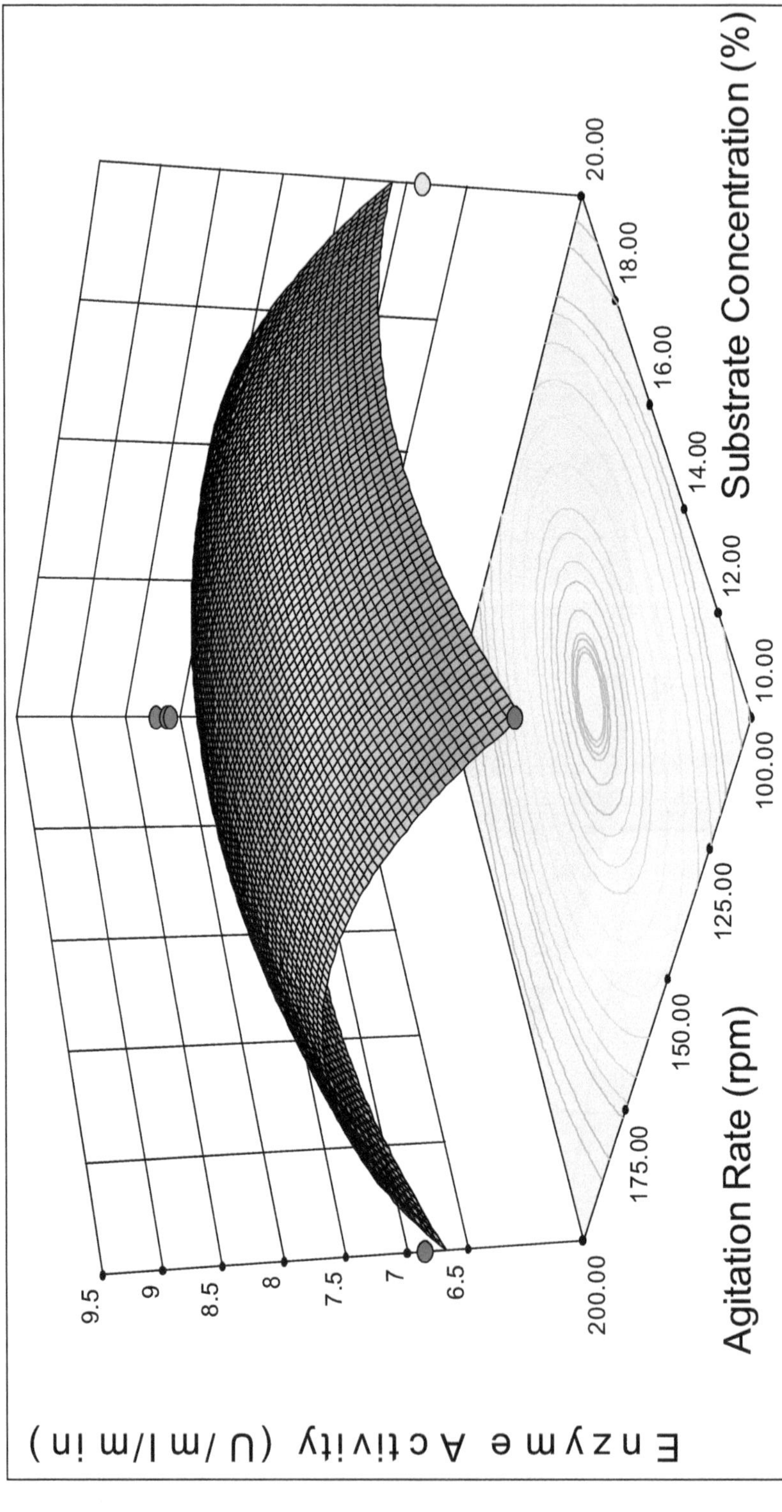

Figure 10.4: Response Surface Model for the Enzyme Activity versus Substrate Concentration and Agitation Rate.

Figures 10.3 and 10.4, the optimal temperature and agitation rate were 40°C and 150rpm respectively.

Table 10.4: Experimental Design and Result of Box Behnken Design Type of Response Surface Methodology.

Run	*Temperature (°C)*	*Substrate Conc. (per cent)*	*Agitation Rate (rpm)*	*Enzyme Production Experimental*	*Predicted*
1	40.00	15.00	150.00	7.92	7.83
2	42.00	15.00	200.00	6.77	7.13
3	38.00	20.00	150.00	7.63	7.25
4	38.00	15.00	200.00	7.20	7.13
5	40.00	15.00	150.00	7.68	8.01
6	40.00	20.00	100.00	6.88	6.66
7	38.00	10.00	150.00	6.22	6.35
8	42.00	20.00	150.00	6.70	6.61
9	42.00	10.00	150.00	7.32	7.28
10	40.00	15.00	150.00	6.88	7.13
11	40.00	15.00	150.00	6.87	6.70
12	38.00	15.00	100.00	6.68	6.81
13	40.00	20.00	200.00	9.06	8.68
14	40.00	15.00	150.00	8.00	8.68
15	40.00	10.00	200.00	8.57	8.68
16	42.00	15.00	100.00	8.98	8.68
17	40.00	10.00	100.00	8.95	8.68

3.2. Kinetic Parameters

The values of V_{max} (4.149) and K_M (0.184). The specific growth rate (μ) of 0.0086 h^{-1} and doubling time t_d of 5.44 showed that the microorganism is growing with doubling time efficiency in the reactor.

4. CONCLUSIONS

The response surface methodology (RSM) in this investigation suggested the importance of various parameters at different level. Box-Benhken maximizes the amount of information that can be obtained, while limiting the numbers of individual experiments. The results of this study endorse this view point. In this study, a high similarity was observed between the predicted and experimental results, which reflected the accuracy and applicability of RSM to optimize the process for enzyme production. This work showed that cassava starch can serve as raw material for the production of α-amylase. *B. subtilis* is capable of producing amylase enzyme from gelatinized cassava starch. The best optimal condition obtained consists of 40°C for temperature, 150 rpm for the agitation and 10 per cent starch. From bioreactor studies, the specific growth μ ($0.0086h^{-1}$), doubling time t_d of 5.44 h of the organism showed the utilization of starch while K_m (0.184mg/ml) and V_{max} (4.149units/ml) reported showed the efficiency of the substrate enzyme system.

ACKNOWLEDGEMENTS

The authors thank Miss. Blessing E. Oliseagulu of Environmental Biotechnology and Bio-conservation of National Biotechnology Development Agency, NABDA and Mrs. Kehinde Adeola Adetunji of Osun State Liaison Office, Abuja respectively for collating and typing the initial draft of the paper; Former Honourable Minister of Science and Technology, Professor Turner T. Isoun, Dr. Bako Zaku and Professor Mohammed Kaoje Abubakar respectively for instituting a strong policy for capacity building in the Nigerian Federal Ministry of Science and Technology; Dr. Sonibare A. and Dr. E. Betiku of Department of Chemical Engineering, Obafemi Awolowo University, Ile-Ife, Osun State for introducing Response Surface Methodology (RSM) into the work; World Bank STEB 'B' for providing money for the purchase of chemicals for the research work.

REFERENCES

1. Aderibigbe A.F. (2005): Development of Hydrolytic Procedures for cassava Starch. An unpublished M.Sc. Thesis of the Department of Chemical Engineering, Obafemi Awolowo University, Ile-Ife.
2. Aiyer, P.V.D. (2004): Effect of C: N ratio on α-amylase production by *Bacillus licheniformis* SPT 278, *Afr. J. Biotechnol.* 3: 519–522.
3. Aransiola E. F. (2005): A study of the Batch and Fed Batch Cultivation of Bakers Yeast (Saccharomyces Cerevisiae). An unpublished M.Sc. Thesis of the Department of Chemical Engineering, Obafemi Awolowo University, Ile-Ife
4. Bajpai, P. and P. Bajpai (1989): High temperature alkaline alpha amylase from Bacillus licheniformis TCRFC-B13. *Biotechnology and Bioengineering* 33: 72-78
5. Bello, R.A. (2002): Industrial enzymes utilization in Nigeria and investment opportunities for its production. Proceedings of international Conference on Biotechnology 35-44.
6. Bello, R.A. (2006): Biotechnology: An alternative Goldmine, inaugural lecture series University of Lagos, 35.
7. Bhumibhamon, O. (1986): Glucoamylases of a fungus isolated from a rotting cassava tuber. *MIRCEN Journal* 2: 473 482.
8. Calleja, G.B, Yuaguchi, M, Levy- Rick, S, Segun, J.R.H, Roy, C. and Lusena, C.V. (1986): Single cell protein production from potato starch by the yeast. *Schwanniomyces alluvius* J. Ferment Technol, Japan, 65: 71 – 75.
9. Daishou Y. (2004): Bioethanol, Kougyou Chyou Sakai, Tokyo 4: 113-117
10. De Vrij, W.G. Speelmans and R.I.R Heyne (1990): Energy transduction and amino acid transport in thermophilic aerobic and fermentative bacteria. *FEMS Microbiology Reviews* 75: 183-200

11. Egelseer, E.I., Schocher and U. Sleytr (1996b): Evidence that an N-terminal S-Layer protein fragment triggers the release of a cell-associated high-molecular-weight amylase in *Bacillus stearothermophilus* ATCC 12980. *Journal of Bacteriology* 178: 5602-5609

12. El-Batal, A.I., Atia, K.S., Eid, M. (2005): Stabilization of α-amylase by using anionic surfactant during the immobilization process, *Radiat. Phys. Chem. 74:* 96–101.

13. El-Tayeb, O., Mohammad, F., Hashem, A., and Aboulwafa, M. (2007): Optimization of the industrial production of bacterial alpha amylase in Egypt. IV. Fermentor production and characterization of the enzyme of two strains of *Bacillus subtilis* and *Bacillus amyloliquefaciens.* Africa Journal of Biotechnology Vol. 7 (24): 4521-4536

14. El-Banna, Abd-Aziz Ahmed, Mohamed I. Abou-Dobara and Reham I. Ibrahim (2008): Optimisation and Immobilisation of alpha amylase from Bacillus species. *Egyptian J Environmental Sciences.* 3 (1): 45-53.

15. Fogarty, M.W. (1983): Microbial Amylases. In: *Microbial Enzymes and Biotechnology,* W.M. Fogarty (Ed.), Applied Science Publishers Ltd., London, UK, 1–92.

16. Grace, M.R. (1997): cassava processing. Plant Prodution and Protection Series No.3. FAO. Rome.

17. Haq, I., Ashraf, H., Iqbal, J., Qadeer, M.A. (2003): Production of alpha amylase by *Bacillus licheniformis* using an economical medium, *Bioresour. Technol. 87:* 57–61.

18. Hayashida, S., Teramoto, Y. and Zhang, C. (1988): Production and characteristics of raw-potato-starch-digesting alpha amylase from *Bacillus subtilis* 65. *Applied and Environmental Microbiology,* 54, 1516-1522.

19. Johansson, T., Kelly, H., Reddy, A.K.N., Williams, R.H and Burnham, L. (1993): Renewable energy. Sources for fuels and electricity, Island Press, Washington 102-115.

20. Kim, S. and Dale, B.E. (2004): Global potential bioethanol production from waste crops and crop residues. Biomass Bioenergy 26: 361-375.

21. Leman, A. and Didry, P. (1950): Hydrolysis of starch with dilute hydrochloric acid, Chemical Abstract, 45,887p.

22. Licht, F.O. (2005): World Ethanol and Biofeuls Report, 3, 15, Agra-net.com

23. Mamo, G., Gessesse, A. (1999): Purification and characterization of two raw-starch-digesting thermostable α-amylases from a thermophilic *Bacillus, Enzyme Microb. Technol.* 25: 433–438.

24. Mathew, G., Padmajo, G. and Moorthy, S.N. (1991): Enhancement of Starch extractability from cassava *(Manihotes culenta* Crantz) tubers through fermentation with a mixed culture inoculum. *Journal of Root Crops* 17 (1)1-9.

25. MOE, Ministry of the Environment (2003): Rennyubumon ni okeru tyau kakuteki taisaku gijyutsu nikansuru tyuukanhappyou, Japan. 31-41

26. Monte Alegre, R., Rigo, M. and Joekes, I. (2003): Ethanol fermentation of a diluted molasses medium by *Saccharomyces cerevisiae* immobilized on chrysolite. *Braz.Arch Biol. Technol.*, 46,751-757.

27. Nordstrom, K.M. (1993): Effect of temperature on fatty acid composition of a white *Thermus* strain. Applied and Environmental Microbiology 59: 1975-1976.

28. Odibo, F.J.C., Okafor, N. And Okafor, B.U. (1996): Purification and immobilization of *Scytalidium* sp. Alpha amylase and its general properties. *J.Gen.and Appl. Microbiol.* 38, 1-11.

29. Ogundero, V.W. and Osunlaja, S.O. (1986): Glucoamylase production and activity by *Aspergilus clavatus* Des, atoxigenic fungus from malting barley. Mycopathology 96, 153-156.

30. Queynh, N.C. and Cecil, J. (1996): Sweetness from starch, a manual for making maltose from starch. FAO, Rome. 37.

31. Radley, J.A. (1976): Starch Production Technology. Applied Science Publishers, London. 587.

32. Rao, J.L.U.M. Satyanarayana, T. (2003): Enhanced secretion and low temperature stabilization of a hyperthermostable and Ca^{2+} independent α-amylase of *Geobacillus thermoleovorans* by surfactants, *Lett. Appl. Microbiol.* 36: 191–196.

33. Reed, G. (1975): Enzymes in Food Processing 2ed. New York: Academic Press Inc. 62-87.

34. Riaz N.I., UL-Haq and Qadeer (2003): Characterization of amylase by *Bacillus subtilis*. International Journal of Agricultural Biology 5 (3): 249-252.

35. Ryan, S.M., Fitzerald G.F., and Sinderen K. (2006): Screening and identification of starch, amylopectin and pullulan degrading activities in Bifidobacterial strains. *Applied and Environmental Microbiology* 72 (8): 5289-5296.

36. Saito N., and Yamamoto K. (1975): Regulator factors affecting alpha amylase production in *Bacillus licheniformis*. *Journal of Bacteriology* 121: 848-856.

37. Sani, A., Awe, F.A. and Akinyanju, J.A. (1992): Amylase synthesis in *Aspergillus flavus* and *Aspergillus niger* on cassava peel. *Journal of Industrial Microbiology* 10, 55-59.

38. Specka, U., Mayer, F. and Antranikian, G. (1991): Purification and properties of a thermoactive glucoamylase from *Clostridium thermosaccharolyticum*. *Applied and Environmental Microbiology* 57, 2317-2323.

39. Stephenson, K., Carter C.R., Harwood, M.F., Petitglatron and Chambert, R. (1998): The influence of protein folding on late stages of secretion of alpha amylase from *Bacillus subtilis*. *FEBS Letter* 430: 385-389

40. Sree, N.K., Sridhar, M., Suresh, K., Banat, I.M. and Rao, L.V. (2000): High alchohol production by repeated batch fermentation using an immobilized osmotolerant sacch.cerevisiae *J. Ind Microbiol.* 24, 222-226

41. Swanson, M.A. and Cori, C.F. (1948): Structure of Polysaccharide I. Acid hydrolysis of starch like polysaccharide, *Journal of Biological Chemistry Baltimore.* 56: 96-104

42. Takagi, T., Toda H., and Isemura, T. (1971): The Enzymes (Boyer, P.D., ed) 3 rd Ed, Academic Press, New York, NY, 5, 235-271.

43. Wind, R.D., Buitelaar and Eggink G. (1994): Characterisation of a new *Bacillus stearothermophillus* isolate: a highly thermostable alpha amylase producing strain. *Applied Microbiology and Biotechnology* 41: 155-162.

44. Yamamoto, T. (1988): Bacterial α-amylase (liquefying and saccharifying types) of *Bacillus subtilis* and related bacteria, Handbook of amylases and related enzymes. Pergamon Press,Oxford, England. Pp 40-45.

Chapter 11

Some Traditional Fermented Foods: Current Status and Future Prospects in Nigeria

A.A. Adekunle[1], O.A. Adetunji[1], G.B. Olukotun[1], M.T. Abdulkareem[1] and J.M. Madu[2]*

[1]Department of Food and Industrial Biotechnology,
[2]Department of Environmental Biotechnology,
National Biotechnology Development Agency, Abuja, Nigeria

ABSTRACT

The word fermentation has been known for its significant contribution to the food technological process mostly in the developing countries which includes Nigeria. Its ability to improve the shelf-life, enhance the nutritive value and also add values to food in terms of flavour cannot be over emphasized. Nigeria as a nation has its own traditional fermented foods which are derived from different agricultural raw materials such as cereal *(ogi)*, legumes *(dawadawa, iru)*, milk *(wara)*, roots, tubers *(lafun, gari, fufu)* and beverages *(burukutu* and *pito)*. Recently,fermentation technology has advanced into isolation and characterization of wide range of microorganisms involved in food fermentation. With this recent technology, the techniques used in the Nigeria cottage industries still remain traditional. The use of simple and non-sterile material is paramount which in turn put a great reliance on the use of natural inoculum under uncontrolled conditions. These had led to variations in the sensory attribute, contamination, shortened shelf-life and poor unattractive packaging for the fermented products. It is essential that modern biotechnological techniques should be integrated into the traditional processing procedures in order to improve the quality and safety of the product. The production and the use of starter cultures and the maintenance of the optimum conditions for microbial activities during fermentation will enhance the qualities of fermented

* E-mail: ayobami_2003@yahoo.com

foods produced in the Nigerian cottage industries. This paper will discuss the processing procedures of some traditional fermented foods in Nigeria as well as the possibility of enhancing them through biotechnology.

Keywords: *Fermentation, Agricultural product, Cottage industries, Isolation, Starter culture, Biotechnology.*

1. INTRODUCTION

Food fermentation has been known as the oldest technology of food processing and preservation. Fermented foods are defined as palatable products, which are prepared from raw and heated materials to acquire their respective characteristics properties by a process that involves microorganisms (Buckenhuskes, 1993). Aworh (2010) described fermentation as a metabolic process in which carbohydrate and related compounds are partially oxidized with the release of energy in the absence of any electron acceptors. Several researchers have reported on food fermentation which has made a great contribution to the whole process. Pederson (1971) reported that in the preparation of fermented foods, microbes are used to prepare and preserve food products, which in turns add value in terms of nutrition, flavour and other qualities associated with edibility. Lactic acid bacteria and yeast were reported to be responsible for fermentation of food products. Lactic acid bacteria are known for producing lactic acid from sugar based products and it has been found to reduce the pH and inhibit the growth of other microorganism which may cause spoilage and diseases (Cooke *et al.*, 1987; Odunfa and Oyewole, 1997).

Fermented foods play a major role in the economy of most developing countries as well as making a major contribution to the protein requirement of the national population (Achi, 2005). Fermented food has contributed greatly as a good source of energy and a key player in protein and fatty acid sources.

In Africa, traditional fermented foods are made under primitive conditions which has led to low yield and poor quality which makes it lack good appeal (Achi, 2005). It is obvious that traditional fermentation processes, though, it has formed part of the culture of the people in Africa, are being carried out by women. This is because African men see traditional fermentation as a domestic work which should be handled by women. Nigeria has a variety of people with different cultures which makes it difficult to pick one national dish. Each area has its own regional fermented food that depends on their custom, tradition and religion (Abdel *et al.*, 2009).

Knowledge of the fermentation processes employed to produce fermented foods in Nigeria are acquired through observation and experience being passed from one generation to another. Achi, (2005) reported that several traditional fermentation from other parts of the world like Asia have been upgraded to high technology production system and there is a need for such revolution in Nigerian fermented foods. It is essential that modern biotechnology be integrated into the traditional processing procedures in order to improve the efficiency and productivity of the product.

This paper reviews some of the traditional fermented food processing as it relates to Nigeria cottage industries.

2. CLASSIFICATION

Several authors have classified fermented foods in different ways. Some classifications are made according to the kind of microorganism involved while other classifications are made based on the type of commodity (Yokotsuka, 1982; Campbell-Platt, 1987).

The different classification from each author's point of view reflects the part of the world which they come from.

Some Nigerian fermented foods classifications are shown in Table 11.1.

Table 11.1: Classification of Nigerian Fermented Foods.

Class of Food	*Fermented Food*	*Raw Material*
Cereal	Ogi	Maize
Legumes	Dawadawa, iru	Locust bean
Milk	Wara	Cow
Roots and tubers	Lafun, Gari, Fufu	Cassava
Beverages	Burukutu, Pito	Sorghum

3. TRADITIONAL METHODS OF PROCESSING FERMENTED FOODS

3.1. *Fufu*

Fufu is a cassava tuber product. The process undergoes peeling, washing and soaking (Aworh, 2008). The peeled and washed tubers are cut into smaller sizes and soaked in earthen pot of water for 4-5 days to undergo fermentation. According to Uyoh *et al.*, 2009, the lactic acid fermentation reduces the pH value which will make the tubers soft and also reduce the potential of toxic cyanogenic compounds. When sufficiently soft, the roots are taken out, broken by hand and sieved to remove the fibers. The sieved product is allowed to sediment in large container for 24 hours after which the water is poured off. The clean sediment which contains mainly starch is dewatered using a high powered press and the cake is then sifted before drying.

3.2. *Gari*

Gari is a food commonly consumed in Nigeria. It can be reconstituted in hot water into a meal and consumed with various soups and stews. *Gari* is a cassava tuber product. To prepare *gari*, fresh cassava tubers are harvested, cleaned, peeled and washed, grated and the pulp transferred into a cloth bag and weighted down with a heavy object at ambient temperature for 4 days to remove waste materials from the pulp while it is fermenting (Uzogara *et al.*, 1990; Oyewole and Isah, 2012). The water extracted from the pulp contains starch which can be cooked into a paste and consumed as "*ozie*" in mid-western Nigeria (Uzogara *et al.*, 1990). Aworh (2008) reported that the process of grating, expressing, pulverizing toasting, and addition of palm oil by some processors are adequate to reduce HCN to a safe level. Oyewole and Isah (2012) also reported that fermentation impacts sour taste to *gari* while toasting extends its shelf–life. Ejifor and Okafor (1981) stated that the lactic acid bacteria induce the characteristic sour taste or flavour of *gari*.

During the fermentation process, the cyanogenic glycosides, linamarin, and lotanstralin present in cassava are detoxified. (Aworh, 2008; Uzogara, 1990).

3.3. *Lafun*

Lafun is a cassava product which is commonly consumed in the western states of Nigeria. During the processing, cassava undergoes peeling and soaking in water for 3-4 days to induce fermentation. The water is drained off and the fermented cassava dried in the sun. The dried cassava undergoes the process of communition (size reduction) using a milling machine to produce "*elubolafun*" (cassava flour). The flour is added into boiling water with constant stirring to produce a paste. The paste can be served with soups such as "*ewedu*" or okro soup. (Anthonio and Isoun, 1982).

3.4. *Ogi*

Ogi is a fermented corn starch produced from fermented dry maize. The maize undergoes soaking in water for 1-3 days to allow the lactic acid bacteria and yeast ferment the maize and develop a characteristic odour (Umoh and Field, 1981). The fermented maize is washed, ground into meal either with mortar and pestle or in a village mill. The ground material is mixed with water and sieved to remove parts of the hull and other fibrous materials. The filtrate (starch suspension) is placed in a pot so that the starchy material sediments. The supernatant is decanted and the wet starch poured into cloth bags, squeezed and dewatered until a semi-solid corn-starch is produced. *Ogi* is served hot as breakfast with sugar and milk to enhance the taste and nutritive value.

3.5. *Iru*

The production of locust bean condiment "*iru*" is commonly practised as a rural cottage industry mainly by women. There are several stages involved in the processing operation as described by Oni (1997). The process includes shelling of the beans, pre-drying, pounding, winnowing or sieving, washing, drying and sorting. The flow chart (Figure 11.1) of a typical traditional method of processing locust bean as reported by Odunfa and Adewuyi (1985) is shown in Figure 11.1.

3.6. *Wara* (Cheese)

The Fulani cattle rearers in the Northern part of Nigeria produced "*wara*" which is soft white unripened cheese (Ogundiwin, 1978). It is produced by Fulani women from unpasteurized cow milk. The traditional method of producing '*wara*' is based on the milk coagulating properties of the juice from the leaves of Sodom apple plant (*Calotropisprocera*) (Aworh, 2008). The juice obtained from the Sodom apple leaves is mixed with fermented cows' milk and gently heated in a pot over a wood fire. After the coagulating process, the loose curd pieces are pound into small raffia baskets and allowed to drain (Osuntoki, 2010).

Africa locust bean seed

↓

Boiling in water for 12 hours

↓

Cooling

↓

Washing

↓

Boiling cotyledons in water

↓

Drain through raffia sieve

↓

Spread while hot in wide calabash tray

↓

Stack strays together, wrap with jute bag

↓

Ferment for 36 hours

↓

Add salt and mould into desire shape

↓

Sun dry

Figure 11.1: Flow Chart of *Iru* (Odunfa and Adewuyi, 1985).

3.7. *Burukutu*

Burukutu is a popular alcoholic beverage consumed in Nigeria and some part of Africa, like, Republic of Benin and Ghana. The preparation of *burukutu* involves steeping sorghum grains in water overnight, following which excess water is drained. The grains are then spread out on a tray and covered with banana leaves for germination to occur. During germination process, the grains are watered on alternate days and turned over at intervals. Germination continues for 4-5 days until the plumule attains certain length. The malted grains are spread out in the sun to dry for 1-2 days, following which the dried malt is ground into a powder. *Gari* (cassava flake) is added to a mixture of the ground malt and water in a ratio of 1: 2: 6 of *gari*, malt and water respectively. The resulting mixture is allowed to ferment for 2 days after which it is boiled for 4 hours and allowed to mature for another 2 days. The resulting product is a cloudy alcoholic beverage called *burukutu*.

3.8. *Pito*

Pito is prepared by soaking cereal grains in water for 2 days, followed by malting and allowing them to stay for 5 days in baskets lined with moistened banana leaves. The malted grains are ground mixed with water and boiled. The resulting mash is allowed to cool and later filtered through a fine mesh. The filtrate thus obtained is allowed to stand overnight, or until it assumes a slightly sour flavour, following which it is boiled to a concentrate which is allowed to ferment overnight. *Pito* is thus obtained.

4. PROPERTIES OF FOOD FERMENTATION

Fermented foods are known for its good tastes which are different from the starting materials (raw materials). Chelule *et al.* (2010) reported that fermentation affects the palatability of food by enhancing its organoleptic properties; that is, aroma, texture and flavour. In terms of preservative properties is a cheap means of preserving local staples for long period. Several reports have been made on the effects of fermentation on the preservation of fermented foods. It has been clearly reported that fermentation lower the pH level of food materials by inhibiting the growth of pathogenic organisms that cause food spoilage, food poisoning and diseases thereby improving shelf-life of fermented foods and makes food safe for consumers (Abdel, 2009, Chelule *et al.*, 2010).

Fermentation as reported by several researchers has the characteristic of eliminating toxic substances. The use of lactic acid bacteria in fermentation detoxified toxins and preserves the nutritive value and flavour of foods (Chelule *et al.*, 2010). Egbere (2008) reported that cooking time of most fermented foods is reduced when compared to that of raw unfermented substrates. The process of destroying any anti-nutrients in any raw food material will reduce cooking time and improve the nutritional quality of fermented foods. It is obvious that most local fermented foods are not expensive and are within the financial capacity of many individuals in the community. Production of fermented food by small scale food processors will therefore contribute to the economy of Nigeria as well as improving the nutrition of consumers (Uzogara *et al.*, 1990).

5. MODERN BIOTECHNOLOGY AND TRADITIONAL FERMENTED FOODS

The relationship between modern biotechnology and traditional fermented foods has not been discussed widely in the literature. One can imagine, however, that biotechnology can be of help in the improvement of fermented foods at various levels:

5.1. Raw Materials

It is obvious that fermented foods are produced from either animal or plant raw materials, and the availability of these raw materials will help in the production of fermented foods. Experts have researched on improving plant and animal production through biotechnological methods around the world and there is a need to do such to agricultural raw materials in Nigeria in order to make available raw materials for production of fermented foods.

5.2. Fermentation Engineering

Recent developments in biotechnology have given rise to great innovations in bioreactor designs. These designs deal with liquid reaction media, it is obvious that a great number of fermented foods are produced through a solid-state fermentation in which the fermenting product is hand mixed. The use of bioreactors in Nigerian fermented foods will help to simulate processes that are needed to upgrade the traditional method of fermentation to a modernized state.

5.3. Microbiology and Enzymology

There are many opportunities for biotechnological innovations in the microbiology of traditional fermented foods. First, the active microorganisms responsible for fermentation in traditional foods should be isolated, characterized, and preserved. Also, the potential of the metabolic role of each of the strains of the microorganisms involved in traditional fermentation should be clearly identified, and studied. The powerful technique of monoclonal antibodies for the characterization of different strains of the same species can be of great help in this area.

Many of these organisms involved in traditional fermentation have the enzyme complement that is capable of producing vitamins and amino acids in fermented foods. This potential can be improved through the technique of recombinant DNA technology to produce strains that are capable of producing and releasing the required amino acid or vitamin into the food. In other to avoid food losses due to spoilage-causing organisms and development of food-poisoning microbes, it is possible to genetically engineer a strain required for the process as a pure culture. Such a strain may bring about all the changes required in the food and grows at a convenient temperature.

6. CONCLUSION

In view of the above, the place of basic biotechnology in the production and up-scaling of traditional fermented foods in Nigeria cannot be over emphasized. In conclusion the use of biotechnological tools will greatly enhance employment generation and also influence both availability and safe food for human consumption.

REFERENCES

1. Abdel A.A. and Dardir H.A., 2009. Hygienic Quality of Local Traditional Fermented Skimmed Milk (Laban Rayb) Sold in Egypt. World Journal of Dairy and Food Sciences, 4 (2), pp. 205-209.

2. Achi O.K., 2005.The potential for upgrading traditional fermented foods through biotechnology. African Journal of Biotechnology, 4 (5), pp. 375-380
3. Anthonio, H.O. and Isoun M., 1982.Nigerian Cookbook. Macmillan Press, London, pp. 172.
4. Aworh O.C., 2008. The Role of Traditional Food Processing Technologies In National Development: the West African Experience. In: Using Food Science and Technology to Improve Nutrition and Promote National Development, Chapter 3, (Robertson, G.L. and Lupien, J.R. Eds), International Union of Food Science and Technology *(IUFoST)*, http: /iufost.org/sites/default/files/docs/case_studies/chapter3_RobertsonLupien.pdf
5. Aworh, O. C. 2010. Food Technology and National Development: A Global Perspective. University Lecture, University of Ibadan. Published by the Ibadan University Press Publishing House, Ibadan, Nigeria.
6. Buckenhuskes H.J., 1993. Selection criteria for lactic acid bacterial to be used as starter cultures for various food commodities. FEMS Microbial. Rev., 12, pp. 253-273.
7. Campbell-Platt G., 1987. Fermented foods of the world a dictionary and guide. London, Butterworths.
8. Chelule P.K., Mbongwa H.P., Carries S. and Gqaleni N., 2010. Lactic acid fermentation improves the quality of amahewu, a traditional South African maize-based porridge. Food Chemistry, 122 (3), pp. 656-661.
9. Cooke R.D., Twiddy D.R. and Reilly P.J.A., 1987. Lactic acid fermentation as a low-cost means of food preservation in tropical countries. FEMS Microbiol. Rev., 46, pp. 369–379.
10. Egbere O.J., 2008. Principles and practice of Food Microbiology.Deka, Jos, pp. 123-139.
11. Ejiofor, M.A.N. and Okafor, N., 1981. Comparison of pressed and unpressed cassava pulp for gari making. In: Perry, E.R., Oduro, K.A. and Caveness, E. (eds.) Tropical Root Crops Research Strategies for the 1980s. IDRC, Ottawa, Canada, pp. 134-145.
12. Odunfa, S.A. and Oyewole, O.B., 1997. African Fermented Foods. In: Microbiology of Fermented Food, Blackie Academic and Professional, London,Vol. II. pp. 713-752.
13. Odunfa, S.A. and Adewuyi, E., 1985. Optimization of process conditions for fermentation of African locust bean, effect of time, temperature humidity. Food chemical microbiology, 9, pp. 118-121.
14. Ogundiwin J.O., 1978. A study of the traditional manufacturing processes and chemical composition of warankasi, a Nigerian soft white cheese. Nigerian Food Journal 2, pp. 72-78.
15. Oni, P.I., 1997. *Parkiabiglobosa* (JacqBenth) in Nigeria. "A resource assessment". An unpublished Ph.D thesis; University of North Wales, Bangor, United Kingdom.

16. Osuntoki A. and Korie I., 2010. Antioxidant Activity of Whey from Fermented Milk, Fermented with *Lactobacillus* Species Isolated from Nigerian Fermented Foods. Food Technology Biotechnology, 48 (4), pp. 505–511.

17. Oyewole O. A. and Isah P., 2012. Locally fermented foods in Nigeria and their significance to national economy: a review. Journal of Recent Advances in Agriculture, 1 (4), pp. 92-102.

18. Pederson, C. S., 1971. Microbiology of food fermentations. AVI Pub Co. Inc., Westport, pp. 537.

19. Umoh V. and Fields M.J., 1981. Fermentation of corn for Nigerian Agidi. Journal of Food Science, 46, pp. 903-905.

20. Uyoh E.A., Ntui V.O. and Udoma N.N., 2009. Effect of Local Cassava Fermentation Methods on Some Physio-chemical and Sensory Properties of FUFU. Pakistan Journal of Nutrition, 8, pp. 1123-1125.

21. Uzogara S.G., Agu L.N. and Uzogara E.O., 1990. A review of traditional fermented foods, condiments and beverages in Nigeria: Their benefits and possible problems. Ecology of Food and Nutrition. 24, pp. 267-288.

22. Yokotsuka T., 1982. Traditional Fermented Soybean Foods. In: Rose A.H., editor. Fermented Foods. London, UK: Academic Press.

Chapter 12

Recent Technical Advancements in the Areas of Industrial Biotechnology in Pakistan

Mudassir Asrar and Saima Nasir

Pakistan Council for Science and Technology,
Islamabad, Pakistan

ABSTRACT

The 21st century is envisioned as an era of Biotechnology and Applied Microbiology. The application of modern biotechnology for the industrial production of chemical substances and bioenergy, using living cells and their enzymes, resulting in inherently clean processes with minimum waste generation and energy use is a rapidly advancing field. Pakistan is also striving hard to keep pace with the global advancement of biotechnology. The present paper reviews the status of industrial biotechnology research in Pakistan. It highlights the problems and issues of industrial biotechnology in Pakistan. The conclusions and policy recommendations focus on identifying the future areas of study.

Keywords: *Biotechnology, Industrial biotechnology, Nanobiotechnology, Bio-energy, Pakistan.*

1. INTRODUCTION

The introduction is too long and talks about general aspects of biotechnology that seems to have been taken from few sources

☆ The 21st century is envisioned as an era of Biotechnology. Biotechnology can broadly be defined as the application of science and technology to living organisms, as well as parts, products and models thereof, to alter living or non-living materials for the production of knowledge, goods and services." In other words, biotechnology is derived from biological knowledge and finally is associated to the evolution of biological sciences (1).Biotechnology is at the frontline of new methods for the efficient and clean production of biological materials and chemicals. These environment friendly processes utilize the power of biology to make antibiotics, enzymes, proteins and chemicals for commercial uses. To common man, the key uses of biotechnology are in medicine, food and agricultural sciences. But precisely biotechnology has been subdivided in three areas:

1. Healthcare Biotechnology that deals with drug/medicine related research and addresses medical needs for the future is known as "Red Biotechnology" (KET.2011).
2. Agricultural Biotechnology focusing on research related with technology to grow food, fodder, fuel and fiber with low input and putting less impact on the environment, referred as "Green Biotechnology". (KET, 2011).
3. Industrial Biotechnology exploits mainly fungi, yeasts, bacteria and/or enzymes to make a number of everyday items including chemicals, detergents, vitamins, paper etc is called as "White Biotechnology" (KET2011).

The interest of the present paper is focused on this third wave of strongly developing biotechnology – the industrial biotechnology. It can be defined as the application of modern biotechnology for the industrial production of chemical substances and bioenergy, using living cells and their enzymes, resulting in inherently clean processes with minimum waste generation and energy use (2).

The importance of industrial biotechnology in economic development is evident from the OECD (2009) report (5) stating that the value of biochemicals (other than pharmaceuticals) could increase from 1.8 per cent of all chemical production in 2005 to between 12 per cent and 20 per cent by 2015, and biofuel production could partly shift from starch-based bioethanol to higher energy density fuels manufactured from sugar cane or to cellulosic ethanol from lignocellulosic feedstock such as straw, grasses and wood (6).A recent report by the World Economic Forum (WEF)concluded that converting biomass into fuels, energy, and chemicals has the potential to generate upwards of $230 billion to the global economy by 2020 (7).

The present paper reviews the status of industrial biotechnology research in Pakistan. It highlights the problems and issues of industrial biotechnology in Pakistan. The conclusions and policy recommendations focus on identifying the future areas of study.

2. BIOTECHNOLOGY IN PAKISTAN

Pakistan has a history of engagement with traditional biotechnology. However, it has not made significant developments in recent fields of biotechnology. Other developing countries, such as Cuba, Brazil, India and China, have been quick to identify the potential benefits of the technology and have established measures both to develop such industries and to extract value, wherever possible and relevant.

A National Commission on Biotechnology was established in 2001 to streamline and promote research in this vital sector and during the last few years billions of Rupees have been invested in R&D in this priority area through various projects approved by the Ministry of Science and Technology and the Higher Education Commission (HEC).

In Pakistan there are 26 institutions engaged in education and research in biotechnology and genetic engineering (Table 12.1). The focus of most of these institutions is on the agriculture and health biotechnology.

Presently, these research institutes have succeeded in producing many Bt crops including varieties of cotton, wheat and cereals (Soomro *et al.*, 2003; Abro and Arain, 2010; Sial *et al.*, 2012). Health biotechnology has also given its output in the form of important products like human interferon (Ali *et al.*, 2012).

In 2005, report of the expert committee on Biotechnology and Genetic Engineering published by Pakistan Council for Science and Technology (PCST), has described biotechnology as a *cross-cutting* technology[7]. The expert committee outlined a precise strategy of biotechnology policy. The document identified short-term (5 years); medium-term (5-10 years) and long-term (15 years) technologies to be developed. But all the focus is on agriculture and health biotechnology, and Industrial biotechnology was a much neglected field.

Recently, the new National Science, Technology and Innovation (S, T and I) Policy 2012 has been launched and is in implementation phase. R&D areas have been determined keeping in view the social, economic and security needs of the country. The National ST and I Policy 2012 has identified 16 Thrust Areas for R&D activities for Pakistan and has suggested measures for enhancing efforts in each of these areas. The thrust areas include Metrology, Standards, Testing and Quality (MSTQ), Environment, Health and Pharmaceuticals, Energy, Biotechnology and Genetic Engineering, Agriculture and Livestock, Water, Minerals, Ocean Resources, Electronics, Information and Communication Technologies (ICTs),Space Technology, Materials Science, Nanoscience and Nanotechnology, Lasers and Photonics and Engineering. The implementation of the ST and I Policy will lead to the new dimensions inimproving R&D institutions, development of research and engineering, effective collaboration between academia, R&D organizations and industry and above all economic development of the country.

Fortunately, biotechnology has been one of the thrust areas of this policy. This policy recommends policy actions for this area and states that

- ☆ Revival of 'National Commission on Biotechnology' and charging it with the task of coordinating national-wide research programmes in different areas where biotechnology can be applied.
- ☆ Reviewing the draft of 'National Biotechnology and Genetic Engineering Policy and Action Plan' and implementing it with the support of relevant organizations.
- ☆ Enacting biotechnology related legislations.
- ☆ Establishment of biotechnology incubation centers

Table 12.1: Institutions Engaged in Education and Research in Biotechnology and Genetic Engineering in Pakistan.

Sl.No.	*Name of Organization*	*Year of Establishment*	*Sector*	*Major Research Areas*
1.	Agricultural Biotechnology Research Institute, Ayub Agricultural Research Institute, Faisalabad	1987	R&D Organization	☆ Marker assisted breeding ☆ Fingerprinting ☆ Genomics ☆ Molecular characterization studies ☆ Soil bacteriology
2.	Atta-ur-Rehman School of Applied Biosciences (ASAB), National University of Sciences and Technology, Islamabad	2007		☆ Plant Biotechnology ☆ Health biotechnology ☆ Industrial Biotechnology
3.	Biomedical and Genetic Engineering Division, Dr. A.Q. Khan Research Laboratories, Islamabad	1900	R&D Organization	☆ Human Genome Diversity ☆ Medical Biotechnology ☆ Genetics of Inherited diseases ☆ Forestry
4.	Center for Molecular Genetics, University of Karachi	1990	HEI	☆ Molecular Biology ☆ Biotechnology ☆ Molecular genetics
5.	Center of Animal Biotechnology (CAB), Veterinary Research Institute, Peshawar	1992	R&D Organization	☆ Animal Biotechnology ☆ Vaccine Development
6.	Centre for Applied Molecular Biology (CAMB) and Centre of Excellence in Molecular Biology (CEMB), Lahore	1987	R&D Organization	☆ Molecular Biology ☆ Recombinant DNA technology ☆ Fingerprinting ☆ Gene cloning
7.	Centre of Agricultural Biochemistry and Biotechnology (CABB), University of Agriculture, Faisalabad	2002	HEI	☆ Agricultural Biotechnology
8.	Centre of Biotechnology, University of Peshawar	2001	HEI	☆ Biochemistry ☆ Agriculture Biotechnology ☆ Industrial Biotechnology ☆ Environmental Biotechnology

Contd...

Table 12.1–*Contd...*

Sl.No.	*Name of Organization*	*Year of Establishment*	*Sector*	*Major Research Areas*
9.	Department of Bio Sciences, COMSATS Institute of Information Technology (CIIT), Islamabad	2003	HEI	☆ Molecular Biology ☆ Microbiology ☆ Immunology ☆ Molecular Genetics ☆ Developmental Biology
10.	Department of Biochemistry, University of Arid Agriculture Rawalpindi	1998	HEI	☆ Biochemistry ☆ Biotechnology ☆ Molecular Biology
11.	Department of Bioinformatics, Mohammad Ali Jinnah University, Islamabad	2008	HEI	☆ Bio-informatics ☆ Genetics ☆ Molecular Biology
12.	Department of Biological Sciences, FC College University, Lahore	2005	HEI	☆ Biological Sciences ☆ Biotechnology
13.	Department of Biological Sciences, Quaid-e-Azam University, Islamabad	1972	HEI	☆ Biochemistry ☆ Animal Sciences ☆ Plant Sciences ☆ Biotechnology ☆ Environmental Sciences ☆ Bioinformatics ☆ Pharmacy ☆ Microbiology
14.	Department of Biotechnology, University of Karachi	1996	HEI	☆ Biotechnology ☆ Biological Sciences
15.	Department of Microbiology and Molecular Genetics, University of the Punjab, Lahore	2002	HEI	☆ Molecular genetics ☆ Microbiology ☆ Molecular biology

Contd...

Table 12.1–*Contd...*

Sl.No.	*Name of Organization*	*Year of Establishment*	*Sector*	*Major Research Areas*
16.	Department of Microbiology, University of Karachi	1957	HEI	☆ Microbial taxonomy ☆ Genetics ☆ Immunology ☆ Physiology
17.	Dr. Panjwani Center for Molecular Medicine and Drug Research, University of Karachi	2004	HEI	☆ Pharmaceuticals ☆ Drug development ☆ Molecular medicine ☆ Rational drug designing
18.	Food and Biotechnology Research Centre, Pakistan Council for Scientific and Industrial Research, Lahore	1980	R&D Organization	☆ Biological Evaluation and Fermentation ☆ Food Technology and Nutrition
19.	Institute of Agricultural Biotechnology and Genetic Resources (IABGR), NARC, Islamabad	1980	R&D Organization	☆ Development of GMOs ☆ DNA finger printing ☆ Cloning ☆ Tissue culture
20.	Institute of Biochemistry and Biotechnology, University of the Punjab, Lahore	1997	HEI	☆ General Biotechnology ☆ Biochemistry ☆ Health ☆ Agriculture
21.	Institute of Biochemistry, University of Balochistan, Quetta	1991	HEI	☆ Biochemistry ☆ Biotechnology ☆ Biological sciences
22.	Institute of Biotechnology and Genetic Engineering (IBGE), KPK Agriculture University, Peshawar	2000	HEI	☆ Biotechnology ☆ Genetic Engineering
23.	Institute of Biotechnology and Genetic Engineering (KIBGE), University of Karachi	2003	HEI	☆ Biological Sciences ☆ Health Biotechnology ☆ Genetic engineering
24.	Institute of Biotechnology and Genetic Engineering, University of Sindh, Jamshoro	2002	HEI	☆ Health and Industrial Biotechnology ☆ Genetics

Contd...

Table 12.1–*Contd...*

Sl.No.	*Name of Organization*	*Year of Establishment*	*Sector*	*Major Research Areas*
25.	Institute of Industrial Biotechnology, Govt. College University, Lahore	2005	HEI	☆ Industrial Biotechnology ☆ Microbiology
26.	Institute of Molecular Biology and Bio-Technology, BZU, Multan	2006		☆ Molecular Biology ☆ Biotechnology
27.	National Institute for Biotechnology and Genetic Engineering (NIBGE), Faisalabad	1992	R&D Organization	☆ Plant Biotechnology ☆ Health biotechnology ☆ Industrial Biotechnology ☆ Environmental Biotechnology
28.	Nuclear Institute for Agriculture and Biology (NIAB), Faisalabad	1972	R&D Organization	☆ Plant breeding and Genetics division ☆ Soil Science Division ☆ Plant Protection Division ☆ Animal Sciences Division
29.	Plant Biotechnology Division, HEJ Research Institute of Chemistry, University of Karachi	1999	HEI	☆ Plant biotechnology ☆ Molecular medicine ☆ Drug research
30.	School of Biological Sciences, University of the Punjab, Lahore	2002	HEI	☆ Life Sciences ☆ Biological Sciences

3. STATUS OF INDUSTRIAL BIOTECHNOLOGY IN PAKISTAN

Although, industrial biotechnology is a neglected area in Pakistan as compared with agricultural or health biotechnology but still work is being done in this area by a few institutes. Areas of research on industrial biotechnology in Pakistan are:

- ☆ Agriculture and food
- ☆ Pharmaceuticals, DNA recombinant technology, vaccinology
- ☆ Livestock, animal health, aqua culture, fisheries
- ☆ Environment and its pollution, engineering, chemicals
- ☆ Forensic medicine, bioinformatics

The major initiatives in this field are

1. **Nanobiotechnology**: The research focuses on developing protocols for size and shape-controlled metal nanoparticles (MNPs) *viz.* Au, Ag, Pt, Pd, Fe, Cu, and explore their applications in biotechnology and new materials fabrication.
2. **Fermentation Technology:** The research focuses on process development for production, purification and characterization of industrial enzymes (alpha amylase, protease and beta-glucosidase).
3. **Industrial Enzymes and Biofuels**: Impressive work is being done on Isolation and purification of local thermophilic fungi for biotechnological purposes.
4. **Bioresources Development for Industry**: Notable research is going on in this area in Pakistan. The R&D work is being conducted in the areas microbial biodiversity and systematics, biotechnology of extremophiles, extremozymes and gene mining.
5. **Bioprocessing of Ores and Fossil Fuels**: Work has been done to develop biotechnological processes for the extraction of valuable metals from low-grade ores or wastes (microbial leaching) and their removal/recovery from leach liquors and industrial waste effluents using microbial biosorbents (bioseparation technology) effectively and economically. Also, bioprocessing of ores and fossil fuels engages biodesulphurization of indigenous fossil fuels *i.e.* coal and petroleum to meet our sulphur free fuel requirements for the future. Existence of sulfur compounds in indigenous fuels limits its industrial application due to environmental as well as technical problems.
6. **Microbial Production to Supplement the Poultry Feed:** The microbial production of antibiotic bacitracin to supplement the poultry feed is successfully being done in Pakistan.
7. **Vaccinology**: Currently vaccines for human's prophylaxis against various infectious and contagious diseases are mainly imported while there is a dire need to develop the institutes and human resources for local production. In contrast to this, the livestock and poultry vaccine are being produced

locally, though quality and quantity required is not up-to the mark. The production of vaccines for animals needs improvement especially in terms of adopting hi-tech and hi-efficiency production systems.

8. **Biotechnological Production of Protease for Detergents and Leather Industries:** Laboratory Scale Bioprocess has been developed and actual production of protease will start soon on commercial scale. Second Phase will include establishment of Bioresource and metabolic Engineering Facilities.
9. **Production of Bio-Energy from Plant Biomass**: Pre- treatment of cellulosic biomass by chemical, physical and biological methods has been completed. The trials after saccharification on pilot scale are in progress for ethanol development.

4. INDUSTRIAL BIOTECHNOLOGY: PROBLEMS AND ISSUES IN PAKISTAN

There are several barriers that hamper the research and translation of R&D to market products in the area of industrial biotechnology. The foremost problem is the limited resources available for R and D. Inadequate stock of trained manpower in this field hold back the development. Other issues that delay the growth of this potential area is a lack of proper coordination among the institutions,poor understanding between academics and industry, the gap between R&D and pre-commercial demonstration and first-of-its-kind production plants and lack of awareness for Intellectual Property Rights and innovation.

5. CONCLUSIONS AND POLICY RECOMMENDATIONS (FUTURE AREAS OF STUDY)

Pakistan is looking forward for prosperity through knowledge based industrial revolution. New technologies must be adopted or developed through R and Dand be linked to innovation and commercialization. There is a need to spend more on education, human resources development, public and private sectors should work in strong collaboration and coordination. Incentives should be given to the researchers and industrialists such as venture capital, funds, matching grants, tax holidays etc. you may mention what incentives are being given to researchers in the field of biotechnology at large and in industrial biotechnology in particular

REFERENCES

1. OECD (2005). Organisation for Economic Co-operation and Development (OECD) A framework for biotechnology statistics.
2. Royal Belgian Academy Council of Applied Sciences Report (2004). Industrial Biotechnology and Sustainable Chemistry.
3. EuropaBio–Industrial or White Biotechnology–Research for Europe.http: //www.bio-economy.net/reports/files/sra.pdf
4. Sea of Dreams: Genetically Modified Microbes will lead to a Revolution in Industrial Biotechnology, *The Economist* 1 May 2004, Vol. 371 (8373).

5. OECD (2009). Organisation for Economic Co-operation and Development (OECD) The Bioeconomy to 2030: Designing a Policy Agenda.
6. World Economic Forum (2010) – The Future of Industrial Biorefineries. http: // www3.weforum.org/docs/WEF_FutureIndustrialBiorefineries_Report_2010.pdf
7. Pakistan Council for Science and Technology Islamabad (2005).Report of the Expert Committee on Biotechnology and Genetic Engineering.www.pcst.org.pk
8. KET (2011).Working Group Report of KET – Industrial Biotechnology, June 2011.http: //ec.europa.eu/enterprise/sectors/ict/files/kets/4_industrial_biotechnology-final_report_en.pdf
9. Soomro, A.M., A.W. Baloch, H.R. Bughio, M.S. Bughio, T. Mohammed and N.N. Mastoi. 2003. A new high yielding mutant aromatic rice variety Khushboo-95. Int. Rice Res. Notes. 28. p. 32.
10. Abro, S. and M.A. Arain. 2010. New cotton varieties of NIA. Sindh Zaraat, 20 (4): 6.
11. Sial, M.A, M.A. Arain and K. A. Laghari 2012. Evolution of new wheat variety NIA-Amber for the general cultivation in Sindh province-A Case Study 2012.Pak. J. Bot., 44 (1): 301-306.
12. Ali A, An SJ, Cui C, Haque A, Carbis R. Preparation and evaluation of immunogenic conjugates of Salmonella enterica serovar Typhi O-specific polysaccharides with diphtheria toxoid. Human Vaccines and Immunotherapeutics 2012; 8: 189–193; PMID: 22426380; http: //dx.doi.org/10.4161/hv.18350.

Chapter 13

Large Scale Cultivation of a Mixed Microbial Consortium for Biofuel Production

Maranda Esterhuizen-Londt and Ben Zeelie***

InnoVenton Institute for Chemical Technology and Downstream Chemicals Technology Station, Nelson Mandela Metropolitan University, Port Elizabeth, South Africa, 6321

ABSTRACT

The use of microalgae for biofuel production has received a great deal of attention due to its numerous advantages over the use of terrestrial plants. However, the production of microalgae biomass has been extensively criticized for its production costs. This has led to research in genetic engineering of microalgae to optimize biomass yield to increase production economy. In nature, algal blooms occur regularly possibly due to the fact that these blooms are not axenic but occur in association with a range of microbes. This co-occurrence functions as a symbiosis where each organism contributes to or supports the optimal growth of another and to some extent buffers against adverse environmental conditions. Microalgae may also inhibit bacterial activity thus retaining dominance in culture. We demonstrate here the growth of a natural microalgae/cyanobacteria-bacteria consortium at large scale and overcoming challenges in large scale cultivation. The consortium was grown in vertical enclosed gas-sparged photobioreactors in a greenhouse with no artificial lighting or heating and used for biofuel production. Such a consortium biomass production system is an ideal self-supporting system with sustainable production year round that is more economic compared to uni-algal culture used to date.

***Keywords**: Microalgae, Cyanobacteria, Bacteria, Consortium, Co-occurrence, Biofuel.*

E-mail: *maranda.esterhuizen2@nmmu.ac.za, **ben.zeelie@nmmu.ac.za

1. INTRODUCTION

Currently the majority of the world's energy demand is produced from oil, gas and coal; however, these fossil fuels are being depleted at an alarming rate. Furthermore, emissions from fossil fuel combustion have led to increased environmental damage (Amin, 2009; Greenwell *et al.*, 2012). Thus, alternate environmentally friendly and renewable energy sources were sought after. Crop derived biofuels were considered but has not been generally accepted due to; ethical concerns that the crops are used for human consumption, the slow growth of the crops, and low yields (Greenwell *et al.*, 2012). Microalgae were considered an option as it has been used extensively for high valuable metabolites production, its CO_2 utilization capacity, rapid growth rates and high photosynthetic efficiency (Shay, 1993; Ahmed *et al.*, 2011). However, the economy of microalgae culture (Christi, 2007) and the use of potable water sources for culturing (DEO, 2009) was a concern and thus biofuel from microalgae has not been widely commercialized (Wu *et al.*, 2012; Greenwell *et al.*, 2012).

To date, large scale microalgae culture has been based on laboratory culture techniques where uni-algal or even axenic microalgae are cultured under sterile conditions using potable water and a carefully calculated chemical feed (Christi, 2007). Optimal microalgae strains have been selected based on growth rates achieved under laboratory conditions and lipid content (Greenwell *et al.*, 2012). Additionally, biofuel has generally been produced from microalgae lipids and this has led to unnecessary extraction costs. Many strategies have been suggested for decreasing biomass production costs such as cultivation in wastewater which will reduce the cost of adding nutrient and reduce freshwater use (Li *et al.*, 2008; Pittman *et al.*, 2011; Wu *et al.*, 2012). Genetic and metabolic engineering has been used to increase the photosynthetic capacity of the microalgae thus increasing biomass production rate and oil content (Christi, 2007).

In nature, microalgae bloom events occur regularly. These blooms are in no way uni-algal or axenic and it is due to the synergism of co-occurrence within the bloom that leads to the development, and adds to the sustainability of the bloom (Fukami *et al.*, 1997). This co-occurrence functions as a symbiosis where each organism contributes to or supports the optimal growth of another and to some extent buffers against adverse conditions.

We demonstrate here the growth of a microalgae/cyanobacteria-bacteria consortium at large scale. Additionally, we investigate the challenges to optimal microalgae biomass production and thereby decreasing the culture expenditure at large scale.

2. MATERIALS AND METHODS

Microalgae comprised of eukaryotic *Scenedesmus* spp. and *Chlorella* sp., and cyanobacteria including *Limnothirix* sp. and *Oscillatoria* sp.were obtained from various sources, combined with symbiotic bacterial genera represented by *Pseudomonas, Aeromonas* and nitrogen fixing bacteriawere cultured non-sterilely over a year period for the communities to establish and stabilize. The consortium was cultured in vertical enclosed photobioreactors (PBR) with airlift sparging supplemented with 5 per cent CO_2 in the InnoVenton greenhouse. The PBR were not in any way supplied with artificial lighting or heating depending solely on the environmental temperature and season. The mixed consortium of microalgae, cyanobacteria and heterotrophic bacteria were fed with a feed mixture based on Carbon Hydrogen Nitrogen and Sulfur (CHNS) analysis of the consortium.

The stable consortium was monitored overtime with bright field microscopy and changes in the populations and ratios were documented. The majority of the dominant strains were isolated and identified. Bacterial species were isolated on nutrient agar and identified using biochemical testing. Eukaryotic microalgae were isolated on JM media (Kessler *et al.*, 1957), modified Bold Basal 3N Media (Stein, 1973) and Z8 media (Kótai, 1972). Cyanobacteria were isolated on BG_{11} and BG_{11}^{o} media (Stanier *et al.*, 1971). Both eukaryotic microalgae and cyanobacteria were identified based on morphology.

A range of standard microbiological methods were evaluated for determining biomass concentration. Based on statistical comparison of the methods, ease of use and economy, turbidity was selected. The growth rate of the consortium was monitored sporadically over a year to determine seasonal variation and also compared to optimal growth rates reported in literature (Sorokin and Krauss, 1958; Brennen and Owende, 2010). The effect of the nitrogen source and concentration as well as micronutrients addition on growth rate was investigated. Additionally, the water from various boreholes as well as sea water (sterile and non-sterile) was tested against fresh water (tap water) to evaluate efficacy for cultivation. In all experiments the growth rate, pH, and media temperature was recorded using a TB 200 turbidity meter (Orbeco) and a Hanna pH meter respectively. Statistical analyses were conducted using Statisica software 2011 Multiple regression analysis with indicator variables was used to determine whether a statistically significant difference (alpha is 0.05) exists between the treatments investigated.

3. RESULTS AND DISCUSSION

At InnoVenton, microalgae growth is a function of the environmental conditions as no artificial light or heating is supplied in the greenhouse. Biotic and abiotic parameter control is essential in microalgae cultivation to ensure maximal yield. However, this control will result in increased production costs. The average doubling time of the consortium growth at InnoVenton is 15 hours which was higher than doubling times achieved with laboratory cultivation (Maxwell *et al.*, 1994). However, with the production capacity at InnoVenton of 2.2 Tons biomass per year, economy and culture sustainability and stability was of greater concern. The dominant microbes identified in the consortium included eukaryotic microalgae *Scenedesmus* spp. and *Chlorella* sp., cyanobacteria include *Limnothirix* sp. and *Oscillatoria* sp. and the bacterial genera include *Pseudomonas, Aeromonas* and nitrogen fixing bacteria. Variation in the species present in the consortium was not seen except for variation in the ratios in with they occur from season to season.

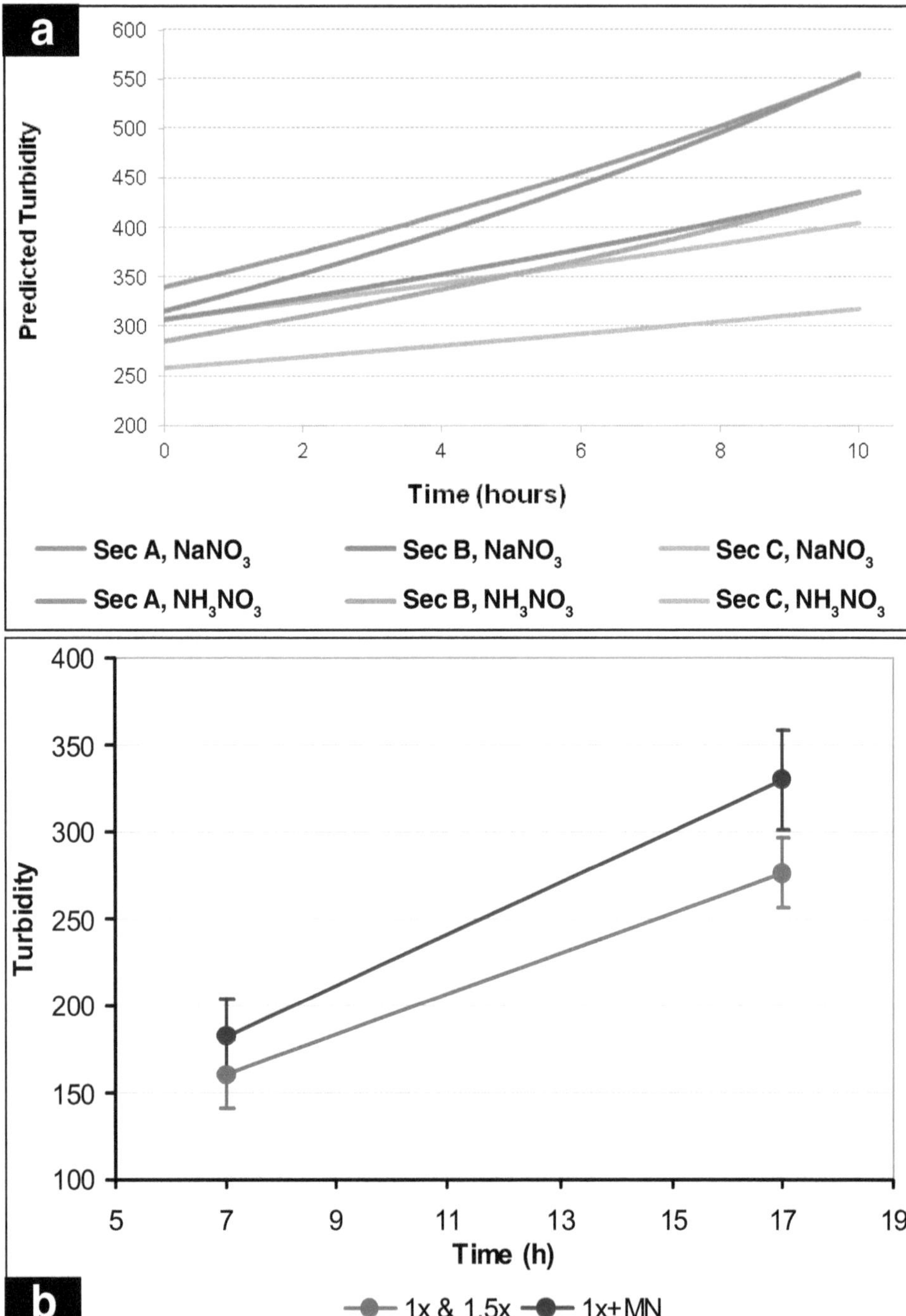

Figure 13.1

a) Microalgae time for two nitrogen sources at various positions within the greenhouse; b) Average daily growth rate of microalgae under two feed concentrations and the addition of micronutrients. Error bars represent 95 per cent confidence intervals.

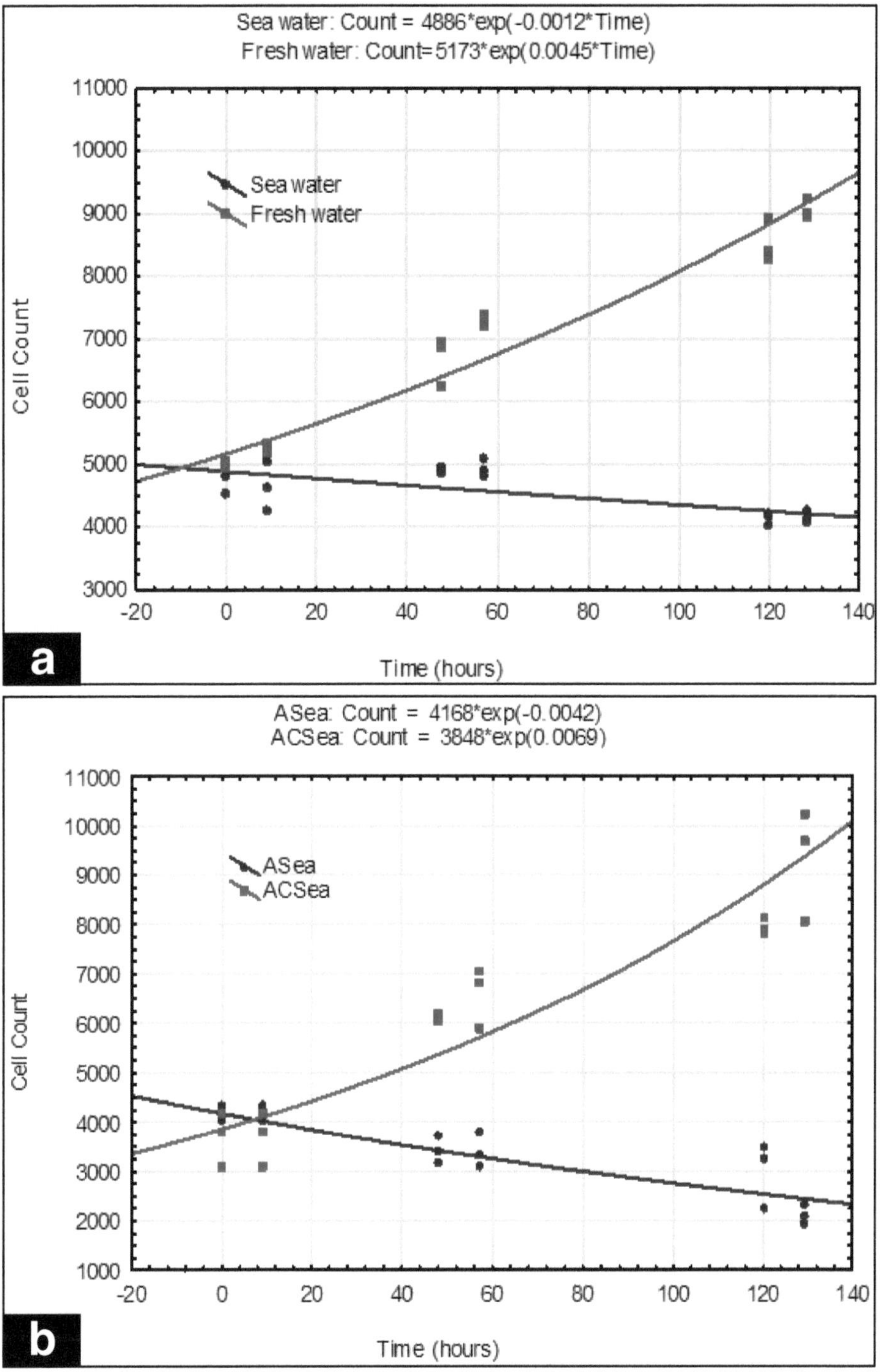

Figure 13.2

a) The growth of microalgae in raw seawater compared to a control of tap water; b) The growth of microalgae in sterilized seawater compared to a control of tap water.

From Figure 13.1a, an increase in the overall microalgae growth rate can be achieved by the use of $NaNO_3$ instead of NH_4NO_3 and the addition of micronutrients (Figure 13.1b) will also statistically significantly increase the growth rate.

All the tested borehole waters promoted microalgae growth when compared to a control, except type 3 (Table 13.1). However, the doubling time was not significantly different compared to its control and thus all the borehole water tested is suitable for cultivation. From Figure 13.2a and b it is clear that seawater is not an ideal water type for cultivation of the consortium used at InnoVenton.

Table 13.1: Average Doubling Time of Each Borehole Type versus its Corresponding Control.

Type	*Control DT**	*Borehole DT**	*Statistically Significant*
1	20	14	Yes
2	33	25	Yes
3	20	32	No
4	28	23	Yes

DT: Microalgae doubling time.

The consortium biomass production system used at InnoVenton is an ideal self-supporting system with sustainable production year round that is more economic compared to uni-algal culture used to date. Biofuel from the cultivated biomass has been achieved by direct liquefaction without the selection for lipid molecules; however, this is outside of the scope of this article.

4. CONCLUSION

In this report, we demonstrate that a mixed consortium of eukaryotic microalgae, cyanobacteria and bacteria can be used to successfully produce biocrude without extractions. Description and discussion of the biocrude production and profiling was, however, outside of the scope of this article. We describe a stable, sustainable system for large scale microalgae production year round with no additional energy usage by controlling biotic parameters.

ACKNOWLEDGEMENTS

InnoVenton would like to thank the Technology Innovation Agency (TIA), the Department of Science and Technology (DST), c*change and ESKOM for funding the project.

REFERENCES

1. Amin, S. 2009. Review on biofuel oil and gas production processes from microalgae. Energy conversion and management 50, 1834-1840.
2. Brennan, L. and P. Owende. 2010. Biofuels from microalgae–A review of technologies for production, processing, and extractions of biofuels and co-products. Renewable and Sustainable Energy Reviews 14 (2), 557–577

3. Department of Energy (DOE), National algal biofuels technology roadmap, 2009.
4. Greenwell, H.C., Laurens, L.M.L., Shields, R.J. Lovitt, R.W. and K.J. Flynn. 2012. Placing microalgae on the biofuels priority list. J.R. Soc Interface 7, 703-726.
5. Kótai, J. 1972. Instructions for preparation of modified nutrient solution Z8 for algae. NIVA B-11/69.
6. Li, Y., Horseman, M., Wu, N., Lan, C.Q. and N. Dubois-Calero. 2008. Biofuels form microalgae. Biotechnol. 81, 815-820.
7. Maxwell, D. P Falk, S. Trick C. C, and N.P.A. Huner. 1994. Growth at Low Temperature Mimics High-Light Acclimation in *Chlorella vulgaris*'. Plant Physiol. (1994) 105: 535-543.
8. Pitman, J.K., Dean A.P. and O. Osundeka. 2011. The potential of sustainable algae biofuel production using wastewater resources. Bioresour. Technol. 102,17-25.
9. Shay, *E.G.* 1993. Diesel fuel from vegetable oils: Status and opportunities. Biomass Bioenerg 4 (4), 227–242.
10. Stanier RY, Kunisawa R, Mandel M and G. Cohen-Bazire. 1971. Purification and properties of unicellular blue-green algae (Order Chroococcales). Bacteriol. Rev. **35**: 171-205.
11. Stein, J. (ED.) 1973. Handbook of Phycological methods. Culture methods and growth measurements. Cambridge University Press. 448 pp.
12. Sorokin C. and R. W. Krauss. 1958. The Effects of Light Intensity on the Growth Rates of Green Algae. Plant Physiol. 1958 March; 33 (2): 109–113.
13. Wu, L.F., Chen, P.C., Huang, A.P. and C.M. Lee. 2012. The feasibility of biodiesel production by microalgae using industrial wastewater. Bioresource Technology 113: 14-8.

Chapter 14

Alpha Amylase Production Using Cassava Root Extract

S.L. Dalpatadu[1], A.K. Nanayakkara[1], N.V. Chandrasekharan[2] and S.G. Senaratne[1]*

[1]Biotechnology Unit, Industrial Technology Institute, Sri Lanka
[2]Department of Chemistry, University of Colombo, Sri Lanka

ABSTRACT

The starch liquefaction process in the brewing industry uses two key industrial enzymes, α-amylase and amyloglucosidase. The high cost of production in Sri Lanka has led to importation of these enzymes from countries such as Denmark and Singapore, resulting in loss of foreign exchange. This study is focused on using locally produced low cost cassava (*Manihot esculenta*) roots as a primary substrate to produce α-amylase using *Bacillus subtilis* subsp. *spizizenii* str. ATCC 6633. The efficiency of enzyme production by *Bacillus subtilis* at room temperature (RT) and 37°C was first analyzed using nutrient broth as fermentation medium. Cassava root extract was produced by milling cassava roots obtained from the local market with distilled water. Cassava root extract (20 per cent w/v) was supplemented with yeast extract (0.5 per cent w/v), pH adjusted to 6.7, autoclaved and inoculated with 500 μl of overnight liquid culture of *Bacillus subtilis*. Fermentation of cassava root extract was carried out at RT in shaker incubators (180 rpm) and α-Amylase activity was analysed at 37°C and 55°C using the Dinitrosalicylic colorimetric method. There was no significant difference between enzyme production by fermentation at RT and at 37°C (RT: 0.11 ± 0.003 U [μmol ml^{-1} min^{-1}] vs. 37°C: 0.12 ± 0.003 U). The enzyme activity at 37°C and 55°C were 1.21 ± 0.011 U and 1.47 ± 0.006 U respectively. Optimization of fermentation conditions indicated 120 hours of incubation and pH 8.5 for culture medium resulted in highest enzyme activity. Furthermore, α-amylase produced in this study had optimum activity at 55°C and pH 5. Results suggest that α-amylase could be efficiently produced using cassava root extract.

* E-mail: sandun@iti.lk

Further optimization of fermentation conditions may result in higher yields of α-amylase. Therefore, we propose locally produced cassava root extract as a substrate for cost effective production of industrial enzymes in Sri Lanka.

Keywords: *Amylase, Bacillus subtilis, Starch, Detergents, Tapioca, Sri Lanka*

1. INTRODUCTION

Enzymes are produced from various biological sources such as plants and microorganisms (Gale *et al.*, 1983; Nahas and Waldemarin, 2002; Bano *et al.*, 2011). Starch hydrolysis can be achieved using chemicals such as acids. However, since recently; amylases obtained from biological sources have completely replaced chemical hydrolysis of starch in starch processing industries due to the low cost of production and environmental friendliness (Tester *et al.*, 2006). Most abundant amylases used in industry today are from microbial sources (Gupta *et al.*, 2003). This is due to the broad spectrum of industrial applications these microbial amylases can be utilized due to the stability of microbial amylases compared to amylases derived from plants or animals (Tanyildizi *et al.*, 2005).

Enzymes are routinely used in many industrial applications. Sri Lanka has numerous industries that require the usage of enzymes. Food and beverage, detergent and textile industries in the country are the main consumers of industrial enzymes. However, Sri Lanka does not produce enzymes locally and the entire enzyme requirement of the country is satisfied by importing from countries such as Denmark and Singapore. This has resulted in a loss of valuable foreign exchange of approximately 2 billion Sri Lankan rupees annually (Senaratne, personal communication). α-Amylase (E.C.3.2.1.1) is an enzyme imported to Sri Lanka and is used extensively in various industries ranging from brewing to detergent manufacturing, α-Amylases catalyse the hydrolysis of internal α-1,4-glycosidic bonds in starch to produce low molecular weight components such as glucose, maltose and maltotriose (Rajagopalan and Krishnan, 2008).

Large scale production of α-amylase is carried out using different species of microorganisms. However, amylases used in industrial applications are mainly produced from the genus *Bacillus* (Gupta *et al.*, 2003; Pandey *et al.*, 2000). The starch processing industry is the main consumer of amylase where it is used to liquefy starch to convert into fructose and glucose syrups. However, α-amylases have a broad range of applications in numerous industrial processes in food, fermentation, textile, paper, detergent, and pharmaceutical industries (Kirk *et al.*, 2002). Generally, α-amylase production use raw material containing high starch content. One main factor that has contributed to industrial enzymes such as α-amylase not being produced in Sri Lanka is the high cost of production that results from using economic crops such as rice or wheat as raw material. An alternative to these economic crops are Cassava *(Manihot esculenta)*.

Cassava is a perennial shrub that produces high yield of tuberous roots within 6 months to 3 years after planting (CGIAR, 2005). In Sri Lanka, cassava is grown chiefly as a food and animal feed, with little significant industrial use. It is mainly grown as a rain-fed crop throughout the island excluding high elevation areas. Cultivation of cassava is mostly concentrated in the wet and intermediate zones and is grown as a backyard crop (DOASL, 2006). However, large scale open-land cultivation in the wet zone (Gampaha, Colombo, Kegalle, Rathnapura and Matara districts) has been reported (DOASL, 2006). In the intermediate zone (Kurunegala district) Cassava is grown as a mixed crop with coconut and pineapple cultivations and large scale cultivations of cassava are present as "Chena" cultivation in the dry zone (Putlam, Anuradhapura, Ampara, Hambantota, Moneragala districts) (DOASL, 2006). Cassava roots have high starch content and have remarkable hardiness, drought resistance, resistance to pest attack and an ability to produce acceptable yields under unfavoured conditions with low inputs and attention. These characteristic of cassava and its low cost of production make it a suitable material to use as a raw material in amylase production industry.

In this study we used cassava root extract as a raw material for α-amylase production using amylase producing bacterium *Bacillus subtilis.* A simple batch fermentation system and dinitrosalicylic colorimetric assay was used to assess the initial fermentation conditions and to optimize parameters such as incubation duration and initial pH of fermentation medium to obtain high enzyme production. Furthermore, enzyme activity was evaluated at different temperatures and pH conditions.

2. MATERIALS AND METHODS

2.1. Culture Medium and Microorganism

Cassava root extract was used in fermentation medium to determine the possibility of using cassava as a raw material for α-amylase enzyme production. Fresh cassava roots were obtained from a market in Colombo, Sri Lanka. The outer layer of the roots was peeled off and the roots were cut into small cubes (approximately 1 cm^3). The cubes were ground into a paste using mortar and pestle, mixed with deionised water (20 per cent w/v) and shaken in a shaker for 1 hour at 180 rotations per minute (rpm) at room temperature (RT).

The mixture was filtered with a cheesecloth and the filtrate was supplemented with yeast extract (0.5 per cent w/v; Fluka Analytical, St. Louis, MO 63103, USA) and pH adjusted to 6.7. Sterilization was done by autoclaving at 121°C for 20 minutes. The sterilized cassava root extract was allowed to return to RT before inoculation. *Bacillus subtilis* subsp. *spizizenii* str. (American Type Culture Collection [ATCC] No. 6633; ATCC, Manassas, VA 20110, USA) was cultured overnight in nutrient broth (Fluka Analytical) at 37°C according to ATCC guidelines. Five hundred micro litres of overnight culture was used to inoculate 50 ml of culture medium. All fermentations in this study were carried out under aerobic conditions.

2.2. Enzyme Assay

A crude enzyme extract was obtained by centrifuging 5 ml of fermented broth at 3000 x *g* for 20 minutes at 4°C and collecting the supernatant. The focus of this study was to evaluate only alpha amylase secreted from bacteria to the culture medium and not total alpha amylase content. Therefore, bacterial cells were not lysed. Dinitrosalicylic acid (DNS) method was used to determine α-amylase activity. In brief, 0.05 ml of enzyme extract was incubated for 15 minutes at 37°C or 55°C with 0.45 ml soluble starch (1.0 per cent w/v; Avonchem Limited, Bradbury, Oxon, UK) prepared in 0.1 M phosphate buffer, pH 6.7. The reaction was stopped and the reducing sugars released were determined by adding 1.0 ml of 3, 5-dinitrosalicylic acid reagent (Sigma Aldrich, St. Louis, MO 6310, USA) and boiling the mixture for 5 minutes. Absorbance was measured at 540 nm using a spectrophotometer (Genesys 10S, Themo Electron Corporation, USA) and D- (+)-glucose (Sigma Aldrich) was used as a standard. One unit (U) of α-amylase activity was defined as the amount of glucose (micro moles) released in 1 ml of final assay solution in 1 minute (1 unit = 1 μ moles/$ml^{-1}min^{-1}$).

2.3. Determination of Incubation Temperature for Use of Cassava Root Extract in Fermentation Medium

The amount of enzyme production by *Bacillus subtilis* at RT and 37°C was compared using nutrient broth (Fluka Analytical) as fermentation medium. Afterwards, an analysis of suitability of cassava root extract as a growth medium for *Bacillus subtilis* was carried out at RT. Both studies had an incubation period of 48 hrs and a shaker speed of 180 rpm. Enzyme assay was carried out at 37°C and 55°C.

2.4. Optimization of Incubation Period, pH of Fermentation Medium and Cell Mass Analysis

Cassava root extract medium (100 ml) inoculated with *Bacillus subtilis* was used in these studies. The incubation period was extended up to 120 hours and 7.5 ml of medium was removed after 24, 48, 72, and 120 hour time interval to analyze pH of the medium, enzyme activity and cell mass.

Five millilitres of fermented medium was centrifuged at 3000 x *g* for 20 minutes at 4°C to obtain a cell pellet. The cell pellet was air dried in an incubator at 60°C for 48 hours and was used to determine the dry cell mass of the medium.

The initial pH of cassava root extract was varied to determine optimum pH of fermentation medium to achieve highest enzyme activity. The pH values used were 5, 6.7, 8.5 and 10.50. Fermentation was carried out in a shaker (180 rpm) incubator at RT for 120 hrs.

2.5. Effect of Temperature and pH on α-Amylase Activity

Modified DNS assay was used with crude enzyme extract obtained after 120 hours of fermentation. Extracellular α-amylase activity was analyzed at different temperatures ranging from 25°C to 80°C by varying the incubation temperature of the DNS assay. By varying the pH of the DNS assay (from pH 5.0 to pH 10.5), extracellular enzyme activity of α-amylase was determined at different pH levels. In the pH study, the incubation temperature of the DNS assay was kept at 55°C.

2.6. Statistical Analysis

All data are expressed as mean ± standard error of the mean (SEM). Statistical analysis was carried out using PASW Statistics 18 (IBM SPSS Statistics; IBM, Chicago,

USA) statistical analysis software. Analysis of difference between two groups was done using student t-test. Analysis of optimization studies (duration of incubation, pH of fermentation medium, cell mass analysis) and analysis of enzyme characteristics (optimum temperature and pH) was done using one-way analysis of variance (ANOVA). For equal variation and unequal variation between groups, Tukey-Kramer Post Hoc test and Tamhane's-T2 Post Hoc test was carried out respectively. Differences were considered significant when P <0.05.

3. RESULTS

3.1. Incubation Temperature and Suitability of Cassava Root Extract Medium for Fermentation

There was no significant difference between enzyme production by fermentation at RT and at 37°C (Figure 14.1A; RT: 0.11 ± 0.003 U vs. 37°C: 0.12 ± 0.003 U). α-Amylase was successfully produced in cassava root extract and enzyme activity at 37°C and 55°C were 1.21 ± 0.011 U and 1.47 ± 0.006 U (Figure 14.1B) respectively.

3.2. Duration of Incubation, pH of Medium and Cell Mass Analysis

A significant increase in enzyme production was observed at 72 hours and 120 hours of incubation compared to 24 hours and 48 hours (Figure 14.2A, 24 hours: 0.04 ± 0.004 U and 48 hours: 0.07 ± 0.005 U vs. 72 hours: 0.14 ± 0.013 U and 120 hours: 0.23 ± 0.018 U; P< 0.05). Furthermore, there was a significant difference between enzyme activity at 120 hours compared to 72 hours (Figure 14.2A, 72 hours: 0.14 ± 0.013 U vs. 120 hours: 0.23 ± 0.018 U; P< 0.05). Enzyme production was significantly

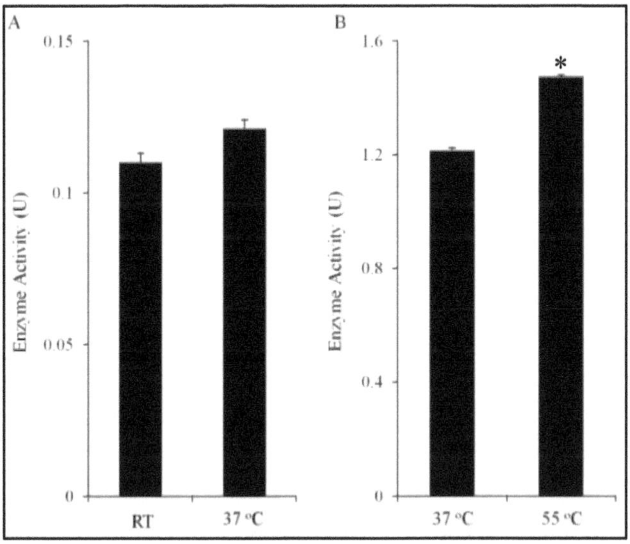

Figure 14.1

(A) Analysis of enzyme activity at room temperature using standard culture media (nutrient agar) (RT) and at 37 °C. (B) Enzyme activity at 37 °C and at 55°C of α-amylase produced from cassava root extract medium; 1 U = 1 μ moles/ml $^{-1}$ min^{-1}; *P*<0.05; Error Bar: Standard Errors of the Mean.

increased in fermentation medium with an initial pH of 8.5 compared to pH 5 and pH 6.7 (Figure 14.2B, pH 8.5: 0.22 ± 0.008 U vs. pH 5: 0.17 ± 0.0053 U and pH 6.7: 0.18 ± 0.0003 U; P< 0.05). However, at pH 10.5 enzyme activity were significantly reduced (Figure 14.2B, pH 8.5: 0.22 ± 0.008 U vs. pH 10.5: 0.13 ± 0.0007 U; P< 0.05). Cell mass analysis showed a significant increase in cell mass at 72 hours and 120 hours compared to 24 hours and 48 hours (Figure 14.2C, 24 hours: 3.2 ± 0.23 mg/ml and 48 hours: 3.57 ± 0.01 mg/ml vs. 72 hours: 6.00 ± 0.32 mg/ml and 120 hours: 7.13 ± 0.14 mg/ml; P< 0.05). However, there was no significant difference between the cell mass values at 72 hours and 120 hours. The pH value of the fermentation medium did not

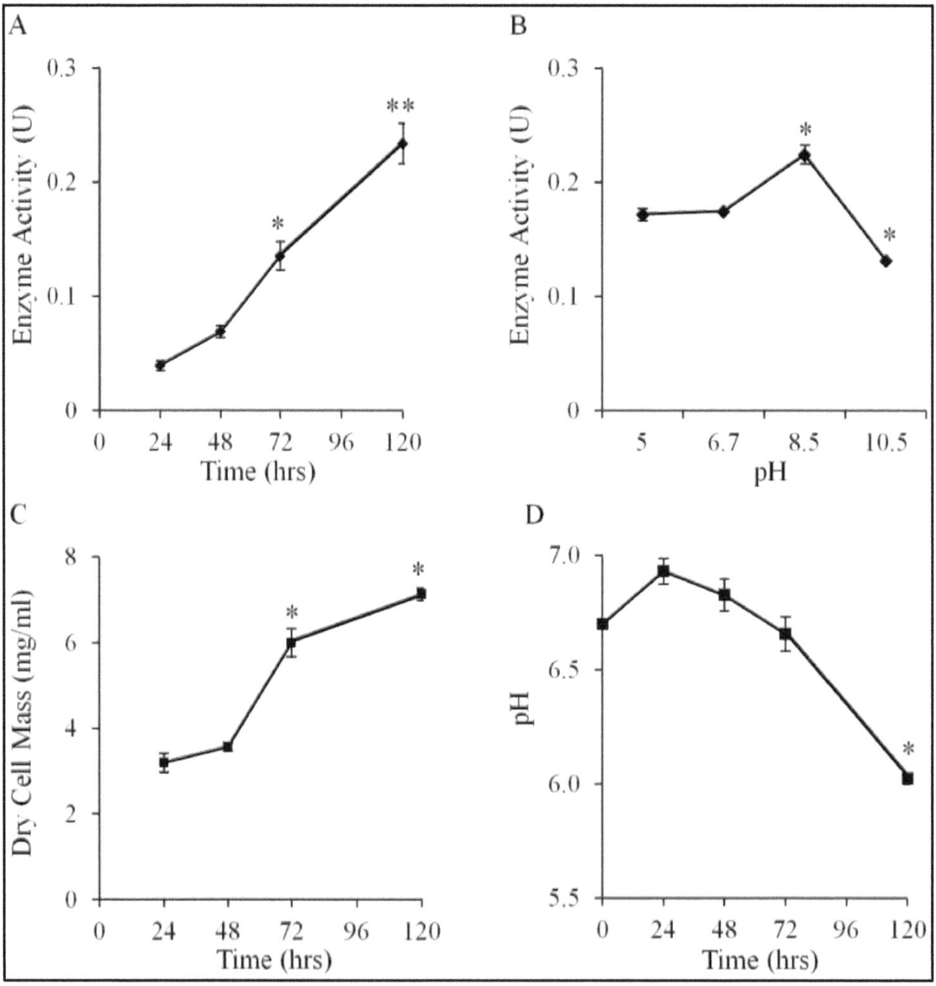

Figure 14.2: Optimization of Fermentation Conditions.

(A) Enzyme activity at different incubation durations and (B) at different pH levels of fermentation medium (incubated for 120 hrs). Analysis of fermentation medium at different stages of incubation, (C) Dry cell mass and (D) pH of the medium; 1 U = 1 µ moles/ml $^{-1}$ min^{-1}; *P <0.05; Error Bar: Standard Errors of the Mean.

significantly change during 0 to 72 hours. However, at 120 hours of incubation the pH level of the medium significantly dropped to pH 6.03 ± 0.02 (Figure 14.2D).

3.3. Effect of Temperature and pH on α-Amylase Activity

Enzyme activity was highest at 55°C (Figure 14.3A, 0.21 ± 0.002 U). There was no difference between enzyme activity at 25°C, 70°C and 80°C (Figure 14.3A). Highest

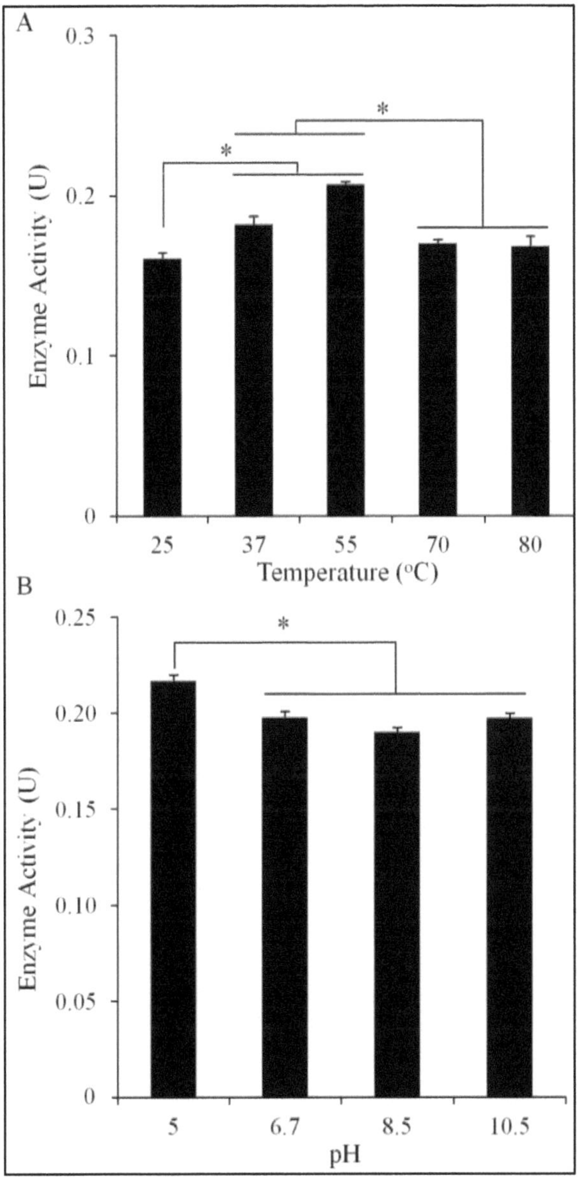

Figure 14.3: Enzyme Activity of α-amylase Produced by Cassava Root Extract (fermented for 120 hours) at different (A) temperature (°C) and (B) pH levels; 1 U = 1 μ moles/ml $^{-1}$ min^{-1}; *P <0.05; Error Bar: Standard Errors of the Mean.

enzyme activity was observed at pH 5, which was significantly higher compared to pH 6.7, 8.5 and 10.5 (Figure 14.3B, pH 5: 0.22 ± 0.004 U vs. pH 6.7: 0.20 ± 0.003 U, pH 8.5: 0.19 ± 0.003 U and pH 10.5: 0.20 ± 0.003 U; $P< 0.05$).

4. DISCUSSION

In this study, cassava root extract was used as a fermentation medium for α-amylase production. However, initially we compared the production of α-amylase at room temperature (RT) and at 37°C in nutrient broth to determine whether *Bacillus subtilis* was capable of producing comparable amounts of enzymes at RT compared to 37°C. Results confirmed the amount of α-amylase produced at RT and 37°C were comparable. Therefore, RT was used as the incubation temperature in all fermentation studies. α-Amylase produced by *B. subtilis* grown on cassava root extract responded well at 37°C and 55°C in our enzyme activity analysis and produced α-amylase at comparable levels to nutrient broth. Any fermentation process would require an optimization procedure since physical and chemical properties of the fermentation medium affects the growth of the organisms. Therefore, following the observations in our initial fermentation studies using cassava root extract, optimizations were carried out for fermentation conditions to increase α-amylase production by *Bacillus subtilis*.

Highest enzyme production was achieved by fermenting the medium for 120 hours. However, cell mass analysis showed there was no significant difference between the levels of dry cell mass at 72 hours and 120 hours of incubation. Therefore, it is likely that the bacterial growth rate has achieved an early stationery phase by 120 hrs of incubation. The optimum pH of the growth medium for maximum production of enzyme was pH 8.5. This suggests *Bacillus subtilis* prefers a relatively basic medium for optimum growth. Analysis of pH at different stages of the incubation period showed a significant decrease in pH levels towards 120 hours. The decrease in pH may be a factor that contributes to a decrease in bacterial growth towards 120 hours of incubation. Therefore, maintaining pH levels at a slightly basic level throughout the fermentation period may result in higher production rate of enzymes.

The rate of production of enzyme and the characteristics of the enzyme depends on the type of environment the organisms prefers to thrive in. For an example, amylases produced by some halophilic microorganisms such as *Chromohalobacter* sp. (Prakash *et al.*, 2009), *Halobacillus* sp. (Amoozegar *et al.*, 2003), *Haloarcula hispanica* (Hutcheon *et al.*, 2005), *Halomonas meridiana* (Coronado *et al.*, 2000), and *Bacillus dipsosauri* (Deutch, 2002) have optimal activity at high salinities and are used in many industrial processes considered to be harsh. The concentrated salt solutions used in these processes would otherwise inhibit many enzymatic conversions. Enzymes such as amylases produced by *Bacillus* species are of special interest for large-scale biotechnological processes because of their notable thermostability (Asgher *et al.*, 2007; Srivastava and Baruah, 1986).

The α-amylase produced in our study showed a broad temperature stability ranging from 25°C to 80°C with an optimum temperature of 55°C. Interestingly, at 80°C the enzyme activity dropped only by 18.7 per cent compared to 55°C. The optimum pH at which the enzyme showed highest activity was pH 5, suggesting that the enzyme functions well in an acidic environment. However, the broad range stability of this enzyme can be observed since only a drop of 8.8 per cent in activity is observed at pH 10.5 compared to pH 5. In industrial enzyme production the properties of α-amylase such as thermostability, pH profile and pH stability should be matched to its application. For example, starch processing industry requires the use of high temperature and low pH values (Asgher *et al.*, 2007) whereas, industries such as detergent manufacture may require enzymes that functions well at lower temperatures (from 25°C–55°C) and basic conditions (Grant *et al.*, 1990; Van Der Maarel *et al.*, 2002). The findings in this study suggest that amylase produced by *Bacillus subtilis* using cassava root extract as a raw material is suitable for low temperature (55°C) starch hydrolysis or brewing industries.

Cassava root extract used in this study confirmed that the cassava plant is a good raw material to be used in enzyme production by *Bacillus subtilis*. Indeed previous studies have used cassava starch as a substrate in fermentation processes (Okolo *et al.*, 1995). These studies focused mainly on using cassava starch as a raw material for ethanol production (Agu *et al.*, 1997; Nellaiah *et al.*, 1988). Few studies have focused on enzyme production using cassava root extract and to our knowledge this study is the first such report from Sri Lanka. Currently, superior varieties of cassava with improved qualities are available in the market. For example, a spontaneous polyploid in cassava has been discovered, with characteristics such as enormous vigour and variation in form of structure and a triploid has been developed known as super cassava (CGIAR, 2005). These varieties have double the yield of existing varieties. Developments have also been made to increase the ability to resist termites, reduce cyonagen capacity and to increase the tolerance towards droughts (CGIAR, 2005). Therefore, low cost of production (Approximately Sri Lanka Rupee 5.00/kg) and the robustness of the plant makes cassava an ideal raw material for industrial enzyme production.

5. CONCLUSION

Industrial enzymes are not produced in Sri Lanka because of high cost of production. This study shows cassava root extract could be used for α-amylase production by *Bacillus subtilis*. With its low production cost in Sri Lanka, compared to traditional crops such as wheat and rice, cassava could be considered as a low cost alternative for alpha amylase production. The results indicate that α-amylase produced could be used in broad range of applications. Further optimization in fermentation conditions, purification and characterization studies of the enzymes may lead to improving the potential to cost effectively produce these enzymes in Sri Lanka.

ACKNOWLEDGEMENTS

This work was supported by TG 11/51 Treasury Grant from the Government of Sri Lanka (S. G. S.)

REFERENCES

1. Agu, R., Amadife, A., Ude, C., Onyia, A., Ogu, E., Okafor, M. and Ezejiofor, E., 1997. Combined heat treatment and acid hydrolysis of cassava grate waste (CGW) biomass for ethanol production. Waste management, 17 (1), pp. 91-96.

2. Amoozegar, M., Malekzadeh, F. and Malik, K. A., 2003. Production of amylase by newly isolated moderate halophile, *Halobacillus* sp. strain MA-2. Journal of microbiological methods, 52 (3), pp. 353-359.

3. Asgher, M., Asad, M. J., Rahman, S. and Legge, R., 2007. A thermostable α-amylase from a moderately thermophilic *Bacillus subtilis* strain for starch processing. Journal of Food Engineering, 79 (3), pp. 950-955.

4. Bano, S., Ul Qader, S. A., Aman, A., Syed, M. N. and Azhar, A., 2011. Purification and characterization of novel alpha-amylase from *Bacillus subtilis* KIBGE HAS. AAPS PharmSciTech, 12 (1), pp. 255-261.

5. CGIAR, 2005. Research and Impact: Areas of Research: Cassava. The Consortium of International Agricultural Research Centers, http: //cgiar.bio-mirror.cn/impact/research/cassava.html (accessed 14 Nov. 2012)

6. Coronado, M. J., Vargas, C., Mellado, E., Tegos, G., Drainas, C., Nieto, J. J. and Ventosa, A., 2000. The α-amylase gene amyH of the moderate halophile *Halomonas meridiana*: cloning and molecular characterization. Microbiology, 146 (4), pp. 861-868.

7. Deutch, C., 2002. Characterization of a salttolerant extracellular α-amylase from Bacillus dipsosauri. Letters in applied microbiology, 35 (1), pp. 78-84.

8. DOASL, 2006. Cassava: *Manihot esculenta*. Crop Recommendations

9. http: //www.agridept.gov.lk/index.php/en/crop-recommendations/1456 (accessed 14 Nov. 2012)

10. Gale, M., Law, C., Chojecki, A. and Kempton, R., 1983. Genetic control of α-amylase production in wheat. TAG Theoretical and Applied Genetics, 64 (4), pp. 309-316.

11. Grant, W., Mwatha, W. and Jones, B., 1990. Alkaliphiles: ecology, diversity and applications. FEMS Microbiol Lett, 75 (2), pp. 255-269.

12. Gupta, R., Gigras, P., Mohapatra, H., Goswami, V. K. and Chauhan, B., 2003. Microbial α-amylases: a biotechnological perspective. Process Biochemistry, 38 (11), pp. 1599-1616.

13. Hutcheon, G. W., Vasisht, N. and Bolhuis, A., 2005. Characterisation of a highly stable α-amylase from the halophilic archaeon *Haloarcula hispanica*. Extremophiles, 9 (6), pp. 487-495.

14. Kirk, O., Borchert, T. V. and Fuglsang, C. C., 2002. Industrial enzyme applications. Current opinion in biotechnology, 13 (4), pp. 345-351.

15. Nahas, E. and Waldemarin, M. M., 2002. Control of amylase production and growth characteristics of *Aspergillus ochraceus*. Revista latinoamericana de Microbiologia, 44 (1), pp. 5-10.

16. Nellaiah, H., Karunakaran, T. and Gunasekaran, P., 1988. Ethanol fermentation of cassava starch by *Zymomonas mobilis* NRRL B-4286. Biomass, 15 (3), pp. 201-207.

17. Okolo, B. N., Ezeogu, L. I. and Mba, C. N., 1995. Production of raw starch digesting amylase by *Aspergillus niger* grown on native starch sources. Journal of the Science of Food and Agriculture, 69 (1), pp. 109-115.

18. Pandey, A., Nigam, P., Soccol, C., Soccol, V., Singh, D. and Mohan, R., 2000. Advances in microbial amylases. Biotechnology and Applied Biochemistry, 31 pp. 135-152.

19. Prakash, B., Vidyasagar, M., Madhukumar, M., Muralikrishna, G. and Sreeramulu, K., 2009. Production, purification, and characterization of two extremely halotolerant, thermostable, and alkali-stable α-amylases from *Chromohalobacter* sp. TVSP 101. Process Biochemistry, 44 (2), pp. 210-215.

20. Rajagopalan, G. and Krishnan, C., 2008. Optimization of medium and process parameters for a constitutive α amylase production from a catabolite derepressed *Bacillus subtilis* KCC103. Journal of Chemical Technology and Biotechnology, 83 (5), pp. 654-661.

21. Srivastava, R. and Baruah, J., 1986. Culture conditions for production of thermostable amylase by *Bacillus stearothermophilus*. Applied and environmental microbiology, 52 (1), pp. 179-184.

22. Tanyildizi, M. S., Özer, D. and Elibol, M., 2005. Optimization of α-amylase production by *Bacillus* sp. using response surface methodology. Process Biochemistry, 40 (7), pp. 2291-2296.

23. Tester, R., Qi, X. and Karkalas, J., 2006. Hydrolysis of native starches with amylases. Animal Feed Science and Technology, 130 (1), pp. 39-54.

24. Van Der Maarel, M. J. E. C., Van Der Veen, B., Uitdehaag, J. C. M., Leemhuis, H. and Dijkhuizen, L., 2002. Properties and applications of starch-converting enzymes of the a-amylase family. Journal of biotechnology, 94 (2), pp. 137-156.

Chapter 15

Research and Application of Biotechnology for Food Industry in Vietnam

*Do Thi Thuy Le**

Food Industries Research Institute (FIRI), Ministry of Industry and Trade, 301 Nguyen Trai Road, Thanhxuan District, Hanoi, Vietnam

ABSTRACT

During the last three decades, the biotechnology of Vietnam has been developed and has obtained significant achievements in constructing the infrastructure and research to achieve national goals and objectives for foodstuff processing, agriculture-forestry-fishery, human health care and environmental protection. Some traditional product like rice spirit, lactic fermented foods (tôm chua, nem chua), are very popular in Vietnam. They are produced by small enterprise, family households. These are research and application of purebred microorganisms for quality improvement of traditional rice spirit and fermented food by some projects. Application of enzymes for production of starch sugar, maltodextrin and oligosaccharides were studied. Maltodextrin and glucose are produce in industry scale. In the recent time, bioactive compounds and functional foods have been researched, but they are produced at pilot scale. This report defines the the latest achievements of biotechnology application for food industry in Vietnam.

Keywords: *Biotechnology, Food Industry, Traditional food, Fermented food, Enzyme, Function food.*

1. INTRODUCTION

In Vietnam, biotechnology has been identified as a prioritized technology to be developed. This stems from the fact that Vietnam is an agricultural country endowed

* E-mail: dothuyle@yahoo.com

with a wide range of biological natural resources, which could be usefully exploited as raw materials for agricultural and aqua cultural production, food processing, health services, pharmaceutical production and others. In 1994, Vietnamese government issued the Resolution N°18, namely "The development of Vietnam's Biotechnology up to the year 2010" with the view to build up a developed biotechnology industry, which are able to produce biotech products enough for domestic users as well as for exports [7].

1.1 Current Status of the Biotechnology Application in Food Industry in Vietnam

In the food industry, through the use of microorganisms; enzyme and protein, fermentation technologies, the starch sugar, glucose syrup, maltose syrup, maltodextrin, etc. were produced and provided the needs for foodstuff processing; the traditional fermentation processes were developed and improved; the methods and Kits in orders to detect pathogenic microbes and poisons in materials and foods were constructed and developed; some of microbial enzymes, bioactive compounds and functional foods were studied in laboratories and produced at the pilot – plant scale.

With the support of Vietnam Government through National Biotechnology Programs, the human resource and research capacity for development of biotechnology in food industry are being improved.

However, some of the products including enzymes, amino acids, vitamins, organic acids, etc. used for food industry are only produced by foreign invested sector or import from developed countries due requirement for high initial capital investments, high-quality technical expertise, imported large-scale fermentation and downstream systems for microbial products.

1.2. Achievement of Biotechnology Application for Food Industry

Research and Application of Microorganisms for Quality Improvement of Traditional Rice Spirit and Fermented Foods

In Vietnam, traditional foods using natural microorganisms through fermentation process such as traditional rice spirit, lactic fermented foods have been very popular since ancient times. Traditional fermentation processes used in the production of these foods are uncontrolled and are dependent on microorganisms from the environment or the fermentation substrate for initiation of the fermentation process. Such processes, therefore, result in products of low yield and variable quality. The traditional rice spirit is manufactured in the village at home – scale or by local small business manufacturing with unique technology giving special spirits with specialty flavors for each locality. However, the technology has many disadvantages such as the quality of spirit depends primarily on the quality of solid – state in tablet form (Banh men), fermentation and distillation. Banh men are made mostly by experience, selected Banh men of the first batch are used for the following batch, and the enzyme activity of starter is often low, unstable, infected with a variety of complex microbes. This leads to the quality of spirit being uneven and does not guarantee food safety and hygiene. In order to promote the traditional spirit of Vietnam, the solutions are: improvement of the quality of Banhmen, and application of purebred mold product instead of Banh men. The technology process for production of purebred mold product of *Aspergillus niger* having cell concentration 10^8 CFU/gram and the use in traditional rice spirit was established [2, 7] (Table 15.1).

Table 15.1: Research and Application of Purebred Microorganisms for Quality Improvement of Traditional Rice Spirit and Fermented Foods.

Products	*Microorganisms for Pure Bred Starter*	*Application Scale*
Rice spirit	"Banh men" with addition of some pure microbes having high enzyme activity *(Endomycopsis fibuliger, Aspergillus oryzae, Rhizopus sp., Mucor sp., Saccharomyces cerevisiae)*	Family households; Small–Medium Enterprises
	Aspergillus niger (10^8 cfu/g product); Use 10 g/kg raw material	
Sour shrimp (Tom chua)	*Lactobacillus plantarum* NCDN4; Use 10^4 cfu/g raw material	Family households
Fermented sour sausage (Nem chua)	*Lactobacillus plantarum* NCDN4; Use 10^4 cfu/g raw material	Family households

Lactic fermented foods constitute an important role in traditional Vietnamese fermented foods with popular products including sour shrimp and fermented sour sausage. The presence of lactic bacteria plays an important role in metabolizing components in the raw materials into foods having high nutritional value, delicious flavor and better characteristics. Lactic acid bacteria reduce the pH of the mixture through which they inhibit and significantly reduce the development of complex bacterial infections.

Fermented sour shrimp (Tom chua) is a famous traditional fermented food in Vietnam, specially in Hue city. This product is usually made by small – scale producers in the traditional manner. Materials used for producing sour shrimp are raw shrimp, vegetable (chili, garlic, galingale), cooked – sticky rice, salt. Because the fermented sour shrimp is produced by manual methods, the quality of the product depends entirely upon environmental conditions and microorganisms available in nature. The production process has many potential hazard to food safety and hygiene and it is difficult to implement it at a large scale.

To create the sour shrimp products with stable, ensuring quality, hygiene and food safety, and technological process for production of starter lactic bacteria and using it into fermentation stage has been studied in Food Industries Research Institute and other institutions and universities. Sour shrimp fermentation process with additional purebred lactic bacteria strains is as follows: The ratio of rice is 50 – 70 per cent of the weight of shrimp, salt 10 per cent, fermentation temperature 30 – 35°C, the ratio of mixing lactic bacteria 10-10^4 CFU/gram [2,4,7]. The fermentation technology for sour shrimp was trained and transferred to many sister owners in Hue city and Quang Binh, Quang Tri provinces.

Table 15.2: Research and Application of Enzymes for Food Industry [2].

Products	*Material*	*Used Enzymes*	*Produce Scale*
Fructooligosaccharides (FOS)	Sucrose	Fructosyltransferase (FTS)	Pilot plant
Xylooligosaccharides (XOS)	Xylan in conrncob	Xylanase	Pilot plant
Galactooligosaccharides (GOS)	Lactose	β-galactosidase	Laboratory
Isomaltooligosacchrides	Cassava starch	Maltogenic amylase	Pilot–plant
Fructose syrup 42 per cent	Cassava starch	Spezyme Prime 42 (Genencor, USA)	Pilot–plant
Glucose	Cassava starch	α-amylase, glucoamylase	Industrial scale
Maltodextrin	Cassava starch	Amylase (Termamyl SP, Novodisk, Denmark); SEBstar – HTL (USA)	Industrial scale

The purebred of *Lactobacillus platarum* NCDN4 strain, which produces heat stable bacteriocins having molecular weight between 14.3 and 20kDa was used as starter for fermented sour sausage (Nem chua) and sour shrimp (Tom chua) with dosage of 10^4 CFU/gram raw material [4]. The results showed the advantage of application of this starter in terms of food hygiene and microbial indicators of the studied products.

Application of Enzymes for Production of Starch Sugar, Maltodextrin and Oligosaccharides

The food processing industry is currently the largest consumer of enzymes. Enzymes are widely applied as processing aids in the food and beverage industry. Nowadays, in Vietnam, Manioc becomes an industrial tree and Vietnam's cassava starch export production capacity is still being pushed up to the third in the world export ranking. The enzymatic modification of cassava starch can produce glucose, glucose syrup, maltose syrup, high fructose syrup, maltodextrin, cyclodextrin and oligosaccharides, etc. Maltodextrin is produced by the application of α-amylase with different molecular weights and have been used in wide range of application. Maltodextrin is produced at the small industrial scale by Minhduong Food Processing Join Stock Company (Hanoi, Vietnam) and used in food processing to produce many kinds of food products such as functional food, baby food, snack milk food and milk products, fruit juice flavors, instant drinking products, etc.

Fructooligosaccharides (FOS), are synthesized by the enzyme fructosyltransferase (FTS) of the fungus *Aspergillus* sp. acting on sucrose. Galactooligosaccharides (GOS), which also can be synthesized by enzyme from. FOS, GOS are available as nutritional supplements in capsules, tablets, and as a powder.

Using enzyme technologies, many food products and oligosaccharides were investigated and developed (some examples are given in Table 15.2).

Research and Application of Enzymes and Microorganisms for Production Bioactive Compounds and Functional Foods

Today, in Vietnam, due to development of molecular biological tools and protein engineering, several strains of microorganisms have been selected to increase the efficiency in producing enzymes at laboratory scale (Table 15.3).

In addition, through microbial fermentation process and enzymatic technology, various bioactive components such as food ingredients, nutritive supplements, food processing aids and functional foods were and are developed (Table 15.4).

2. CONCLUSION

The Vietnamese government has a number of scientific programmes on biotechnology in food processing, but the efficiency is still low and can not meet the needs of society. Vietnam has to research the creation of advanced biotechnology in the country, production in industrial scale enzyme products (including recombinant enzymes), the microbial products, and bioactive compound response needs to develop processing industries.

Table 15.3: Microbial Enzymes were Studied and Produced in Laboratory Scale [1,4,7].

Sl.No.	*Enzyme*	*Microorganisms*
1.	Fructosyltransferase (FTS)	*Aspergillus flavipes* VVTP84
2.	Pectinase	*Aspergillus awamori* L1
3.	Glucooxydase	*Aspergillus niger*
4.	β–galactosidase	*Aspergillus oryzae*
5.	Fibrinolytic enzyme	*Bacillus subtilis, Aspergillus oryzae*
6.	Lipase	Lipase genes from *Ralstonia* sp. M1 (AY 364601) and *Geotrichum candidum* DTQ -26.3 (EF061458) were expressed in *E.coli* BL21 (DE3) and *Pichia pastoris*
7.	β–glucanase	β – glucanase from *Aspergillus niger* VTCC – F021 (GU445334) was over-expressed in *Pichia pastoris* GS115
8.	Xylannase	Genes encoding a xylanase from *Aspergillus niger* DMS1957 (xylanase A: EU848304, xylanase B: EU848405) and *Aspergillus oryzae* VTCC-F187 (xylanase G2: EU848307) were over-expressed in *Pichia pastoris* and *Aspergillus niger* VTCC-F017)

Table 15.4: Using Microorganisms and Enzymes to Research and Produce of Bioactive Compounds and Functional Foods [3,4,6,7].

Sl.No.	*Products*	*Microorganisms/Enzymes*	*Production scale*
1.	Food pigments	*Blakeslea trispora, Monascus purpureus*	Pilot–sclae
2.	Bacteriocins	*Lactobacillus plantarum, Lactococcus* sp.	Pilot–sclae
3.	Angiotensin Converting Enzyme Inhibitory Peptides	*Fermented milk by Lactobacillus bulgaricus* and *Saccharomyces cerevisiae* Green bean protein hydrolyzed by Papain	Pilot–sclae
4.	Chromium enriched yeast	*Saccharomyces cerevisiae*	Pilot–sclae
5.	Isoflavon form soybean	Converted glucosid isoflavone to aglucone isoflavone by β – glucoside (Sumizyme FP)	Pilot–sclae

In the next stage, Vietnam needs application of modern biotechnology in industrial processing and access and rapid development of modern biotechnology to create new strains of good quality, performance fermentation and stability in industrial production of recombinant enzymes.

Need to strengthen the research and application in food processing to promote value-added processing industry to meet the target by 2020. Biotechnology is expected to contribute to over 40 per cent of the total contributions of science and technology in Vietnam.

ACKNOWLEDGMENT

I deeply thank my Advisor, Assoc. Prof. Dr. Nguyen Thi Hoai Tram for the help, support and advice.

REFERENCES

1. Abstract of Asian Core Program (2009-2013) "Nest – Generation Bioproduction Platform Leveraging Subtropical Microbial Bioresources", October 14-15, 2010, Hanoi, Vietnam.
2. Proceedings of the International Workshop on "Agricultural and Bio-system Engineering". December, 8-9, 2009 Hanoi, Vietnam:
3. Proceedings of the 11th Asean Food Conference 2009 "Food Science and Technology: Innovative Approaches and Opportunities for Global Market". October 21-23, 2009, Bandar Seri Begawan, Brunei Darusalam.
4. Proceedings of the National Conference on Biotechnology 2009 "Biotechnology in Agro-Forestry and Aquaculture, in industry and food and feed processing industry, in medicine and Pharmacy, and in Environment protection". November 26-27, 2009, Thai Nguyen, Vietnam.
5. Proceedings of the 4th National Scientific Conference on "Biochemistry and Molecular Biology for Agriculture, Biology, Medicine and Food Industry". October 15-17, 2008, Hanoi, Vietnam.
6. Proceeding of the 10th Asean Food Conference 2007 "Food for mankind – Contribution of Science and Technology". August 21-23, 2007, Kuala Lumpur, Malaysia.
7. Asean–Russia Workshop on The modern food biotechnology, 2011, Vietnam.

Chapter 16

Status of Biotechnology in Zimbabwe: Towards a More Sustainable Biotechnology Era in Zimbabwe

Muvhunzi Faith[*1] and Mufandaedza Jonathan*[2]*

[1]National biotechnology Authority of Zimbabwe, Zimbabwe
[2]Department of Faculty of Science, Great Zimbabwe University, Masvingo, Zimbabwe

ABSTRACT

This paper highlights the current status of biotechnology in Zimbabwe with respect to research, development, applications and management. The management of biotechnology and related modern technologies such as nanobiotechnologies is the responsibility of the National Biotechnology Authority (NBA). However the national adoption of biotechnology opens an era of opportunities for Zimbabwe to transform it's largely raw material based agro-economy to a more knowledge based industrial economy. A rapid and sustained social and economic transformation of Zimbabwean economy was anticipated given the perceived potential of the technology to address most of the economic, social and environmental problems. However a lot more challenges hampered this rapid application of technology in Zimbabwe. At the centre of this review are the national biotechnology policies which serve as the guiding framework for any future research and applications and the significant roles of agencies and stakeholder with view towards the improvement of public sector implementation of biotechnology research. Additionally these institutions have a fundamental role to provide public understanding and knowledge of biotechnology. Currently several research groups have adopted modern biotechnology techniques and tools. Universities

* E-mail: faithmuvhunzi@gmail.com

and public research institutes have dominated biotechnology research particularly in crop improvement and food biotechnology industries. However the use of enzymes biotechnologies in wastewater treatment with view to upscale biogas and biofuels production from municipal, industrial and agricultural waste is still in its infancy. Challenges including low adoption of modern biotechnology and limited funding have been identified as the major setbacks.

Keywords: *Biotechnology, Nanobiotechnology, Modern biotechnology, Agro-economy, Biofuels.*

1. INTRODUCTION AND BACKGROUND

The ever declining agricultural productivity coupled with climate change and the insistent increase in the population has put great pressure on the global food basket hence threatening food security. Conventional breeding techniques are however time consuming and not quite as specific as should be. This challenge therefore calls for another set of techniques which can address the need for improved crop varieties to meet the demand rate.

Biotechnology is one of the most important and technological revolutions of this century and has greatly influenced various aspects of human life. The new tools of biotechnology offer great potential for improvement in the agricultural sector, including horticultural plantation crops and forest trees in a timely and more precise manner. Some of the solutions offered by biotechnology have included crops resistant to pests and diseases, tolerance to herbicides and environmental stresses and also some whose nutritional content has been fortified.

The Zimbabwean government realized the great potential of biotechnology in increasing land productivity and hence was urged to put in place an institutional framework for harnessing biotechnology to address challenges in agriculture, health, provision of energy, cleaning the environment, promoting industrial development, creating employment and growing export receipts. Consequently by 1998 the National Biosafety Framework was put in place. Since then, the government has made concerted efforts in building human and infrastructural capacity; source funds for research and development and strengthening biotechnology governance and regulatory frameworks. Additionally efforts have been put towards increasing public awareness and education on issues relating to biotechnology and biosafety and encouraging investment in biotechnology R&D through public-private sector partnerships.

1.1. Definition of Biotechnology

In simple terms, biotechnology can be defined as any set of techniques that uses living organisms to make goods and services to meet human needs. The UN Convention on Biological Diversity scientifically defines Biotechnology as: any technological application that uses biological systems, living organisms, or derivatives thereof, to make or modify products or processes for specific use (article 2). The technologies are mainly classified as either Conventional biotechnology or Morden biotechnology.

1.2. Conventional Biotechnology

Conventional Biotechnology or rather traditional Biotechnology refers to early techniques used to produce new products or modify existing ones. These techniques archived the development and or modifications at the organism level rather than at the molecular level. Techniques involved include composting, fermentation, and drug and vaccine development. Traditional biotechnology has been in application since time immemorial to make or modify existing products, for instance brewing of beer and turning milk to yoghurt. Mankind has used selective breeding to collect wild plants for cultivation and wild animals for domestication since ancient times.

With the advent of technology, innovation and discovery, these skills have greatly improved over several years and generations to achieve desired traits. Consequently mankind learned to control the natural processes that occur within living cells and scaling them up from domestic to largely industrial applications and products.

1.3. Modern Biotechnology

Modern biotechnology refers to techniques and applications that are achieved at a molecular or genetic level in a predictable and controlled environment. Examples of modern biotechnology include recombinant DNA technologies *i.e.* genetic transformation and mutagenesis.

According to the Chemical Heritage Foundation, the field of modern biotechnology is generally thought of as having been born in 1971 when Paul Berg's (Stanford) experiments in gene splicing had early success. Herbert W. Boyer (Univ. Calif. at San Francisco) and Stanley N. Cohen (Stanford) significantly advanced the new technology in 1972 by transferring genetic material into a bacterium, such that the imported material would be reproduced. However some scientists like Verma AS *et al.* (2011) believe that the discovery in 1953 by JD Watson and FHC Crick for the first time cleared the mysteries around the DNA as a genetic material and hence paved the path for modern biotechnology and to its current status.

Advances in information and communication technologies and other sciences like biochemistry, bioinformatics, physiology and nanotechnology have opened up the possibilities for new applications of biotechnology which were previously unheard of in traditional biotechnology. Knowledge of the genes and cells being transformed has greatly reduced the time required to obtain similar results with traditional biotechnology, consequently modern biotechnology has found applications in various other sectors of human influence other than food production such as the environment (bioremediation); human and animal health (vaccine development, gene therapy and diagnostics) and energy (biofuels).

2. BIOTECHNOLOGY IN ZIMBABWE

Zimbabwe regards biotechnology as a very useful science capable of making a significant contribution to national economic and social development, through its application in agriculture, human health, environmental management and industrial processes. As such the National Science and Technology Policy emphasizes the need for the country to embrace biotechnology, develop its own capacity to utilize the science and also ensure that the application of modern biotechnology do not compromise human health and environmental quality.

In June 2012, the Ministry of Science and Technology Development (MSTD) launched its Second Science and Technology Policy, a decade after the initial one. The policy underscored the need to adopt an innovative approach focusing at the emerging technologies in biological science like biotechnology and nanotechnology for national development. It stipulated the need to strengthen research aimed at optimising manufacturing processes through the use of biotechnology and also to exploit the biodiversity using biotechnology processes. It further indicated nanotechnology as a potential enabling engine for development of products with significantly improved properties such as durability, efficiency and precision hence the focus on nanobiotechnology.

Industrial biotechnology involves the application of biotechnology for industrial purposes, including manufacturing, alternative energy (or "bioenergy"), and biomaterials. Inevitably, because of its crosscutting nature, industrial biotechnology tends to overlap other fields of biotechnology like pharmaceutical biotechnology, food biotechnology, environmental and agricultural biotechnology. Hence, Industrial biotechnology, particularly the development of large-scale bioenergy refineries, will likely involve dedicated genetically modified crops as well as the large-scale bioprocessing and fermentation in some pharmaceutical production.

2.1. Biotechnology Applications in Zimbabwe

Biotechnology techniques and applications in Zimbabwe range from traditional tools, modern agricultural biotechnology and applications in industry, environment, food and agriculture. The economy is mainly agrarian and hence biotechnology research is mainly biased towards agricultural biotechnology, mainly to address food security issues through disease resistance and drought tolerance. However, in recent years, the research focus has spread to other fields which include improving manufacturing techniques, clean energy production, vaccine development and environmental management. These constitute most of what is industrial biotechnology in Zimbabwe.

2.2. Industrial Biotechnology in Zimbabwe

Applications in this sector vary from industry to industry but are all currently applying the traditional and basic application of biotechnology. This includes the use of enzymes to enhance natural biochemical processes. There is virtually no application of modern techniques like genetic manipulation of enzymes used in the various processes. Importation of genetically manipulated organisms may boost production of various products.

One most important player who is focusing on this sector and others that includes the environmental sector in carrying out research is the Food and Biomedical Technology Institute (FBTI) under the Science and Industrial Research and Development Centre (SIRDC). The Food and Biomedical Technology Institute (FBTI) was established in the year 2002 as an autonomous technical department of the SIRDC. Previously housed under the Biotechnology Research Institute, the FBTI has been mandated to undertake focused research and development to rejuvenate growth and sustainable expansion in the food and biochemical industries and to discover new compounds and techniques of pharmaceutical and medical importance through scientific and technological exploration of Zimbabwe's vast biodiversity. Other players in this sector are those in the food industry and even these mainly focus on quality control of the products they manufacture. Examples include Dairibord of Zimbabwe, Cairns foods, Nestle and brewing companies such as Chibuku, Natbrew and Ingwebu to mention a few. The mentioned and many others are only using traditional approaches to try to improve their various processes like the use of enzymes to enhance natural biochemical processes.

2.2.1. Simple Sugars from Starch

Glucose can be made from maize cheaply but glucose is less sweet and less soluble than fructose. Enzymes can be used to isomerise the glucose to fructose, which is commercially used in the confectionery industry. Some fermentation processes are also being employed in the brewing and dairy industry *e.g.* in the production of sour milk and yoghurt in the dairy industry.

2.2.2. ATP Bioluminescence

This technique is particularly used in some breweries and other food industries as a means of assessing and controlling plant hygiene. It involves detection of ATP (assumed to be of microbial origin). Various commercial kits are available for this type of assay.

2.2.3. In Beer Maturation

Diacetyl is a product of the yeast in the biosynthesis of the amino acid valine. It arises spontaneously from alpha-acetolactic acid. Yeasts and other microorganisms produce more acetolactate that can be converted into valine. As a result the acetolactate is released into the beer where it is shortly converted into vicinyl diketone-Diacetyl. This compound is later on taken up by yeast cells and degraded via acetone to butanediol. The degradation of acetolactate can be accelerated by shunting it directly to acetoin without formation of diacetyl by adding appropriate amounts of the enzyme acetolate decarboxylase isolated and purified from bacterial sources.

2.2.4. Immobilised Cells

In this technology yeast cells are immobilized on a bed used to ferment wort to beer in a continuous rather than batch production. This is particularly applied in continuous fermentation of low alcohol beer and continuous diacetyl removal and some waste water treatment plants. These are usually on sintered glass, ceramic cells, Diethylaminoethyl cellulose (DEAE C) systems and ceramic membrane separation. The main advantage of immobilised cell systems is high productivity rates and high efficiency.

2.2.5. Waste Treatment

The key technology is the use of anaerobic digestion of low soluble organic matter content effluent to yield methane and a low Biochemical Oxygen Demand

Table 16.1: Summary of Potential Industrial Enzymes and Carbohydrates Isolated in Zimbabwe.

Types of Enzymes	*Source*	*Potential Industrial Applications*	*References*
Proteases			
Serine proteases	*Bacillus subtillis* CHZ1 (hot springs)	Food, detergent industry	Zvidzayi and Zvauya, 2001
Cellulases			
Endo-β-1,4 glucanase	*Bacillus* species (hot springs)	Hydrolysis of cellulotic biomass	Mawadza *et al.,* 1996
Cellulases	*Bacillus* species (hot springs)	Hydrolysis of cellulotic biomass	Mawadza *et al.*, 2000
Endo-β-1,4 glucanase	*Bacillus* species (hot springs)	Hydrolysis of cellulotic biomass	Zvauya and zvidzai, 1995; zvidzai *et al.,* 2
Cellulase	*Aureobasidium pullulans*	Hydrolysis of cellulotic biomass	Kudanga and Mwenje, 2005
Polygalacturonase Endo-β-1,4 glucannase	Capnodium isolates	Food industry	Mwenje and Mguni
xylanase	*Bacillus* species (Indigenous fruits)	Pulp and paper, food manufacturing	Chivero *et al.,* 2001b
Polygalacturonase	Zimbabwean wild fruits	Food industry	Muchuweti *et al.,* 2005
Lipases			
Lipase	*Vernonia galamensis*	transestrification	Ncube *et al.,* 1995, Ncube and Read 1995
Lipase	*Jatropha curcas L*	Hydrolysis of triglycerides	Staubmann *et al.,* 1999
Esterases	*Aureobasidium pullulans*	Food detergent pharmaceutical industries	Kudanga *et al.,* 20007
Polysaccharides			
Mucilage	*Dicerocaryum zanguebarium* (ruredzo)	Food industry (emulsification)	Benhura and Mavhudzi, 1996; Benhura and Marume, 1993a, 19993b, Benhura and Mavhudzi, 19996, Benhura ad Marume, 2006
polysaccharide	*Cordia abyssinica*	Food industry (emulsification)	Behura and Chidewe, 2002; Benhura and Katayi-Chidehwe, 2002

(BOD) effluent usually on an immobilised biomass reactor or in a large reactor buffer tank. The key outcome desired is elimination of chemical oxygenation demand which is one of the key criteria used by local authorities for determination of payable levies for effluent. Chibuku breweries have such a plant operating. This technology could be used in dairy and meat industry effluent as well.

Significant research has been explored for new potential enzymes from various sources within the country as reviewed by Pawarira (2008) a summarised in Table 16.1. The potential target benefits include food production efficiency; reduced consumption of energy, water and raw materials; improved quality and efficiency of production; reduced generation of waste and environmental pollutants; bulk reduction and inevitably cost reduction.

2.3. Environmental Biotechnology

In Zimbabwe, biotechnology has the potential to contribute to national development if applied in water purification, waste water management at lower cost, production of bio-pesticides for weed control and energy production. There is a serious need to encourage research which focuses on current and future environmental problems. Table 16.2 shows a summary of environmental biotechnology research in Zimbabwe.

Table 16.2: Summary of Environmental Biotechnology Research in Zimbabwe.

Area/Techniques	*Application*	*References*
Aerobic digestion	Treatment of opaque beer Undergraduate	Pawarira *et al.*, 2005
Anaerobic digestion	Biogas production from agricultural waste	Pawarira 2004, Pawarira *et al.*, 2004, 2006
Anaerobic digestion	Potato processing waste water	Pawarira 2006, Manhokwe *et al.*, 2009
Anaerobic digestion	Treatmet of opaque beer brewery water	Zvauya *et al.*, 1994
Biological nutrient removal	Municipal waste water treatment	Makaya *et al.*, 2007
Duck weed system	Municipal waste water treatment	Nhapi *et al.*, 2003
Fungal degradation	Decolouration of textile dyes waste water	Tekere *et al.*, 2001a
Fungal degradation	Decolouration of textile dyes waste water	Nyanhongo *et al.*, 2002
Fungal degradation	Decolouration of textile dyes waste water	Muzariri *et al.*, 2001
Fungal degradation	Bioremediation of PAH contaminated soils	Tekere *et al.*, 2005

Source: Pawarira and Khosa 2009.

2.4. Food Biotechnology in Zimbabwe

Food biotechnology is widely used in Zimbabwe's food industries especially in the production of milk products, alcoholic beverages and mushrooms. The technology is seen to be very useful especially with regards to improving the livelihoods of the Zimbabwean community. The techniques used are the traditional fermentation processes that have been used in the production of beer, wine, bread and milk products.

The fermentation processes employed are mediated by naturally occurring microorganisms which include properly identified and selected bacteria and yeast cells. Tissue culturing is another biotechnology used in food biotechnology in Zimbabwe in the production of mushrooms. Table 16.3 shows the extent to which biotechnology is being applied in the food industry.

Table 16.3: Application of Food Biotechnology in Zimbabwe.

Sector	*Examples of Major Players*	*Technique Employed*	*Products Manufactured*
Dairy	Dairiboard Zimbabwe Limited, Kefalos, Dendairy	Fermentation	Sour milk, Yoghurt, and cheese
Brewing	Natbrew and Chibuku	Fermentation	Clear and opaque beer
Winery	AFDIS and Mukuyu wineries	Fermentation	Wine and spirits
Bakery	Proton bakeries and Bakers Inn	Fermentation	Bread and cakes
Mushroom	Biotechnology Research Institute	Tissue culturing	Mushrooms

There is a steady growth in the number of players who are involved in biotechnology, but operating at different levels of production, especially in the dairy industry. This development has seen the creation of employment for the locals and an increased supply of biotechnology products. In terms of economic contribution of food biotechnology products, there is a significant contribution that is realised through the local market and exports of some of the products to the regional markets.

Through research and development, food biotechnology can be applied in the production of a wide range of food products that can be important for food security. Food biotechnology plays the role of increasing the value of agricultural products, enhancing the nutritional quality of foods and decreasing the cost of production. It has the potential to address the challenges of food security and food safety facing the developing world. Of importance to note are the potential adverse effects that the technology may have on human health or the environment. This means that safety aspects of food biotechnology must be taken into consideration to ensure that maximum benefits are derived while minimising the potential adverse effects that may come with the technology.

2.5. Nanobiotechnology in Zimbabwe

The world's industrial architects have, in recent years, shifted their attention to a more efficient, economic and space saving technology- nanotechnology. Consequently nanotechnology has found application in material science, ICT and even biotechnology as smaller becomes better. Zimbabwe has recently experienced an increase in the number of scientists, young and old, who are developing interest in nanotechnology. Consequently the Ministry of Science and Technology Development (MSTD) launched the Zimbabwe National Nanotechnology Programme recently in October 2012. The programme encourages research and development and management schemes.

Table 16.4: Food Biotechnology Research in Zimbabwe.

Type of Food	*Aspects of Food Addressed*	*References*
Fermented milk		
Sour milk (Mukaka wakakora)	General properties, microbiological and biochemical processes, safety, starter cultures	Mutukumira 1995, Mufandaedza *et al.,* 2006, Feresu 1992
Cereal based fermented foods		
Mahewu (on-alcoholic beverage)	General properties, microbiological processes and safety of traditionally prepared mahewu, anti-nutritional properties	Mutasa and Ayebo 1983, Dhlamini *et al.,* 2007
Chibuku (alcoholic beverage)	Extension of shelf life	Kutyauripo *et al.,* 2009
Fermented Wild Fruits Products		
Mukumbi (marula fruits)	General properties, microbiological and biochemical processes	Madovi 1981, Okagbue 1995, Zvauya *et al.,* 1997
Masau wine	General properties, microbiological and biochemical processes	Trdgold, 1986 Nyanga *et al.,* 2007
Food Safety		
Bioassay of bacteriocins	Rapid detection of bacteriocins in foods	Magochi *et al.*, 2001
Characterisation of bacteriocin AMA-K	Identification of antimicrobial properties of fermented milk	Todrov *et al.,* 2007

2.6. Energy Biotechnology in Zimbabwe

Energy supply in Zimbabwe is a major problem affecting all walks of life. The extensive use of fire wood has led to deforestation while the national electricity supply is far too low to meet the nations demands; hence production capacity is failing to meet consumption level. As of 2001, Zimbabwe had 30 billion tonnes of coal in 21 know deposits, however, coal is non-renewable and will be depleted. Hence the way to go has been renewable energy. Hydropower is the main power supply in the Zimbabwe.

Over the recent years government has made efforts to move towards more sustainable biomass utilisation strategies for green fuels and other renewable energy generation. This has consequently led to the promotion of various projects, though in their infancy, which have strong government support. Examples include *Jatropha cacus* by Finealt Engineering which has produced Biodisel and other associated by products; Ethanol by Green Fuel which has resulted in E10, a blend between petroleum and ethanol.Biogas has been in the pipelines for some time now and a lot of research has been carried out but implementation has not been significant. Energy biotechnology seems to be the best way to go these days especially with the advent of climate change and exhaustion of energy reserves. Zimbabwe acknowledges the potential in adoption energy biotechnologies by training several scientists in the field, and allowing several research projects on energy generation, however the issue of inadequate funding ad resources hamper progress.

3. MANAGEMENT OF BIOTECHNOLOGY IN ZIMBABWE

Zimbabwe is one of two countries in the region with an operational biosafety framework with legal mechanisms for biosafety which ensures the safe and effective development and applications of biotechnology. A well-functioning regulatory system can instil confidence in the public that the risk assessment used to evaluate biotechnologies are science-based, as stated under Article 15 and Annex III of the Cartagena Protocol on Biosafety (Convention on Biological Diversity (CBD) Secretariat, 2000). Zimbabwe is a signatory to the Cartagena Biosafety Protocol, an addendum to the Convention on Biodiversity, which governs safety in biotechnology.

The Government of Zimbabwe has implemented several strategies in support of biotechnology. To begin with was the Research Council of Zimbabwe (RCZ) with one of its primary goals being to formulate policy guidelines for the use of biotechnology for crop and livestock improvement and expansion of the genetic base. Several initiatives for capacity building in biotechnology research and biosafety were rolled out resulting in several masters and post-doctoral graduate students and the setting up if the Biotechnology Research Institute (BRI) under the SIRDC. The broad priority areas identified for the BRI are; development of commercial-scale micropropagation systems for important vegetatively propagated crops (sweet potato, Irish potato and cassava) which are primarily grown by smallholders farmers; research into applied plant and animal genetics designed to supplement conventional plant and animal improvement techniques, particularly crop varieties for the resource-poor farmers; develop expertise and techniques in food processing; development of new diagnostic tools and vaccines for animal and human health; and to take the initiative in adapting biotechnology to local needs and applications (Pawarira and Khosa, 2009).

Emphasis on biotechnology started in 1992, with the Special Programme on Biotechnology which led to the Biotechnology Forum (BF) being formed in 1992 which lead to the national planning in biotechnology in Zimbabwe (Falconi, 1999). After identified priorities by the BF, the Zimbabwe Biotechnology Advisory Committee (ZIMBAC) was established in 1996 and its mandate was to advise the government and the Dutch supported special programs on developing agricultural biotechnology through identification, management and implementation of high priority projects.

In 1998, the Research Act was amended for provide for the management of potentially harmful technologies and undertakings. In 2000 the Research (Biosafety) Regulations were developed and gazetted and the Biosafety Board was established. National policy on biotechnology and its safe use was developed in 2005. Consequently in 2005, the Government through the National Policy on Biotechnology agreed to allocate 0.5 per cent of GDP towards biotechnology research, development, application and regulation. To reinforce the policy framework, a new law establishing the National Biotechnology Authority into place – the National Biotechnology Authority Act [*Cap 14: 31*] was gazette. The NBA Act of 2006 replaced the Research Amendment Act of 1998 and repealed the Research (Biosafety) Regulations of 2000. The Act is administered by the Minister of Science and Technology Development through the National Biotechnology Authority (NBA) in which the Biosafety Board has been incorporated. The mandate of the NBA is to support and manage biotechnology, research, development and application in Zimbabwe; to ensure safety and security in the development and deployment of biotechnology in all fields of human development including crop research; and to advise government on all aspects concerning the development, production, use, application and release of products of biotechnology and ensures that such activities are done in accordance with the provisions of the NBA Act.

Like most developing countries, however, the capacity of the regulatory body to asses environmental ad food safety risks ad approve the release of transgenic is quite limited. Food safety and biosafety assessments are expensive and require extensive laboratory, contained filed / greenhouse and commercial scale experiments. This lack of biosafety capacity in developing countries is a major constraint to the transfer of modern biotechnology thus limiting the potential of countries to benefit from the benefits promised by the technology. At the same time, unregulated movements of modern biotechnology products into countries continues to become more of a reality thus placing more pressure on regulatory authorities.

Zimbabwe, however, has the human expertise to implement the biosafety regulations and has some laboratories with the capacity to detect genetically engineered organisms. The development of plans and policies to guide the evolution of biotechnology in Zimbabwe has been made successful because of the high level of expertise in issues of science and technology policy of her scientists. In Zimbabwe, there was still a critical mass of trained scientists who fully understand biotechnology issues and can knowledgeably contribute to the debate on the development and introduction of genetically modified organisms since more than 80 Master and Doctoral postgraduate students have been trained in various aspects of biotechnology. There has also been a favourable political will which allowed and guided a harmonious interaction between science and technology activities and institutions on the one hand and the regulatory system on the other.

Nevertheless, over the past decade, the nation has experienced a great exodus of its trained scientists who left for greener pastures and well-equipped laboratories in the SADC region and abroad. This has hampered progress in many scientific institutions with the regulatory body not being spared. With the recent stabilisation of the economy, there has been, however, a return of some of these experts, be it ever slowly.

3.1. Challenges to Biotechnology Adoption and Implementation in Zimbabwe

In as much as biotechnology research and development holds much prospect for Zimbabwe's social and economic development, there are several constraints to its full application. As biotechnology industries are knowledge- and resource-intensive, two of the major drivers of its growth are effective and sustainable research and development and innovations (Gastrow, 2008). Poor infrastructure, and funding (from national and international sources) are considered to be stifling sustainable biotechnology research and development in Zimbabwe. Whether a country is an innovator in biotechnology or whether it adapts technology developed elsewhere, modern biotechnology is associated with high development costs and getting involved will entail new investments in research infrastructure, training and management for research institutes personnel. Biotechnology is a rapidly growing and changing endeavour, and capacity and investments must adjust accordingly.

Development of trained personnel in biotechnology was initiated at University of Zimbabwe which has been offering an M.Sc. degree in Biotechnology since 1991. However, the programme had since collapsed after donors withdrew funding but is now trying to make a comeback in 2013. To date several tertiary institutions have taken up biotechnology offering it as either a diploma (National University of Science and Technology) or as a bachelor's degree (Chinhoyi University of Technology, 2005 and Harare Institute of Technology). As much as more trained graduates are being churned out of universities as a result of adoption of biotechnology by research institutes, there is still strong need to improve human and resource capacity to drive the research and development if Zimbabwe is to benefit from biotechnology.

While adequate infrastructure is a critical factor for the advancement of biotechnological research and development, there is need for industry to fully adopt the technology as well. Adoption of biotechnology by industry will enable injection of funds into R&D and also encourage collaboration between public sector and private companies. Consequently, active involvement of industry in biotechnology and its applications will also result in employment creation hence retaining of the young and trained scientists, who are currently either changing fields or going abroad in search of employment.

The probably greatest, challenge to biotechnology in Zimbabwe has to do with public awareness and understanding of biotechnology. The NBA in 2012 carried out a series of surveys to evaluate the general understanding of biotechnology by the ordinary Zimbabwean. From the findings, it was realised that there is great misconception over what biotechnology is all about, the potential benefits and risks of its products. Regrettably, this has generated a lot of negative view towards the technology, more so on genetically modified organisms which some believe to be the only products of biotechnology. This anti-biotechnology campaign has unfortunately generated fear, among the general public and law makers and has made the decision process of adopting biotechnology products an unduly slow and complex process.

To address the knowledge deficit and also the misconceptions, the NBA together with local stakeholders intends to intensify biotechnology public education and awareness programmes. This programme intents to reach out to all classes of the society from grassroots level providing biotechnology and biosafety education and understanding consequently addressing their fears and concerns and also encouraging public participation in decision making through dialogue. In addition, the campaign could also be used to generate new research areas which are more need based.

Thus far according to Pawarira and Khosa (2009), biotechnology research in Zimbabwe has been generally been science-driven and ad hoc. This ad hoc approach to biotechnology research may have some advantages, at least in the short term. The obvious of these is the free rein given to the scientific community to advance scientific frontiers in their particular field, provided sufficient financial resources can be raised and the appropriate research infrastructure is in place. However, there are some disadvantages inherent with this research approach. These include the dispersal rather than concentration effort on disparate, unrelated projects and programmes and, as a result, a risk of duplication of effort or even of 'reinventing the wheel'. The net result is likely inefficient use of scarce resources, both human and financial. Additionally, scientists are likely to work on projects of their own design, in their areas of personal interest, with little effort focussed on research leading to technologies for which demand may be strongest. A third risk arises when biotechnology research is essentially science-driven and remains increasingly concentrated in universities which, in Zimbabwe and other developing countries, have little tradition of interaction with farmers or with the private sector. It is therefore likely that research will be unrelated either to the perceived needs of agricultural producers, or to the development of technologies which are perceived as having strong market potential and therefore of interest to private firms and national goals of development.

However the Research Council of Zimbabwe (RCZ) has addressed this through laying out National Research Priority Areas which will foster a more coordinated and strategic approach within the identified areas. These are briefly quoted in the 9th Zimbabwe international research symposium book of abstracts for 2013.

4. CONCLUSION

Biotechnology remains one of the most promising tools that can be used to empower developing countries attain national and household food security, ensure a more predictable and sustainable economic and social development, reverse environmental degradation, improve health delivery, exploit environmentally friendly renewable energies, guarantee the provision of clean affordable water and fight other social ills.

In addition biotechnology like Information and Communication Technology (ICT) acts as an enabler *i.e.* it expands the country's horizons in the field of sustainable development. Coupled with ICT, biotechnology accelerates the transformation from a raw material-based to a knowledge-based economy. Unless the benefits of biotechnology for development are well articulated the opportunity to apply these technologies to benefit the poor in developing countries may be missed. Zimbabwe has the human resources, genetic resources and institutions for biotechnology research and development, the enabling legislation to guide the research, and the National Biotechnology Authority to supervise the research and field trials. Zimbabwe should fully embrace biotechnology and tread the path China, India, Malaysia, Brazil and South Africa have taken. Just as the provision of research grants is a major issue, entrepreneurship and financing for biotechnology companies should also be high on the government policy and educational agenda.

REFERENCES

1. http: //www.chemheritage.org/discover/online-resources/chemistry-in-history/themes/pharmaceuticals/preserving-health-with-biotechnology/berg-boyer-cohen.aspx
2. Second Science, Technology and Innovation Policy March 2012, Ministry of Science and Technology Development, 2012.
3. Benhura MAN, Katayi-Chidewe C (2004). The emulsifying properties of a polysaccharide isolated from the fruit of *Cordia abyssinica*. Inter. J. Food Sci. Technol. 39: 579-583.
4. Benhura MAN, Marume M (1993a). The mucilaginous polysaccharide material isolated from ruredzo *(Dicerocaryum zanguebarium)*. Food Chem. 46: 7-11.
5. Benhura MAN, Marume M (1993b). Emulsifying properties of the mucilage extracted from ruredzo *(Dicerocaryum zanguebarium)*. Biosci. Biotech. Bioche. 57: 1995-1998.
6. Benhura MAN, Mavhudzi I (1996). Use of cross linked mucilage prepared from ruredzo *(Dicerocaryum zanguebarium)* in the purification of polygalacturonase extracted from tomato. Food Chem. 56: 433-437.
7. Benhura MAN, Marume M (2006). Viscosity behaviour of the mucilage extracted from ruredzo *(Dicerocaryum zanguebarium)*. Starch 46: 106- 108.
8. Chetsanga CJ (1991). Current status of agricultural biotechnology in Zimbabwe. The Hague: International Service for National Agricultural Research.
9. Chetsanga CJ (1992). Science and Research in Africa. Scand. J. Immunol. 36 (11): 5-7.

10. Chikwamba R (1995). State of the art of biotechnology research in Zimbabwe. Afr. Crops Sci. 3 (2): 24-31.
11. Chirara M, Chetsanga CJ (1994). Genetic diversity of Hepatitis B virus isolated in Zimbabwe. J. Med. Virol. 42: 73-78.
12. Chivero ET, Mutukumira AN, Zvauya R (2001). Partial characterisation and characterisation of a xylanase enzyme produced by a microorganism isolated from selected indigenous fruits of Zimbabwe. Food Chem. 72: 179-185.
13. Derera J, Tongoona P, Vivek BS, van Rij N, Laing MD (2007). Gene action determining *Phaeosphaeria* leaf spot disease resistance in experimental maize hydrids. S. Afr. J. Plant Soil 24 (3): 138-141.
14. Dlamini NR, Taylor JRN, Rooney LW (2007). The effect of sorghum type and processing on the antioxidant properties of African sorghum-based foods. Food Chem. 105: 1412-1419.
15. Falconi C (1999). Agricultural Biotechnology Research Indicators: Zimbabwe. Discussion Paper. International Service for National Agricultural Research (ISNAR), the Netherlands.
16. Feresu SB (1992). Fermented milk products in Zimbabwe. In: Applications of Biotechnology to Traditional Fermented Foods National Academy Press, Washington, DC, pp. 80-85.
17. Gadaga TH, Mutukumira AN, Narvhus JA (2001b). Growth characteristics of *Candida kefyr* and two strains of *Lactococcus lactis* subsp. *lactis* isolated from Zimbabwean naturally fermented milk. Inter. J. Food Microbiol. 70: 11-19.
18. Gadaga TH, Viljoen BC, Narvhus JA (2007). Volatile organic compounds in naturally fermented milk and milk fermented using yeasts, lactic acid bacteria and their combinations as starter cultures. Food Technol. Biotechnol. 45: 95-200.
19. Mufandaedza J, Viljoen BC, Feresu SB, Gadaga TH (2006). Antimicrobial properties of lactic acid bacteria and yeast-LAB cultures isolated from traditional fermented milk against pathogenic *Escherichia coli* and *Salmonella enteritidis* strains. Int. J. Food Microbiol. 108: 147-152.
20. Mugochi T, Nandakumar MP, Zvauya R, Mattiasson B (2001). Bioassay for the detection of bacteriocins in fermentation broth. Biotechnol. Letters 23: 1243-1247.
21. Mugochi T, Parawira W, Mpofu A, Simango C, Zvauya R (1999) Survival of some species of *Salmonella* and *Shigella* in *mukumbi,* a traditional Zimbabwean wine. Int. J. Food Sci. Nutr. 50: 451-455.
22. Mwenje E, Mguni N (2001) Cellulolytic and pectinolytic activities of *Capnodium* isolates (sooty mould) from Zimbabwe. Canadian J. Bot. 79: 1492-1495.
23. Muchuweti M, Moyo E, Mushipe S (2005). Some properties of the polygaturonase from four Zimbabwean wild fruits (*Uapaca kirkiana, Zizphus mauritiana, Tamarindus indica* and *Berchemia discolour* fruits). Food Chem. 90: 655-661.
24. Parawira W, Murto M, Zvauya R, Mattiasson B (2004). Anaerobic digestion of solid potato waste alone and in combination with sugar beet leaves. Renew. Energ. 29: 1811-1823.

25. Parawira W (2004). Anaerobic treatment of agricultural residues and wastewater: Application of high-rate reactors. Doctoral thesis. Department of Biotechnology, Lund University, Sweden.

26. Parawira W, Kudita I, Nyandoroh MG, Zvauya R (2005). A study of industrial anaerobic treatment of opaque beer brewery wastewater in a tropical climate using a full-scale UASB reactor seeded with activated sludge. Process Biochem. 40: 593-599.

27. Parawira W, Murto M, Zvauya R, Mattiasson B (2006). Comparison of performance of a UASB reactor and an anaerobic packed-bed reactor when treating potato waste leachate. Renew. Energ. 36: 893-903.

28. Pawarira W, Khosa EM (2009). Biotechnology research, development, applications and management in Zimbabwe: Review. Scientific Research and Essay vol. 4 (9) pp 825-841.

29. Verma AS, Agrahari S, Rastogi S, Singh A (2011). Journal of Pharmacy and Bio Allied Sciences. J Pharm Bioallied Sci 2011 Jul-Sept; 3 (3): 321-323.

30. Zvauya R, Zvidzai CJ (1995). Constitutive production of endoglucanase by a *Bacillus* sp. isolated from a Zimbabwean hot spring. World J. Microbiol. Biotechnol. 11: 658-660.

31. Zvauya R, Parawira W, Mawadza C (1994). Aspects of aerobic thermophilic treatment of Zimbabwean traditional opaque-beer brewery wastewater. Bioresour. Technol. 48: 273-274.

32. Zvidzai CJ, Zvauya R (2001). Purification of a protease from analkalophilic *Bacillus subtilis* CHZ1 isolated from a Zimbabwean hot spring. J. Food Biochem. 25: 1-13.

33. Zvidzai CJ, Sithole-Niang I, Zvauya R, Hatti-Kaul R, Delgado O (2002). Cloning, sequencing and expression of endo-β-1,4-glucanase gene of a *Bacillus subtilis* CHZ1. J. Appl. Sci. Southern Afr. 8: 1-12.

34. Zvauya R, Mugochi T, Parawira W (1997). Microbial and biochemical changes occurring during production of *masvusvu* and *mangisi*, traditional Zimbabwean beverages. Plant Foods Hum. Nutr. 51: 43.

www.ingramcontent.com/pod-product-compliance
Ingram Content Group UK Ltd.
Pitfield, Milton Keynes, MK11 3LW, UK
UKHW041133071026
15587UKWH00009B/475

9 789351 302711